ORTHODOX CHRISTIANITY

THE BASICS

Resplendent icons, brilliant vestments, fragrant incense, and sonorous chants – the sights and sounds of the Orthodox Church have captured the imagination of people for centuries. *Orthodox Christianity: The Basics* is a compelling introduction to Orthodoxy's origins in the apostolic era, historical development, doctrines, spiritual and liturgical practices, and the social challenges of the twenty-first century. Topics covered include:

- Alexandria, Antioch, and the apostolic age
- Christology, Pneumatology, and Life and Death Orthodox Spirituality
- The Liturgical Tradition
- Orthodox Ecclesiology
- Orthodoxy and Culture Wars

With suggestions for further reading at the end of each chapter, along with a glossary, *Orthodox Christianity: The Basics* is the ideal starting point for those exploring Christianity, Orthodox Christianity, Church History, Eastern Orthodoxy, and Theology.

Nicholas Denysenko is Emil and Elfriede Jochum Professor and Chair, Valparaiso University, USA.

"Denysenko demonstrates with grace that understanding of any one element of Orthodoxy requires some knowledge of the interconnected whole, and that will be of significant pedagogical value (to non-specialists and specialists alike)."
– **Robert Saler**, *Christian Theological Seminary in Indianapolis, IN, USA*

"Nicholas Denysenko has impressively accomplished the formidable task of briefly charactering Orthodoxy. He has composed an accessible but not bland and balanced but not belaboured depiction of the history, theology, spirituality, liturgy, lived experience, and current challenges of the Orthodox Church. His expositions of the schism between Christian East and West as well as the past and current issues of church autocephaly are particularly cogent, and his attention to the domestic and daily realities of Orthodox Christians breathes life and fullness into this portrait of Orthodoxy. Perhaps most laudable is unapologetic avoidance of oversimplification; he accurately conveys the organic, sometimes self-contradictory complexity of the Orthodox Church."
– **Carrie Frederick Frost**, *Western Washington University, USA*

The Basics

JUDAISM
JACOB NEUSNER

RELIGION (second edition)
MALORY NYE

BUDDHISM
CATHY CANTWELL

ISLAM (second edition)
COLIN TURNER

CHRISTIANITY
BRUCE CHILTON

CHRISTIAN THEOLOGY
MURRAY RAE

ROMAN CATHOLICISM (second edition)
MICHAEL WALSH

THE QUR'AN (second edition)
MASSIMO CAMPANINI

RELIGION IN AMERICA
MICHAEL PASQUIER

MORMONISM
DAVID J. HOWLETT AND JOHN-CHARLES DUFFY

RELIGION AND SCIENCE (second edition)
PHILIP CLAYTON

THE BIBLE (second edition)
JOHN BARTON

QUEER THEOLOGIES
CHRIS GREENOUGH

CHRISTIAN ETHICS
ROBIN GILL

BAHA'I FAITH
CHRISTOPHER BUCK

QUAKERISM
MARGERY POST ABBOTT AND CARL ABBOTT

THOMAS AQUINAS
FRANKLIN T. HARKINS

BIBLE AND FILM
MATTHEW S. RINDGE

RELIGION AND FILM
JEANETTE REEDY SOLANO

SECULARISM
JACQUES BERLINERBLAU

NEW RELIGIOUS MOVEMENTS
JOSEPH LAYCOCK

FILM MUSIC
KENNETH LAMPL

JEWISH ETHICS
GEOFFREY D. CLAUSSEN

QUAKERISM (second edition)
MARGERY POST ABBOTT AND CARL ABBOTT

SIKHISM
NIKKY-GUNINDER KAUR SINGH AND ELEANOR NESBITT

ORTHODOX CHRISTIANITY
NICHOLAS E. DENYSENKO

For more information about this series, please visit: https://www.routledge.com/The-Basics/book-series/B

ORTHODOX CHRISTIANITY
THE BASICS

Nicholas Denysenko

Designed cover image: maylat, Getty Images

First published 2026
by Routledge
4 Park Square, Milton Park, Abingdon, Oxon OX14 4RN

and by Routledge
605 Third Avenue, New York, NY 10158

Routledge is an imprint of the Taylor & Francis Group, an informa business

© 2026 Nicholas Denysenko

The right of Nicholas Denysenko to be identified as author of this work has been asserted in accordance with sections 77 and 78 of the Copyright, Designs and Patents Act 1988.

All rights reserved. No part of this book may be reprinted or reproduced or utilised in any form or by any electronic, mechanical, or other means, now known or hereafter invented, including photocopying and recording, or in any information storage or retrieval system, without permission in writing from the publishers.

Trademark notice: Product or corporate names may be trademarks or registered trademarks, and are used only for identification and explanation without intent to infringe.

British Library Cataloguing-in-Publication Data
A catalogue record for this book is available from the British Library

ISBN: 9781032559773 (hbk)
ISBN: 9781032559780 (pbk)
ISBN: 9781003433217 (ebk)

DOI: 10.4324/9781003433217

Typeset in Bembo
by codeMantra

To my students
past, present, and future

CONTENTS

Acknowledgments		xi
List of Figures		xii
	Introduction	1
1	Origins: Alexandria, Antioch, the Apostolic Age	9
2	History	28
3	Orthodox Theology: Christology, Pneumatology, Life and Death	72
4	Conceptualizing Orthodox Spirituality	110
5	Mysteries in Orthodoxy	134
6	Orthodoxy's Liturgical Heritage	154
7	Orthodox Ecclesiology: Communities, Leaders, People	195

8	**Orthodoxy in the Twenty-First Century**	**224**
	Conclusion	**248**
	Bibliography	258
	Index	273

ACKNOWLEDGMENTS

I took on this book project somewhat randomly without looking to develop a textbook on Orthodoxy. I worked slowly at first and gradually gained momentum throughout 2024. Writing this book was like embarking on a journey with multiple stops. I had visited many of the sites before and was delighted to see them again, and also see how they had evolved. The journey took me to new places, challenging my assumptions and motivating me to answer questions I had not previously considered. The personal renewal I experienced in writing this book was unplanned, unexpected, and most welcome. Reviewing some of the most tumultuous events in Orthodox Church history renewed my appreciation for Orthodoxy's desire to be true to Christ, the apostolic tradition, and the Orthodox way.

A semester sabbatical at Valparaiso University provided me with time, space, and the mental and emotional bandwidth to begin and develop this book. I am particularly grateful to three friends who reviewed chapters and gave me essential feedback: Rev. Dr. Mark Roosien, Rev. Dr. Jacob Van Sickle, and Dr. Will Cohen. I am also grateful to Rebecca Clintworth, Publisher of the Religion division at Routledge Publishing, and Katie Beaumont, editorial assistant, for walking me through the publication process and responding to numerous queries. Special thanks to my colleagues at Valparaiso University and numerous friends and colleagues in the academy for your encouragement and support of this project.

LIST OF FIGURES

6.1　Interior Orthodox Church Altar, Odessa, Ukraine.　158
6.2　Painting on the Wall of Hagia Sophia Church, Trabzon, Turkey.　158
6.3　Liturgy of the preparation.　171
6.4　Plashchanitsa (Burial Shroud) at the Gorodets Local History Museum.　188
6.5　Paschal candles at a service in Annunciation, Toronto, Canada.　190
6.6　Greek Orthodox Christian Easter ceremony procession in Athens, Greece.　190

INTRODUCTION

Strangers gather and try to make conversation at a social event. In my case, someone inevitably asks what I teach at the university. I usually respond that I teach theology or religion and politics, and in some cases, people ask more probing questions. What is your specialty? When I respond that I teach about Orthodoxy and have been serving the Orthodox Church as an ordained deacon for over twenty years, reactions are all across the board. Many people have never heard of Orthodoxy before because they have no religious background or have never attended a church other than their own. Others have heard of Orthodoxy through someone they know – a coworker, student, neighbor, or friend. A few folks have heard about Orthodoxy because it has been in the news in recent years on account of Russia's invasion of Ukraine.

I have taught some version of a course on Orthodoxy for over ten years. In that time, I have perused numerous texts, and usually compile an impressive array of *lectio selecta* for my courses. I have tried a few different textbooks in their entirety. A friend recommended David Bell's *Orthodoxy: Evolving Tradition*, and students found it readable.[1] *The Orthodox Church* by Kallistos Ware is a classic, reprinted several times, and I find myself returning to it over and over again.[2] John McGuckin's recent *The Eastern Orthodox Church: A New History* is excellent, especially the care with which he explains Orthodoxy's fervent devotion to true apostolic teaching above all else.[3] Colleagues in the field continue to use Alexander Schmemann's seemingly timeless thin book, *For the Life of the World*.[4]

There is plenty to choose from, more than enough, and here you are, early in the process of moving through my tome. What does my book have to offer that one cannot find in the other sources?

The purpose of this book is to deliver a source that fuses the title with the subtitle. It is a book about Orthodoxy, and it cuts to the heart of what everyone needs to know. How do we sort through the dozens of potential topics and put it all together in a package that tells you only what you need to know about Orthodoxy?

It is not an easy task. This book has two objectives. The first and primary task is to give an updated account of Orthodox Christianity by taking a tour of the Church's story – her origins, history, structure, liturgy, spirituality, and the main issues confronting the church in the twenty-first century. The second primary objective is to make a significant contribution toward shaping the public narrative on Orthodoxy. In the era of digital media and a plethora of self-publishing tools, it is possible for anyone to lay claim to representing Orthodox Christianity.

Let's take a deeper dive into the enterprise of creating a narrative by considering how the apostles told the story of Jesus and how that story resulted in the creation of intentional communities devoted to being servants of Christ. One of Orthodoxy's distinguishing characteristics is its preference for the *local* nature of a church – the Orthodox Church in Greece, Romania, Bulgaria, Ukraine, and America – and how we went from apostles telling communities about their memories of Jesus Christ, what it was like to be his disciple, the details on his passion, death, burial, and resurrection, and the stories of their own travails in sharing this story. Twenty-first century apostles can create their own YouTube channels, becoming social influencers and unofficial sources of information, going viral and speaking on their own behalf. Pastors continue to shape the narrative in their ministries. Pastors introduce visitors and inquirers to Orthodoxy by giving them tours, meeting them one-on-one and in small groups, giving them literature, and communicating with them through a variety of media – e-mails, bulletins, texts, and videos. Church leaders communicate with the public through the same venues. One way of looking at the sources of information that tell us about Orthodoxy is to see it as a selection of streaming services. The inquirer can select from information provided by a national church body, a diocese, a parish, a local parish pastor, a bishop, a professor, an author, a teacher, or someone else they choose.

The purpose of this book is to make a significant contribution toward shaping the narrative by telling an updated story of Orthodoxy. This book does not cast aside the contributions of beloved authors like Ware and Schmemann, but seeks to build upon their contributions by explaining with detail and in everyday language the whos, whats, wheres, and hows of Orthodoxy.

Learning about Orthodoxy requires both an international tour and a quick course on vocabulary. The remainder of this introductory chapter performs two essential tasks. The first one is a quick run-through of essential vocabulary, terms that will appear repeatedly in the book because they are anchors of Orthodox history and identity. The second is to provide a preview of what is to come in the chapters, a teaser that says a lot about the big picture while inviting the reader to dig deeper into the details.

COMMUNITIES

There are two families of Orthodox churches in the world: the Eastern Orthodox Church and the Oriental Orthodox Church. The Eastern Orthodox Church consists of seventeen *autocephalous* Orthodox churches. An autocephalous church is completely self-governing in its activities and administration. The autocephalous churches maintain connections with one another by coming together for special occasions that usually include the celebration of one or more Divine Liturgies – the title used for the Orthodox ritual celebration of the Eucharist. There is also a handful of autonomous Orthodox churches. These churches are mostly self-governing, and depend in some way, usually symbolic, on a larger, mother church.

The Oriental Orthodox Church is a more loosely organized group of churches that is both non-Chalcedonian and miaphysite, which means they believe that Christ has one nature that is both divine and human. The communities constituting these churches accept the definitions of faith in Jesus Christ made by the first three ecumenical councils, but they do not accept the declaration of the fourth one at Chalcedon in 451. Their common confession of faith is the anchor of their bond of unity, but they are not united with the Eastern Orthodox churches.

Leaders of religious communities carry a variety of titles. An imam is the religious leader of a mosque, and a rabbi oversees the life of a Jewish community. Almost everyone knows the Pope, the leader of the global Roman Catholic Church. Orthodoxy has a variety of important people who carry out ministries. They wear clothing that says something about their role in the community.

The main Orthodox leader is the bishop. The bishop is literally an overseer, a literal translation of the Greek word for bishop – *episkopos*, one who oversees. Orthodox bishops oversee the life of a defined region that is anchored in a city, and this region is called either a diocese or an eparchy. We will use diocese for the sake of convenience in this book. Orthodox bishops must be both celibate (unmarried) and monastic (tonsured monks). The bishop wears one or more long, black robes with an icon of Mary, the Mother of God, in a small enclosed case hanging around his neck. The bishop wears a monastic black head covering called a *klobuk*, often for public or church-sponsored events.

The Orthodox Church also has higher ranking bishops: archbishops, metropolitans, and patriarchs. The use of these titles varies among the local Orthodox churches. Technically, an archbishop is the head of bishops. For many Orthodox churches, an archbishop is the chief bishop of all the bishops in the church and is based in the capital city of the region, like the archbishop of Athens. Some churches use the title of metropolitan to describe the senior bishops of either a synod or a major metropolis. Patriarch is reserved for regional or national churches that have been given the dignity of carrying the title of patriarchate. Five ancient churches held this distinction for centuries: Rome, Constantinople, Alexandria, Antioch, and Jerusalem. The Orthodox Church gave the privilege of patriarchate to the churches of Russia, Georgia, Serbia, Bulgaria, and Romania as well. The head of the church in Alexandria (Egypt) is also known as the pope, and this title has also been given to the head of the church in Georgia, along with the title "Catholicos."

The overwhelming majority of Orthodox Christians know their minister as a priest. The word "priest" comes from the Hebrew Bible, the Old Testament, as the priest would offer sacrifices to God for the forgiveness of the sins of the people. The technical Orthodox term for the pastor of parish communities is presbyter, which means elder. Readers should note that most Orthodox Christians know their pastor as a priest, but in this book, we will use the term presbyter to refer to parish pastors. Presbyters usually wear long black robes, distinctive vestments, and, in some cases, a wooden or metal cross around their necks. Almost every parish has a presbyter because he is the ordinary pastor of a community.

The apostles appointed deacons to handle the caretaking of widows in the book of Acts. Deacons became assistants to the bishop, and their service evolved into leading prayer during the divine services. People recognize deacons by the long stole they wear over their shoulders when they lead prayer. Deacons perform a lot of the chanting in the church. One of the most familiar sounds of Orthodox liturgy is the dialogue between the deacon and the singers when the deacon invites the people to pray for a specific purpose that ends with "let us pray to the Lord" or "let us ask of the Lord." The deacon typically chants these petitions, while the singers respond to a specific melody or harmonized setting. Many parishes do not have deacons because a person has to be ordained a deacon before he is eligible for ordination to presbyter. Some parishes have higher ranking deacons known as protodeacons or archdeacons. These deacons have larger orarions (known as a double orarion) and have seniority among the other deacons. Deaconesses also performed ministry in Orthodoxy, and the Church is currently in the process of renewing this order.

There are other people wearing robes and participating in the services of the church. These people are not ordained but are servers who are blessed to help the presbyter and deacon. Some parishes have subdeacons, who wear the orarion folded over their chest like an X. Subdeacons are one of the so-called minor orders, which also include readers. Readers and subdeacons are blessed to perform specific ministries. The subdeacon is usually the leader of the servers and is expected to be knowledgeable about the small tasks that need to be done in the service. Readers typically have training for chanting psalms, the lesser hours, and fundamental musical performance. Like deacons, readers are expected to have a basic level of musical competence.

BOOK OUTLINE

The rest of this book presents a survey of what you need to know about Orthodoxy. Let's start with one of the Orthodox Church's core beliefs about its origin and founding. Orthodoxy traces its beginning to Jesus' appointment of the apostles to go and preach the Gospel to all nations. The Orthodox Church identifies itself as the one, holy, catholic, and apostolic church. This is not a typo – it is as bold as the claim sounds. The Orthodox Church does not apologize for claiming exclusivity – Orthodoxy alone is the one true church.

Orthodoxy explains this bold claim by tracing its origins to apostolic preaching. The claim is similar to the one made by the Roman Catholic Church, but not identical. Apostles founded communities when Jesus sent them out to preach the coming of the kingdom of God. The first chapter of this book discusses the importance of two Christian centers for Orthodox teaching: Antioch and Alexandria. Orthodoxy inherited a great deal of the community tradition used in Antioch for prayer, and Alexandrian theology perhaps made the greatest contribution to Orthodox theology. Orthodoxy also favors the idea that the church is completely present in one place, like Antioch or Alexandria.

The second chapter provides a survey of Orthodox history. This chapter begins with a review of the seven ecumenical councils and then turns to a select presentation of the most significant events in the history of the Orthodox Church. These events include missionary activity among southern and Eastern Slavs, the so-called Great Schism of 1054, the dynamics involved with the Fall of Constantinople and the rise of the Russian empire, the role of the patriarch of Constantinople as a governor of people in the Ottoman Empire, the Orthodox Church in the Soviet era, and Orthodoxy in the so-called diaspora. The history chapter discusses the most recent events having an impact on Orthodoxy, including the creation of the Orthodox Church of Ukraine (OCU) and Orthodoxy's reaction to Russia's invasion of Ukraine.

Chapter 3 presents the fundamentals of Orthodox theology. This chapter focuses on the teachings of the ecumenical councils because they form the core of the Orthodox Church's beliefs on Jesus Christ and the Holy Trinity. The chapter also explores specific features of Orthodox theology, including Orthodox views on salvation, life and death, and the legacies of theologians such as Sergius Bulgakov.

The fourth chapter surveys Orthodox spirituality by focusing on the popular practices of venerating icons, pursuing inner silence (hesychasm), reciting the Jesus Prayer, and practices associated with theosis – the process of becoming like God. We devote space to exploring more recent trends of spirituality, such as the liturgical renewal movement and the neo-patristic way.

Chapter 5 presents the Orthodox mysteries. Readers familiar with Christian literature might think of the mysteries as the sacraments, but this chapter is written differently to show how specific liturgical rites of the church initiate and sustain people in one and the same mystery – eternal life shared with the living God.

The next chapter is devoted to the liturgical tradition and takes the reader on a journey of Orthodox worship by introducing them to the basics of architecture, music, and a textured description of the Divine Liturgy and its inner meaning. This chapter includes an analysis of the Orthodox liturgical year with attention to both the fixed cycle – feast days celebrated on the same day of the calendar each year – and the movable cycle, governed by Pascha (Easter).

The chapter on Orthodox ecclesiology takes the description of churches and peoples and explains, with some detail, the Orthodox view on the church. This chapter begins with the premise introduced earlier – Orthodoxy takes the exclusive approach by defining itself as the one, holy, catholic, and apostolic church. The rest of the chapter goes into some detail on how the autocephalous churches relate to one another, non-Orthodox churches and religious communities, and the world.

The final chapter takes on the issues confronting all churches and religious communities: the culture wars. Presently, the Orthodox Church ordains only men as bishops, presbyters, and deacons. Orthodoxy had deaconesses – women deacons – at one point in history. Orthodoxy's views on gender have also evolved over the centuries. This chapter presents diverse Orthodox perspectives on women, the possibility of ordaining women, same-sex marriage and the LGBTQ community, and the crisis of extremism afflicting church and society.

Most of the world knows Orthodoxy because of its outer appearance. The beautiful vestments, complex rituals, and sonorous chants look and sound truly otherworldly. The Orthodox Church is sometimes in the news and causes controversy. The inner core of Orthodoxy is ancient, because the church has remained remarkably faithful to its theological heritage. There is more to Orthodoxy than meets the eye, and the rest of this book invites you, the reader, to come and meet the Orthodox Church in its fullness.

NOTES

1 David Bell, *Orthodoxy: Evolving Tradition* (Collegeville, MN: Liturgical Press, 2008).
2 Timothy Ware, *The Orthodox Church: An Introduction to Eastern Christianity* (London: Penguin, 2015).
3 John McGuckin, *The Eastern Orthodox Church: A New Introduction* (New Haven, CT: Yale University Press, 2020).
4 Alexander Schmemann, *For the Life of the World: Sacraments and Orthodoxy*, 2d rev. ed. (Yonkers, NY: St. Vladimir's Seminary Press, 2000).

ORIGINS
Alexandria, Antioch, the Apostolic Age

Experts on Eastern Orthodoxy use many adjectives to describe its particular features. Some of these common adjectives include Eastern, Byzantine, patristic, and Greek. To be sure, the Orthodox Church has a strong affinity for the patristic tradition, also known as the legacy of the fathers. One can venture into an Orthodox parish and hear parishioners talking about a discussion group on St. Athanasius's "On the Incarnation." It is also quite common to hear people describe Orthodoxy as the "Church of the fathers."

These diverse references point to one core feature. Orthodoxy values a sense of tradition that developed during the patristic age, with the sermons and writings of the Church fathers. These writings are inscribed in Orthodoxy's primary confession of faith, the Nicene-Constantinopolitan Creed. The first version of this creed was composed at the gathering of bishops in Nicaea in the year 325 CE. Several sentences (articles) were added to the Creed at the next major gathering in the year 381 CE, in Constantinople. This Creed is obviously very important – the Roman Catholic Church uses it, along with a number of Protestant churches. For the Orthodox, the Nicene-Constantinopolitan Creed does not exhaust its sense of the legacy of the fathers. The Orthodox Church points to the seven ecumenical councils as defining its faith. The canons and declarations of these councils are like arteries in the heart of Orthodoxy. The councils do not make any new claims. They clarify the belief that the worldwide communion of Orthodox holds dear to its heart – that Jesus Christ is the only-begotten son of God, true

DOI: 10.4324/9781003433217-2

God of true God, incarnate of the Virgin Mary, sent into the world to save humankind.

The councils did not invent this idea. The Orthodox Church believes that they inherited it from their predecessors, like the stories children receive from their parents and grandparents, telling them who they are and where they come from. The first ecumenical council was in the fourth century – from whom did the teachers and pastors gathered there receive this beloved tradition? And why did it need to be clarified?

Converts to the Orthodox Church identify a number of features that drew them into the communion and sustained them during the process of becoming Orthodox. One dimension that deserved further exploration is the apostolic quality of the Orthodox Church. The apostolic quality of Orthodox is one of authenticity, origins, stability, and steadiness. People view Orthodoxy as unchanging, even though it has changed through the course of its history. Like other features and dimensions of faith, non-Orthodox Christians also view apostolicity as a treasure. It is one of the four marks of the church expressed by the Creed – the Church is one, holy, catholic, and apostolic. Orthodoxy does not have a monopoly on apostolicity, but many Orthodox people believe it retains apostolicity like no other Christian communion.

Every church claiming to be apostolic points to one of the people Jesus himself commissioned to accompany him and to preach the coming of his kingdom. The original twelve disciples Jesus selected were also his first apostles. Peter, James, and John were the best known of these, mentioned most frequently in the private company of Jesus. The story of the apostle Paul and his evangelical activity constitutes most of the book of Acts, written by Luke. Speaking of the writers of the New Testament, the four authors of the four gospels in the canon – Matthew, Mark, Luke, and John – are also apostles. Barnabas was Paul's companion and partner until they parted ways over a disagreement (Acts 15:36).

The apostles were Jesus' companions, eyewitnesses of his teaching, healing, passion, death, and resurrection. The apostles were the original storytellers who told others about Jesus and called others to join them in worshipping him as the only-begotten son of God. Apostles are the most important figures in the memory of all Christians because they depicted Jesus for all future generations. The apostolic act of sharing this story and inviting others to worship him is life-giving for Orthodoxy. Apostolic witness and preaching create and sustain communities. In other words, the Church as a community is founded upon this apostolic witness, these stories, and the commitment to worship the one who sent them. Paul describes his apostolic storytelling as akin to conceiving children, describing himself metaphorically as a father since his preaching gave birth – and therefore life – to Christian communities (1 Cor. 4:15).

Orthodoxy understands apostolicity in both Christological and pneumatological terms. Jesus Christ appointed and sent apostles to preach the coming of the kingdom to the people living in cities and in the countryside. This is the Christological aspect of apostolicity. Apostolic authority is anchored in their connection to Jesus himself. Their eyewitness accounts form the core of the Church's belief in Jesus. The pneumatological aspect of apostolicity is in its succession. When the apostles preached Jesus, the Holy Spirit descended upon them and the communities they formed. More particularly, the Holy Spirit descended upon the people who constituted these new communities.

Orthodoxy is not alone in its adherence to these two aspects of apostolicity. The book of Acts says that baptism is not perfected until the apostles lay their hands upon those who have been baptized (Acts 8:17). This ritual of apostolic handlaying is of special importance to Christians of the West and is the very reason that Roman Catholics require bishops to preside at Confirmation because the bishop laying his hand upon the head of a baptized Christian continues the practice described in Acts.

Orthodox Churches identify their authenticity and legitimacy in their apostolic constitution. This means that they begin their historical narratives with the events of apostolic preaching in their native lands. Historical examples abound. Greek and Slavic Orthodox claim that St. Andrew, the first-called apostle, preached the good news of Jesus risen from the dead to their native peoples. Armenian Christians say that the apostle Thaddeus founded the church among their people. Christians in Egypt, Alexandria in particular, claim that the apostle Mark founded their ancient community. The Syrian community points to the preaching of the apostle Peter.

Many communities trace their origins to Christian figures who founded communities. Ukrainians, Belorussians, and Russians attribute the permanent founding of Christianity to St. Volodymyr.

Georgians credit the creation of their national church to St. Nino. These later figures were not among the original apostles, but their activity of creating church communities that have continued for several generations, over millennia, made them the apostles' equals. The Orthodox Church gave them the title of equal-to-the-apostles (*isapostoloi*) accordingly.

Apostolic preaching has staying power. These church communities that have sustained life and endured foreign invasions, famines, persecution, and many other calamities credit their sustenance to the staying power of apostolic preaching. The more common phrase used to describe this phenomenon is apostolic succession. Roman Catholic and Orthodox Christians tend to define apostolic succession through the person of the bishop.[1] The rationale of this definition is that apostles handed on the ministry of preaching, presiding, and leading Christian communities to bishops, as Paul's letters to Timothy suggest. Bishops are the successors to the apostles in this scheme, so the bishop is the person who bears or carries apostolic succession in his ministry.

Orthodoxy's view on apostolic succession is a bit more extensive. John Zizioulas popularized the notion that it isn't just the bishop who has apostolic succession, but it is the entire community that bears it.[2] The bishop is the personal symbol of apostolic succession as the community's leader, much like a president presents all the core values of the nation that elects them, at least in principle.

There are two schools of thought on apostolic succession. The first school of thought operates like a genealogy or family tree. Every one of Jesus' apostles had a successor, someone who continued the initial ministry of establishing a church and presiding over its life. The bishops who inherited ministry from the apostles that established churches in major cities like Rome, Antioch, and Alexandria were linked to the apostles because they were continuing the original ministry of preaching Christ and the message of his resurrection from the dead. Early Christians considered this ministry essential. Local churches maintained lists of the bishops of other major metropolises, and those lists played an important role in sustaining Christian unity over a distance.[3] The list eventually evolved into a living document called diptychs. Diptychs functioned as a checklist of church leaders, and the local bishop would pray for all the other bishops, and their churches, as a way of maintaining Christian unity through ritual.

The second school of thought explained by Zizioulas is noteworthy because it is a hallmark of the Orthodox Church's belief that each local church, with its urban capital, was fully church because it had been established by an apostle and continued the ministry of the founding apostle through a legitimate bishop.[4] The act of continuing the apostolic ministry was one of the main features of legitimacy that allowed a church to claim that it was the church of the apostles. Zizioulas argued that an entirely local or regional church, understood as a number of church communities constituting a network with a capital (like Rome) as its center, possessed apostolic succession.[5] No bishop could claim to possess that feature of apostolicity on his own – the regional church possessed it, and the bishop, as the president of the regional church, represented his apostolic church by exercising the ministry of his office.

Zizioulas was very careful to avoid reductionism in his explanation of the church as a communion of believers. He stated that Orthodoxy does not disregard the church's universal nature but instead adheres to the simultaneity of the local and universal.[6] Communion, a common adherence to the one truth, expressed in dogma and in the liturgical rite of the Eucharist, is how the fullness (catholicity) of the Church can be in both the local and universal church. The universal church is not the sum of the local churches – it is the one in the many, regardless of the number of the many.

Earlier, we mentioned that the Roman Catholic Church also values apostolic succession. How does Rome's understanding of apostolic succession differ from Orthodoxy's? The Roman Church believes that the bishop of Rome is the successor to Peter, who was the chief of Jesus' apostles, and therefore has a special authority over the global church.[7] Orthodoxy believes that Rome was given the privilege of being first but contends that the bishop of Rome (or the Pope) has strict limits on the exercise of this authority.[8] For example, the Pope has to confirm a new bishop every time he is elected and appointed. In Orthodoxy, the Pope would not have this privilege – it would be all the bishops of a regional church that would confirm the election and installation of the new bishop. Orthodoxy does not believe that there are degrees of apostolicity that make one church more authoritative than another. This does not mean that Orthodox do not believe in rank and order – they do, and they call it taxis. Every regional church and its presiding bishop on the list of apostolic churches possesses the fullness of apostolic succession, no matter where they fall on the list.

Orthodoxy adheres to a balance of regionally independent structures within an ordered system of seniority, with Rome functioning as "the elder brother" on the basis of history. Other regional centers made significant contributions to the formative years of Orthodoxy's history. Two church centers were of particular importance because of the theologians they produced: these were Antioch (in Syria) and Alexandria (in northern Africa). The following section introduces some of the most important theologians who left their mark on Orthodox practice and theology that hailed from these regions.

ESTABLISHING THE CONTEXT

A brief introductory note on the early Christian community can help us understand how Antioch and Alexandria fit into the context of the Christian community of the apostolic age. We are accustomed to imagining a structured Christian world, with some kind of regional center providing guidance to the global Christian church. The early Christian community was local in nature, consisting of Jesus' apostles preaching the news of his resurrection and communities establishing Christian life around these apostolic preachers and their successors.

Christians living in cities like Antioch, Rome, and Alexandria needed to gather in places that were convenient and safe. It was neither convenient nor safe for Christians to gather in synagogues because their confession of Jesus as Lord posed a threat to the Roman emperor (who was the only legitimate 'lord') and the Jewish authorities. Christians gathered in homes and established house churches in these first communities.

The emergence and spread of Christianity as a local phenomenon helps us understand the fragile nature of Christian unity. It is not as if Peter or one of the other apostles bought a large building in a major city, raised funds to create a wide-ranging budget, and began to issue edicts that instructed Christians in all of the other cities on how they were supposed to conduct their affairs. Robert Wilken described Christian unity in the beginning of the second century as unity within a loose organization.[9]

Antioch and Alexandria were two of the local communities that ultimately shaped Orthodox thinking and practice. The ultimate question for Christians – who is Jesus? – proved to be contentious in both locations.

ANTIOCH AND ANTIOCHENE THEOLOGY

Antioch was a significant Christian center from the very beginning. Peter preached in Antioch, and Paul reports that he visited Peter for a period of three years to receive a crash course on Jesus. Luke states that Jesus' followers became Christian and therefore became known as Christians for the first time in Antioch (Acts 11:26). Some of the most important eyewitness accounts of Christian life come from Antioch or nearby regions. The bishop and martyr Ignatius testified to the organization of Christian communities in Antioch in the second century (approximately 117 CE).[10] He writes of the importance of the bishop in the life of the church community and describes how the bishop presides over an ordered community gathered around him in remembrance of Christ. The bishop is considered essential to the community, so much so that Ignatius cannot imagine church life without the bishop.

IGNATIUS OF ANTIOCH

We turn to Ignatius to begin the process of looking at some of the issues that are most important to Orthodox Christians. These begin with Orthodoxy's doctrine of Christ, that Jesus is both human and divine and is God's only son. The term used to describe the doctrine of Christ is Christology. The second major issue that Ignatius helps us understand is the significance of the Church as a community, with specific reference to its organizational structure. The teaching of the church is called ecclesiology.

Ignatius' writings open a window into Antiochene Christology and the ecclesiology of the second century. Ignatius describes Jesus as of the "race of David," having taken on flesh, and also the "son of God," who was born of the Virgin.[11] Ignatius describes Jesus as a historical figure, asserting that he was "truly nailed to the cross" under Pontius Pilate and Herod.[12] Ignatius emphasizes the purpose of Jesus' appearance in the world and his passion – it is for "our" sake, "so that we might be saved."[13] Ignatius pleads with the Smyrneans to hold to the true teaching of Jesus, distinguishing reality from appearance, because of the allure of false teachings, especially those who would deny Jesus.[14]

His reference to his own sufferings – imprisonment and beatings – underscores the cost of discipleship.[15] Remaining faithful to true teaching is costly, to the point of losing one's well being, and for some, one's life. Ignatius' reference to his own sufferings for the sake of true, authentic belief is an early appearance of a value that the Orthodox continue to prioritize today. This is martyrdom – not calling attention to one's self and asking for persecution, but enduring rejection to the point of losing everything for the sole sake of remaining faithful to Christ.

Ignatius's letter to the Smyrneans calls attention to the necessity of maintaining unity in the church community. He identifies the order of the church and describes the roles and ministries of the ordained officials for the purpose of maintaining fragile unity. Ignatius exhorts the Smyrneans to follow the bishop as Jesus followed the father, to remain faithful to presbyters, and to "reverence the deacons."[16] Ignatius teaches that the bishop is the glue that holds the church community, especially its unity, together.

Ignatius's early teaching on the authority of the bishop is one of many contributors to the Orthodox Church's preference for a hierarchical organizational structure, with an almost absolute authority given to the bishop. One of Ignatius's passages from his letter to the Smyrneans expresses this sense of authority:[17]

> Let the Eucharist be held valid which is offered by the bishop or by one to whom the bishop has committed this charge, Wherever the bishop appears, there let the people be; as wherever Jesus Christ is, there is the Catholic Church. It is not lawful to baptize or give communion without the consent of the bishop.

This passage is significant for many reasons. First, it represents the kind of authority a paterfamilias or overseer of a household would possess and exercise in antique to late-antique Christianity. It would not be unusual for a community leader to exercise this kind of authority. Second, the instruction itself suggests that others are challenging the authority of the bishop. Gatherings, meetings, and deliberations that exclude the leader can lead to disputes and splinter communities. Ignatius is acutely aware of the fragility of the Christian community because of its novelty. Identifying the bishop as the source of authority and making him inseparable from the Church is a way of protecting unity threatened by others.

Catholics and Orthodox identify this passage from Ignatius' letter as a reflection of the role and ministry of a bishop in the church. The problem with this text and the teaching to which it contributes is the matter of the degree of authority borne and exercised by the bishop. Can a bishop act unilaterally, and do passages like these undermine the role of the others in the community? Is this a source for clericalism, for placing more distance between lay people and clergy, especially since presbyters and deacons are also mentioned as authoritative figures in the community? Orthodoxy certainly affirms Ignatius' teaching on the ministry of the bishop as president of the community, but there is no consensus among Orthodox on just how much authority the bishop possesses.

Why does the bishop's ministry become so important at such an early time in the history of the Christian church? Ignatius's letters illustrate some of the variant teachings on Jesus circulated by certain teachers. Ignatius' emphasis on Jesus' true birth and true crucifixion is an argument refuting docetists, who taught that Jesus only appeared to be the son of God.[18] False teaching like docetism caused divisions and schisms in both belief and practice. Ignatius condemns the docetists and points out that they refuse to partake of the Eucharist because they do not believe that the Eucharist is the true body of Christ.[19]

Orthodox theologian John Behr illuminates the inseparability of the apostolic faith in Jesus Christ as true human and true God with the Eucharist in the preaching of Ignatius. Behr notes that Christian unity itself, manifest in the assembly's gathering to celebrate the Eucharist, depends on a "prior unity in the apostolic faith."[20] Behr also mentions that which is central to Orthodox Christian identity: the confession of faith to bearing witness and (as Behr notes), for Ignatius himself, to martyrdom.[21] Ignatius of Antioch personifies a core Orthodox value: there is nothing more precious than true faith in Jesus Christ. This communal faith supersedes everything else – including one's own earthly life.

Ignatius is one of our first eyewitnesses to the Christian community's response to the problems that appeared in response to our leading question, who is Jesus? Ignatius adhered to the teaching that Jesus was truly human, born of Mary, and crucified, having experienced suffering and death. The Eucharist observed by the community each week was the primary expression of this faith. For Ignatius, the Eucharist and true faith were inseparable. Participating in the Christian community's Eucharist was the primary way of showing one's unity with the Christian community. This is why Ignatius admonishes the people to avoid schisms and adhere to the one Eucharist.[22] Ignatius's teachings identify true faith with participation in the Eucharist. Ignatius' second-century teaching is one of Orthodoxy's primary core values to this day.

THE DIDACHE: THE FIRST "CHURCH ORDER"

Another significant testimony comes from the Didache, an early instruction manual that guides bishops on how to manage the fundamentals of church life. The Didache holds a place of special reverence throughout the whole church because of its great age – it originated from the first century and is therefore around the same age as many of the writings of the New Testament. The author of the Didache is unknown. The writer claims that the instruction is based on the teachings of the apostles handed down, a common attribution of authority in ancient writings. Similar manuals with greater detail emerged over the course of time, and many of these referred to the Didache as something of a blueprint.

The Didache is significant for our purposes because of its Syrian origin and rare insight into how the early church prayed. While no single Church, including the Orthodox, claims to use the Didache as its main sourcebook for prayer today, Orthodoxy respects the Didache and some of its successors as showing the Church one of the oldest patterns for worship.

Orthodoxy embraces many specific rules of the Didache. For example, the Didache addresses fasting and instructs the Church to fast on Wednesdays and Fridays. The reason for the selection of weekdays is to avoid adopting a living Jewish practice. The larger point is the expectation that Christians would observe a regular fast in a weekly rhythm. The Orthodox Church maintains the practice of fasting from meat and dairy products on Wednesdays and Fridays, an observance traceable to the Didache instruction.

The Didache contains a short passage instructing the church on how to gather for the Eucharist. The short texts in the Didache do not have much in common with the current Orthodox Eucharistic tradition. The instruction points to Eucharistic exclusivity. In the community of the Didache, only those who had been baptized were permitted to participate in the Eucharist. This instruction was common for the early church, restricting participation in the Eucharist to the baptized, a principle the Orthodox Church has adopted to apply to all of those outside of the Orthodox Church.[23]

From the very beginning, there were differences in the forms and content of Christian liturgy, as we shall see in the chapter on Orthodox worship. The Didache's brief instructions to the bishop did not represent the entire church, nor did they become permanent fixtures of Orthodox liturgy. They do, however, introduce important principles from early Christianity in Antioch, especially when paired with the evidence from the letters of Ignatius. True faith, baptism, unity in the faith, the fusion of faith with the Eucharist, and respect for the authority of the bishop, presbyters, and deacons were important values of the Antiochene community that have remained in Orthodoxy. Many aspects of the Divine Liturgy that originated in Antioch would shape Orthodox liturgy for the rest of its history, an issue we will take up in Chapter 5.

THE MARTYRDOM OF POLYCARP

If Ignatius was one of the most important voices of Antiochene Christianity, whose teachings on Christ and the church figured prominently in Orthodoxy, the story of Polycarp, one of Ignatius's disciples, must be mentioned. Polycarp was the bishop of Smyrna in the second century. Polycarp learned about Christianity from Ignatius, but also from the firsthand accounts of the Apostle John.[24] Polycarp's sufferings for bearing witness to the truth of the apostolic faith became sensational in the literary stories of the lives of early Christian saints. Polycarp refused to offer sacrifices to the gods and was sentenced to death by burning. The eyewitnesses to his death by burning shared the prayer attributed to him and also reported that his burning flesh emitted a pleasant fragrance, akin to the smell of silver or freshly baked bread.

The account of Polycarp's martyrdom grants us access to the early Church's method of storytelling and prayer tradition. The author of the account embellishes Polycarp's steadfastness in faith and courage, depicting him as refusing to bend to the proconsul's will when the authority threatens to use wild beasts for the bishop's execution.[25] Polycarp also began to undress in preparation for the burning, an image projecting archetypal Christian courage.[26] The fire did not consume him but surrounded him, a miracle that led the authorities to execute him with a dagger instead.[27] The story depends on plotlines constituting classical Christian hagiography and Orthodox identity to this day.

These include unfavorable comparisons of the cowardice of the executioners with the courage and holiness of the martyr and the Christians in the crowd, the devil as the antagonist working behind the scenes, and Jews acting as collaborators with the authorities and enemies of Christians. Writers of the lives of the saints in late antique Christianity used these kinds of literary devices as tools to evangelize prospective Christians. Orthodoxy has inherited and sustained these devices and the themes, often without removing anti-Semitic themes from the lives of the saints and liturgical texts.

The account of Polycarp's martyrdom includes passages of his prayer to God as he prepared to die. Polycarp asks God to receive him as "a rich and acceptable sacrifice" and petitions God that God would grant Polycarp "a part, along with the martyrs, in the chalice of Thy Christ."[28] Liturgical historians value this passage as potential evidence of a late-antique Christian Eucharistic prayer. The prayer's references to Polycarp's death as an acceptable sacrifice illustrate the development in Christian thinking on the Eucharist. Christians are offering themselves to God in a spirit of martyrdom. Polycarp's prayer is something of a blueprint for all Christians – everyone must be willing to offer their very lives to God to be included in the cup of salvation. This particular idea of self-offering, especially a communal offering, is an identity marker of sainthood and a theme of the Eucharist. The story of Polycarp's martyrdom brings these two themes together. Polycarp's prayer expresses the notion of the Church's self-offering to God when it gathers on Sundays for the Eucharist.

AN ORTHODOX CONSENSUS ON THE SUPREMACY OF THE HOLY SCRIPTURES

The earliest church communities were formed by people who shared their eyewitness accounts of Jesus Christ. People gathered to hear a story – which means that the first Christians were persuaded by an oral tradition passed down from apostles to their disciples and then repeated within local communities. Oral tradition was privileged and held primacy among Christians before written accounts began to emerge. There was no established collection of writings the Christian communities and their leaders considered to be authoritative in the second century. People interested in learning more about Christianity went to places like Alexandria, which had a reputation as a center for learning. Valentinus was among those who traveled to Alexandria and later went to Rome, where he came into conflict with Christian teachers.[29]

Disciples gathered around Valentinus because of his message that God the Father could be known through the word of God, delivering those who came to know God from ignorance. The Valentinians expressed this thought in a writing known as the Gospel of Truth. Valentinian teachings circulated alongside other narratives about Christ, but the differences among them caused both confusion and division. Valentinians believed that the God of the Old Testament was unkind to humans and inferior to the Father of Jesus Christ. The Father sent Christ to illuminate humankind and draw them to himself. The notion of the Father delivering humankind from the manipulative God of the Old Testament was deeply problematic for early Christian communities of the second century.

Irenaeus of Lyons was among the Christian teachers who moved the Church toward a consensus on its beliefs and the identification of trustworthy and authoritative sources. Irenaeus, who learned from Polycarp, was born in Smyrna of Asia Minor, educated in Rome, and became a bishop in southern Gaul. He became familiar with the confusing teachings circulating among the people in his church.[30] Irenaeus's identification of a legitimate collection of writings that expressed the faith held by the Christian communities of the early church was among his most important contributions.[31] Irenaeus adhered to the faith he had received in the community – a belief that the God who created the universe and created a covenant with Abraham, Isaac, and Jacob was the Father who sent his only-begotten son to save humankind, in fulfillment of the promise he made to Israel. Irenaeus connected this rule of faith to a body of New Testament writings. In other words, a common core could be identified in the faith handed down orally and the teachings in a collection of writings. Irenaeus's review of the Scriptural confirmation of the rule of faith was the beginning of the formation of a canon of Scripture – a list of books, letters, and accounts Christians considered legitimate. This delicate balance of oral and written tradition is one of Orthodoxy's most cherished core values, and Irenaeus played a pivotal role in helping to clarify and confirm the Orthodox faith when gnostics who favored personal interpretation and experience challenged it in the second century.

ALEXANDRIA'S "SCHOOL"

The Mediterranean coast in Egypt proved to be one of the locations attracting Christian thinkers in the second century. Accessible by sea, Alexandria had cultivated philosophical learning and was the place where 700 scholars translated the Hebrew Bible into Greek.[32] Christians established a school of sacred learning there that attracted young men who wanted to dig more deeply into the intricate questions the Scriptures had not expounded.[33] Clement of Alexandria was a respected teacher who prepared the faithful for baptism, and he was succeeded by figures such as Pantaenus and Origen. We will turn briefly to Origen, whose teachings on Christ as the word of God and the relationship of the Father and the Son proved to be both influential and consequential for Orthodox Christianity.[34]

Alexandria produced thinkers known as gnostics. There was no single school or cohort of Christians who subscribed to gnosticism. We tend to use the term gnostics to identify people who believed that people who acquired a specific kind of knowledge would grant them access to God. One of the most notorious gnostics whose teachings circulated and who caused controversy learned in Alexandria. Valentinus was a teacher who probably wrote the Gospel of Truth, claiming that knowledge of God through his son was a gift given to some.[35] Wilken notes that gnostics tended to view the world negatively, as a place alien to Christians, created by a "malevolent deity."[36] This particular notion of the world was alien to the Christian foundation of incarnation and the confession of faith in Christ's humanity.

Origen's context is crucial for understanding why his teaching was adopted and also heavily criticized. Origen was teaching in an environment wrought with confusion about the authority of sources. Valentinian teaching was prevalent in Alexandria, highlighted by Valentinus's notion that the personal experience of God superseded the testimony of the Scriptures.[37] Origen formed a group of disciples in the early third century during a period of fierce persecution of the church.[38] The political and cultural context of third-century Alexandria was difficult and demanding of a Christian teacher.

After a stay in Rome and a return to Alexandria, Origen settled into a life of teaching and writing in Palestine. Origen's teaching emphasized the presence of Christ in the Scriptures and in the Christian people, who see the divine nature in the Word himself and are in a process of becoming Christs that is only perfected at the end of time.[39] Origen insisted that the Word of God was with the Father from the beginning, and his writings emphasize both the humanity and divinity of Christ. Behr states that Origen was averse to describing the son as the same essence of the Father since their relationship was not one of materiality.[40] He insisted on the Son's dependence on the Father and that one could not speak of anyone being in the same class as the Father while maintaining the fullness of the Son's divine nature. Behr notes that Origen's exegesis of Wisdom literature to identify Christ as the Wisdom of God included descriptions of Christ as a creature, although Behr suggests that Origen's language is difficult to interpret.[41]

Behr concludes that Origen's legacy is quite complex since the later condemnations of him and his teaching seem to aim at variants Behr refers to as "Origenism."[42] Origen's activity and broad influence, and the opposition to him in Alexandria and also in Rome, testify to the importance of Alexandria for Orthodoxy's legacy. On the one hand, Origen's early teachings reject ditheism and preserve monotheism while insisting on the eternal activity of Jesus Christ from the beginning, along with the capacity for humans to become like Christ when they receive the Word of God. On the other hand, Origen did not and could not have arrived at the consensus reached at the Council of Nicaea approximately seventy years after his death, and some of his speculations made him a target for accusations of heresy. Origen sheds light on the serious theological problems that challenged the early Christian community and the kind of creative theological thinking that ultimately led to an Orthodox doctrinal consensus in places that became important sacred centers for the Orthodox Church: Alexandria and Palestine.

CONCLUSION: EVOLVING ORTHODOXY

The evidence we have on and from the first 300 years of Christian communal life and thought illustrates a global community with important centers slowly coming into being. Antioch and Alexandria are of particular importance because they were cities that bore witness to the thorniest theological problems and also happened to produce brilliant thinkers who helped the Church arrive at a consensus on its faith in Christ. By no means were Antioch and Alexandria the only important centers, and it would be difficult to argue that Orthodoxy holds them in higher esteem than other sacred sites. Antioch was important from the very beginning because the apostle Peter preached there, Paul and Peter argued there, and the community was first known as Christian in Antioch. The figures and sources presented here, namely Ignatius, Polycarp, and the Didache (the oldest of the church orders), bear witness to the pillars of the Orthodox faith. These pillars are a confession in Jesus Christ as preached by the apostles, the concrete identification of the church as a community that gathers in Eucharist with a presider, and a willingness to remain faithful to the true Christ when challenged (the account of Polycarp's dramatic martyrdom). These pillars of faith survived the troubles of early Christianity and remained the cornerstones of Orthodox Christianity through the imperial age, the Rum Millet, Bolshevik persecution, and the unique challenges confronting the church in this post-modern epoch.

Alexandria was home to one of the first schools of Christian thought and life, building upon its heritage as a philosophical center. Origen's legacy of study, travel, exegesis of Scripture, identification of Christ as the eternal word of God and the word who abides in his disciples exemplifies the kind of creative theology Orthodoxy eventually marshaled to clarify the vexing questions posed on the identity of Christ in the age of the councils. Alexandria symbolizes Orthodoxy's struggle for the pursuit of the truth. The councils because of his speculative cosmology and his hints that the word of God was a creature. Both Alexandria and Antioch were home to theological controversies, as Arius was a native of the Egyptian city, and a third-century council gathered in Antioch to condemn Paul of Samosata for his teaching of Christ's "mere" humanity.[43] The figures who taught and the events that transpired in the two cities led to a convenient categorization of Antioch as the place of a school promoting Christ's humanity, while Alexandria emphasized his divinity. What's important for Orthodoxy is that the communities in both cities bore witness to these pillars of Orthodox Christian faith: a community that confesses Christ as true God and true human, that gathers to remember him as he commanded in Eucharist, and that bears witness to this truth, even to the point of death, for one reason alone – that God loves the world and sends his only-begotten son to it.

NOTES

1 See Jaroslav Pelikan, *The Christian Tradition: A History of the Development of Doctrine*, vol. 1: *The Emergence of the Catholic Doctrine* (100–600) (Chicago, IL: University of Chicago Press, 1971), 109–120. For a sort concise definition, see David Carter, "Apostolic Succession," in *The Oxford Dictionary of the Christian Church* (Oxford: Oxford University Press, 2022). (accessed October 3, 2024).

2 John Zizioulas, *Being as Communion: Studies in Personhood and the Church*, foreword John Meyendorff (Crestwood, NY: St. Vladimir's Seminary Press, 1985, 2002 reprint), 116.

3 Zizioulas, *Being as Communion*, 126–142.

4 See the description of the whole church in one place by John Zizioulas, *Eucharist, Bishop, Church: The Unity of the Church in the Divine Eucharist and the Bishop During the First Three Centuries*, trans. Elizabeth Theotikroff (Brookline, MA: Holy Cross Orthodox Press, 2001), 90–91.

5 Zizioulas, *Being as Communion*, 168.

6 Zizioulas, *Being as Communion*, 133.

7 See Second Vatican Council, "Lumen Gentium," no. 18, Lumen gentium (vatican.va) https://www.vatican.va/archive/hist_councils/ii_vatican_council/documents/vat-ii_const_19641121_lumen-gentium_en.html (accessed October 2, 2024).

8 See paragraph no. 41 in "Ecclesiological and Canonical Consequences for the Sacramental Nature of the Church: Ecclesial Communion, Conciliarity and Authority," Ravenna Document | Ecclesiological and Canonical Consequences of the Sacramental Nature of the Church. Ecclesial Communion, Conciliarity and Authority (christianunity.va) https://www.

christianunity.va/content/unitacristiani/en/dialoghi/sezione-orientale/chiese-ortodosse-di-tradizione-bizantina/commissione-mista-internazionale-per-il-dialogo-teologico-tra-la/documenti-di-dialogo/testo-in-inglese.html (accessed October 23, 2024). This common statement of Catholic and Orthodox theologians is known as "The Ravenna Document."

9 Robert Louis Wilken, *The First Thousand Years: A Global History of Christianity* (New Haven, CT: Yale University Press, 2012), 39.
10 Helmut Löhr, "The Epistles of Ignatius of Antioch," in *The Apostolic Fathers: An Introduction*, ed. Wilhelm Pratcher (Waco, TX: Baylor University Press, 2010), 95.
11 Ignatius of Antioch, *The Apostolic Fathers*, vol. 1, trans. Francis X. Climm et al. (Washington, DC: The Catholic University of America Press, 1962), 118. From the letter to the Smyrneans.
12 Ignatius of Antioch, *The Apostolic Fathers*, 118.
13 Ignatius of Antioch, *The Apostolic Fathers*, 118.
14 Ignatius of Antioch, *The Apostolic Fathers*, 118–119.
15 Ignatius asks rhetorically, "why, then, did I give myself up to death, to fire, to the sword, to the wild beasts," if Christ only appeared to be human? In Ignatius of Antioch, *The Apostolic Fathers*, 119–120.
16 Ignatius of Antioch, *The Apostolic Fathers*, 121.
17 Ignatius of Antioch, *The Apostolic Fathers*, 121.
18 "He did not suffer merely in appearance, as some of the unbelievers say," from Ignatius' letter to the Smyrneans, in *The Apostolic Fathers*, trans. Climm et al., 119.
19 Ignatius of Antioch, *The Apostolic Fathers*, 121.
20 John Behr, *Formation of Christian Theology*, vol. 1: *The Way to Nicaea* (Crestwood, NY: St. Vladimir's Seminary Press, 2001), 83.
21 Behr, *Formation of Christian Theology*, 92.
22 Letter to the Philadelphians, in *The Apostolic Fathers*, trans. Climm et al., 114.
23 R.C.D. Jasper and G.J. Cuming, *Prayers of the Eucharist: Early and Reformed*, 3d ed. (Collegeville, MN: Liturgical Press, 1990), 23–24.
24 Robert Louis Wilken, *The First Thousand Years: A Global History of Christianity* (New Haven, CT: Yale University Press, 2012), 41.
25 *The Apostolic Fathers*, trans. Climm et al., 156.
26 *The Apostolic Fathers*, trans. Climm et al., 157.
27 *The Apostolic Fathers*, trans. Climm et al., 159.
28 *The Apostolic Fathers*, trans. Climm et al., 158.
29 Wilken, The First Thousand Years, 40–41.
30 Wilken, The First Thousand Years, 42.
31 On Irenaeus, see also Wilken, *The First Thousand Years,* 40–46, and Behr, *Formation of Christian Theology,* 129–133.
32 Michael D. Coogan, "Septuagint," in *The Oxford Companion to the Bible* (Oxford: Oxford University Press, 1993). (accessed September 30, 2024).

33 Wilken, *The First Thousand* Years, 39–40.
34 This section follows Behr's presentation in *The Way to Nicaea*, 163–206.
35 Wilken, *The First Thousand Years*, 40.
36 Wilken, *The First Thousand Years*, 40.
37 Wilken, *The First Thousand Years*, 20–22.
38 Wilken, *The First Thousand Years*, 165.
39 Wilken, *The First Thousand Years*, 184.
40 Wilken, *The First Thousand Years*, 187.
41 Wilken, *The First Thousand Years*, 195–196.
42 Wilken, *The First Thousand Years*, 201.
43 Behr, *Formation of Christian* Theology, 213.

HISTORY

Where does one begin writing the history of the Orthodox Church? Orthodoxy defines itself as the one, holy, catholic, and apostolic church, so the typical approach to writing history goes to the very beginning – the birth of Jesus Christ. We will adopt a simpler approach since we have already established that the Orthodox Church prefers to understand herself as the church gathered in a particular place.

The first conciliar gathering of the church was in Jerusalem, in Acts 15, to clarify the requirements for communal belonging and whether or not circumcision was required. A number of other councils took place before the ecumenical councils counted by Orthodoxy, and we need to state quite clearly that most Christians cherish the ecumenical councils. These gatherings were tumultuous and revealed disputes that would come to divide the global Christian community. This next section will explain how certain events within the larger framework of the ecumenical councils came to shape the Orthodox understanding of theology, the church, and authority in the church. I will tell the story from the Orthodox perspective, with a critical view of events, in so much as we know the details of how they unfolded.

The rule governing this presentation is that the Orthodox Church believes that there is one church that gathers in many places throughout the world. Orthodoxy does not begin its definition of church by defining itself as Byzantine, or with reference to the liturgies of Saints Basil and John Chrysostom, or through the aesthetics of icons and differing calendars, even if these features are visible and noticeable traits. A church community that looks and sounds completely different could be Orthodox depending on its profession of faith and concept of the church.

DOI: 10.4324/9781003433217-3

The Roman Catholic Church could be considered a church, and there are some Orthodox who would define the communities of the Roman church as Orthodox, with some revisions to their definitions of faith. The Roman church's use of its own liturgical tradition, the Mass of the Roman Rite, and the iconography of the Roman church are Orthodox. Rigorous adherence to the filioque clause in the Creed and a series of declarations on the ministry of the Pope – especially his universal jurisdiction and the infallibility of his teaching in extraordinary form – are not Orthodox. Let's say, for example, that the Roman church convened a Vatican III council and made decisions to revert to the original text of the Nicene-Constantinopolitan Creed while also removing the Pope's claims to universal jurisdiction and infallibility. The Orthodox Church would be considerably closer to renewing communion with the Roman Catholic Church. The Roman church does not need to adopt the Byzantine rite of liturgy or hold the same liturgical and theological emphases as the Orthodox Church to be "Orthodox."

THE ECUMENICAL COUNCILS

FROM NICAEA (325) TO CHALCEDON (451): AN ORTHODOX INTERPRETATION

The first gathering at the Council of Nicaea (325) already tells us a great deal about different Christian interpretations of the council. The emperor Constantine demanded the convocation of the council to settle the affair concerning Arius, the Alexandrian presbyter who was teaching that Jesus was not equal to God. The Nicene Council took up several other topics, including when one should resume kneeling in church and the method for calculating the date of Pascha. We note here that an emperor convened the council, not the bishop of Rome, a detail that contributes largely to the Orthodox interpretation of this council.

The emperor Constantine moved the imperial capital east to the coast of the Sea of Marmara. The new capital took on the name of Constantinople, after the emperor who founded it, and was also known as the new Rome. Constantine's legalization of Christianity in 313 CE and the ensuing growth of Christianity eventually resulted in the Roman Empire's adoption of Christianity. Constantinople became a new center of pilgrimage and gathering, often at the expense of the imperial budget, so it also grew into a major Christian metropolis quite quickly. Constantinople rivaled the authority Rome had previously as the place of the martyrdom of the apostles Peter and Paul. Alexandria retained its reputation as a place of learning and as a metropolis near the Egyptian monastic movement.

The theological controversies that catalyzed the next three ecumenical councils tested Christianity's acceptance of communities in major metropolises that carried the authority of their apostolic founders. Alexandria continued to be one of the hotspots of prominent church leaders with large parties accompanying them. The second ecumenical council took place in 381 in Constantinople. The bishop of the imperial city at the time was Gregory of Nazianzus, and the council adopted Gregory's teaching that the Holy Spirit proceeds from the Father.[1]

The council's adoption of Gregory's teaching and their stamp of approval by adding it to the existing Nicene Creed is a detail that is often forgotten in our view of church history. Gregory's teaching was his and his alone until the entire church adopted it in the conciliar gathering. This essential fact reveals a core tenet of Orthodoxy – no theologian produces anything on his own or by his own authority. The first council in Constantinople ratified the rising authority of the city of Constantinople by designating it as the new Rome, enjoying privileges of "honor' after the bishop of Rome.[2] The Council of Constantinople also expressed its continuity with the council in Nicaea in canon 1, a core value of Orthodoxy – the church does not undo what it had done before but upholds and sustains it.[3]

The next theological controversy necessitating an ecumenical council took place in 431, in Ephesus. The primary problem necessitating this council was the teaching of Nestorius, the archbishop of Constantinople. Nestorius was trying to explain the difficult teaching of Christ's two natures, human and divine. A fervent cult devoted to the Virgin Mary had become established in Constantinople, and they referred to Mary as Theotokos – mother of God. Nestorius wanted to defend God against anthropomorphizing tendencies and worried that claiming Mary had given birth to God instead of Christ or Jesus could lead to further humanizations of God, especially those of emotion or suffering. Nestorius' teaching exacerbated an existing problem about Christ. His steadfast defense of Christ's divine nature suggested that two different persons coexisted in one body, the word of God and Jesus being two different persons.

Nestorius' teaching became unpopular with many, including the empress Pulcheria, who was an advocate of the cult of Mary in Constantinople. Cyril, bishop of Alexandria, took on Nestorius in the dispute to preserve the tradition of veneration that had emerged among the people. The dispute concerned the bishops of Constantinople and Alexandria and came to involve appeals to neighboring sees, such as Antioch and Rome.

The Council in Ephesus (431) supported Cyril's position. John McGuckin notes Cyril's meticulous preparation to support his argument during the council.[4] He brought a corpus of testimony with him to show that the teaching he asserted was anchored in apostolic tradition and therefore belonged to the church. McGuckin notes that Cyril's documented support for his arguments became part of Orthodox and Catholic tradition. Here, we will note two things. First, Constantinople's prestige did not prevent a theologian from a smaller metropolis from challenging a false or misleading teaching, even if Alexandria was vulnerable to imperial politics. Second, Cyril's teaching was the church's teaching and became official doctrine once the entire church adopted it. It was never about Cyril, but Cyril's investigation of the church's beliefs and practices that led him to his assertions. Cyril insisted on the unity of Christ, stating that the church confessed faith in one "Christ and in one Lord" without worshipping the human nature.[5]

Another dynamic we will note here is the interplay of political positioning and the perception of apostolic sees and their authority. The state had involved itself in church affairs, and political dignitaries did not hesitate to enter the fray. Heretical and schismatic groups did not simply hang their heads and walk away – they appealed to the emperor for assistance, and Emperor Constantine exiled Athanasius of Alexandria early in his tenure, in 335 CE, just after the Council of Nicaea.[6]

The exile of the bishop of one of the most important Christian metropolises reveals the instability characterizing the church during this time. The Orthodox Church views correct theology as providing stability and righting the course of the church, even if it took some time to arrive at that point. It takes time, though, for the church to commit to correct theology. The Council of Ephesus functioned as one of the breaking points when followers of Nestorius did not agree to the conciliar declarations. A handful of Nestorian communities continue to exist today, primarily in the Middle East.

Cyril's steadfast defense of right theology did not resolve the debate on how Jesus Christ's two natures came together in one person. The dispute on Christ raged, boiling over with the teaching of Eutychius that Christ had one nature, both divine and human. Once again, the parties involved began to appeal to other bishops, especially when Bishop Flavian of Constantinople removed Eutychius from the ranks of the clergy.[7] Emperor Theodosius asked for the convocation of a second council in Ephesus, and it took place under the presidency of Dioscurus of Alexandria. Pope Leo of Rome had sent several letters to the council, and he explained his understanding of Christ's two natures in Letter 28, which became known as the Tome of Leo.[8] The council reported that Eutychius had accepted the Nicene faith and was reinstated, but that Leo's tome was not read, so Leo declared the council to be illegitimate and pushed for yet another meeting.[9]

This council took place in Chalcedon two years later, in 451. Drama consumed this council as well, with a new emperor in place, Rome under attack, and Pope Leo trying to impose his theological understanding of Christ's two natures on the council, while he also resisted the proposal of making the church of Constantinople equal to Rome.[10] Leo did not attend the council but sent a delegation from Rome. The council's first declaration was its confession of faith in Christ.[11]

The Council of Chalcedon mentions the two versions of the Creed that defined the church's confession of faith in Jesus Christ at the Council of Nicaea and then one at Constantinople, granting pre-eminence to the confessions of these two councils. The purpose of this kind of statement is to indicate that Chalcedon is in continuity with the teachings of previous councils and is not annulling them in any way.[12] Chalcedon also granted additional privileges to the church of Constantinople by permitting a cleric or bishop in a dispute with the metropolitan to appeal to the archbishop of Constantinople in canons 9 and 17.[13] The council in Chalcedon increased the authority of Constantinople, building upon the council of 381 by stating that the church should grant the see of Constantinople the same authority enjoyed by the church in Rome on account of the imperial prestige of the capital. Canon 28 essentially elevated the church in Constantinople, an act that reconfigured the evolving power structure in the Christian church.[14]

The Council of Chalcedon leaves a complicated legacy. On the one hand, the council's attempt to clarify remaining confusion on Christ's natures and person by adding precise language functioned as one of the pillars of Christian faith held by Catholics, Orthodox, and Protestants. On the other hand, disagreements among Christians had simmered before the council and established a divisive tone for the period following. Christians in Egypt, Armenia, and Syria rejected the Council of Chalcedon, creating a schism that remains in place to this day. Furthermore, the church of Rome rejected the new privileges granted to the church of Constantinople, revealing a rivalry for authority that also persists to this day. Another dimension of canon 28 of Chalcedon is less known but equally significant. There is significant disagreement among Orthodox on just what kinds of privileges the church of Constantinople enjoys. It is an issue that came to a head in the early twenty-first century when the Russian Orthodox Church broke communion with Constantinople and all of the churches that supported its creation of a new Orthodox Church in Ukraine, an issue I will cover a bit later.

NON-CHALCEDONIAN ORTHODOX CHRISTIANITY

The rejection of the Council of Chalcedon was experienced most bitterly in Egypt. It is essential to keep in mind the central role of Alexandria in upholding and clarifying Orthodox faith. Athanasius was the chief ideologue behind the composition of the Creed at Nicaea, and Cyril's refutation of Nestorius's confusing Christology set the tone for the Council of Ephesus. Athanasius's reward for his orthodoxy was exile, on multiple occasions, by the decrees of emperors who succumbed to Arian complaints and appeals.

Cyril's definition of one Christ and one Lord left limited wiggle room for explaining the semantics of two natures coming together in one person. The Egyptian Christians resisted Chalcedon's attempt to clarify a point they believed had been settled definitively and authoritatively by Cyril and the council in Ephesus. The Council of Chalcedon occurred during a time of competing priorities for the bishop of Rome (Leo), the emperor, and the bishop of Alexandria. Rome was under siege, its political power removed with the migration of the empire eastward, and its church authority challenged by the new privileges granted to Constantinople. The Egyptians had risen to the occasion to maintain the orthodoxy of the church, and the empire had betrayed them, so they did not trust the imperial apparatus. Everything came to a head with Chalcedon when Pope Leo attempted to use his authority to force the Egyptians to accept the conciliar declarations. The Egyptians resisted with violence, rejected the exile of their elected patriarchs, and refused to accept both the Chalcedonian definition of the faith and the bishops the empire attempted to impose upon them.[15]

In the late fifth and early sixth centuries, a series of political events transpired that led to a brief attempt to resolve the issue. It began with an annulment of both the Tome of Leo and the Council of Chalcedon, but this did not satisfy the archbishop of Constantinople, who did not want to relinquish the new privileges Chalcedon had granted to his church.[16] Emperor Zeno issued a *henotikon* that essentially upheld the teachings of the first three ecumenical councils but excluded the Chalcedonian definition of faith.[17] The Church of Armenia affirmed the *henotikon* and expressed its allegiance to the first three ecumenical councils while rejecting the teachings of Nestorius and the Council of Chalcedon.[18] Once again, the bishop of Rome refuted the *henotikon*, and a new emperor (Justin) also rejected it in 519.[19]

Succeeding Roman emperors attempted to impose Chalcedonian Christology on non-Chalcedonian Christians in Egypt, Armenia, and Syria. The emperor Justinian used the power of his throne to depose the archbishop of Alexandria in the sixth century.[20] Justinian's wife, Empress Theodora, was the daughter of a miaphysite priest and used her influence to protect non-Chalcedonian Christians in the empire, despite the impetus to coerce them into union with the Eastern Orthodox.[21] The Roman Empire's decline began in the sixth century and accelerated in the seventh, with two external forces establishing power in the Middle East – the Persians and the Arabs. The empire and bishops of both Romes failed in their quest to use coercion to sway the non-Chalcedonian Christians, and were then unable to reach them since the communities in Egypt and Syria were no longer ruled by the Roman Empire.

ORIENTAL ORTHODOX AND MIAPHYSITE CHRISTOLOGY

Historians and theologians use a number of different words to describe Christians that belong to communities that reject the Council of Chalcedon. "Oriental" is the word most often used to describe this loosely affiliated group of churches, probably to differentiate them from the Byzantine or Eastern Orthodox. "Non-Chalcedonian" is one of the terms used to describe these churches that adhere to the first three ecumenical councils but consistently rejected the Council of Chalcedon for theological reasons. Theologians have also used the terms "monophysite" and "miaphysite" to describe the communities that rejected the Council of Chalcedon, and we will use "miaphysite" in this book. Miaphysites profess one nature in Christ (as opposed to the diaphysite doctrine of the Council of Chalcedon – two natures). The people of these communities believe that Christ is both human and the only-begotten son of God. They object to the semantics of speaking of two natures because of the problems caused by suggesting that Christ had multiple personalities.

Our analysis here has focused on the Christians in Egypt, and they are one of three major families of "miaphysite" churches now known as the Coptic Orthodox Church. The Coptic church has a patriarch of Alexandria who also bears the title of Pope, so there are two churches anchored in Alexandria: the Orthodox Patriarchate of Alexandria (Chalcedonian) and the larger Coptic church (miaphysite). We have also alluded briefly to the Christians in Armenia, who also rejected the definition of faith of the Council of Chalcedon. Armenian rejection of Chalcedon was ratified with the breaking of communion with Greek Christians in 555 and with the Church in neighboring Georgia in 608–609.[22]

The Syrian Christian tradition may be the most complicated one, as they have multiple allegiances and associations. The Syrian Orthodox Church rejects the Council of Chalcedon along with the Armenians and the Copts. They are occasionally known as the Jacobite church as well.[23] The Syrian Orthodox Church is not the same as the Patriarchate of Antioch, which accepts the Chalcedonian faith. The Antiochian Orthodox are also occasionally known as Melkites because of their fidelity to the Roman Empire. Some of the Melkites entered into communion with the Roman Catholic Church in 1724, long after the split of the Orthodox and Catholic Churches (more on this to come soon). There is also a Maronite church, named after the founder of a monastery in Bet Maroun. This church maintained strong relations with Rome and was eventually Latinized. A number of Christian communities in Southern India were originally governed by the patriarch of the Church of the East but have formed into eight different church communities, all Chalcedonian, and some in communion with Rome.[24]

The Ethiopian Orthodox Church is the largest of all the Oriental Orthodox Churches, with approximately 36 million faithful comprising 43% of Ethiopia's population.[25] Ethiopian Orthodox trace their origins to the eunuch of Ethiopian Queen Candace (Acts 8:26–30), and in terms of the appointment of a bishop, to the late fourth century, when none other than Athanasius ordained Frumentius bishop of the Ethiopians.[26] The Ethiopian church depended on the Coptic church for bishops for much of its history until 1959, when the Coptic church granted them independence. In 1991, the Eritrean Orthodox Church separated from the Ethiopian church, in conjunction with Eritrea's national independence. The Ethiopian and Eritrean churches observe unique Judaic customs, such as the weekly Sabbath and circumcision of males, based likely on a close interpretation of the Old Testament.[27]

The Oriental family of churches – Coptic, Armenian, Syrian, Ethiopian, and Eritrean – tend to have mutually exclusive customs because they developed internally and outside of the orbit of the Roman Empire. Some of the churches do have elements of Byzantine and Latin customs – especially the churches that maintained strong connections with Latin missionaries that established communities nearby, like the Maronite church. The existence of these churches in environments as religious minorities with occasional periods of persecution resulted in resilient emigre communities and a strong sense of national identity in the church. For example, the Armenian genocide carried out by the Ottoman Turks in 1915 and followed by a long period of Soviet repression of religion led to Armenian émigré communities functioning as outposts for the retention of religious, cultural, and political practices. The Oriental churches have maintained their christological viewpoints throughout their histories of persecution, isolation, and migration, though segments of their communities united with the Roman Catholic Church.

The history of the development of the Oriental churches reveals the sharp divisions on the precise language used to describe Jesus Christ as both God and human within the Christian community and the historical role of the state in attempting to coerce non-Chalcedonian groups into their version of Orthodoxy. Theological consultations have made significant progress in bridging the gap between the Oriental and Eastern Orthodox in the twentieth century and beyond, but at the official level, the churches remain separated. The Eastern Orthodox insistence that councils are the highest authority in the church and all succeeding councils retain and sustain previous teachings is an obstacle to unity.

ICONOCLASM, THE SEVENTH ECUMENICAL COUNCIL, AND THE TRIUMPH OF ORTHODOXY

The fifth and sixth ecumenical councils continued to deal with christological issues. Emperor Justinian insisted on the convocation of the second council in Constantinople in 553, with its primary purpose to condemn Theodore, bishop of Mopsuestia, for allegedly claiming that the word of God and the human Jesus were two distinct persons. The council was significant for a number of reasons. We highlight consistency with a pattern established with the second council of Constantinople – the text of the fifth ecumenical council validates the theology of the preceding councils and states its continuity with their teachings.[28] The political environment of the council included the emperor Justinian placing immense pressure on Pope Vigilius to approve its convocation. This small detail is noteworthy because tensions between the state and religious actors – especially the emperor and the bishops of old and new Rome – are manifest in the negotiations leading up to the council.[29]

Imperial and church politics contributed to the shaping of the sixth ecumenical council, which convened in Constantinople in 680–681. Emperor Constantine IV sought to put an end to the monothelite controversy – the teaching that Christ had one will, even though he had two natures. Emperor Heraclius sought to reunite the church and was willing to concede the teaching that

Christ's divine nature alone directed both his activity (monoenergism) and his will (monothelitism). Maximus, a monk in Constantinople, fervently opposed this teaching, arguing that Christ's episode in the garden of Gethsemane revealed his voluntary submission of the human will to the divine. The emperor and patriarch of Constantinople punished Maximus with torture for his teaching, with such cruelty that they reportedly amputated his tongue and his right hand.[30] Maximus's opposition to theologies that would compromise the doctrine of Chalcedon is notable because it comes from a monk.

The seventh ecumenical council was held in Nicaea in 787 following periods of iconoclasm directed by emperors and patriarchs of Constantinople. The decline of the Roman Empire, its inability to respond to Arabic victories led to an internal question of theodicy: was God punishing the Christian empire for its misdeeds, and if so, what had they done to offend God? The emperor Leo confronted these questions and found a bishop, Constantine, who argued that the veneration of icons had violated God's commandment and had displeased God.[31]

Iconoclastic emperors and patriarchs removed icons from the churches, arguing that the cross, the celebration of the liturgy itself, and the consecrated bread and wine were the authentic symbols denoting divine presence.[32] Bishops were able to enforce the removal of images through parish clergy, but laity and monks were able to sustain the practice of icon veneration within the privacy of their homes and cells.

Once again, monasteries produced the theologians who wrote the apologies in favor of restoring the veneration of icons. John of Damascus and Theodore the Studite are the two best-known defenders of icon veneration, and they came from different environments. John wrote from St. Sabas monastery in Palestine, where he was accustomed to theological jousting with Islamic interlocutors. Theodore was the abbot of the Studite monastery in urban Constantinople.

The iconoclastic controversy took place in two waves. The first wave ended when the empress Irene convened a council in 787 to restore icon veneration. The council used the theology of John of Damascus to restore icons and call for their veneration in churches, public, and domestic settings – essentially everywhere.[33] The seventh council's definition also made an important clarification – venerating the image is a way of expressing honor for the person depicted in the image.[34] The council drew from the teaching of John of Damascus and also cited Basil of Caesarea, who had distinguished *latreia* as worship offered to God alone from *proskynesis*, veneration for other holy and pious people.[35]

The seventh ecumenical council did not stop the cycle of iconoclastic emperors. Another wave of iconoclasm surged in 813 with Emperor Leo V and ceased only when Empress Theodora oversaw the restoration of icons in 843. This restoration occasioned the appointment of the first Sunday of Lent as the one of Orthodoxy, the victory of icon veneration, one that persists until this day. It is noteworthy that two Orthodox women, the empresses Irene and Theodora, led the Orthodox Church to defend its Christology and defeat the iconoclasts. The seventh ecumenical council remained consistent with its predecessors in referring to the initial councils and their confessions of faith. The definition upholds the Christology of the incarnation of Christ and legitimizes the private and public rituals of worshipping God and venerating saints through the mediation of art.

OBSERVATIONS ON ORTHODOXY'S RECEPTION
OF THE ECUMENICAL COUNCILS

The Orthodox Church receives the first seven ecumenical councils as legitimate. A number of patterns emerge that reveal what's central to Orthodox faith in this survey of the conciliar tradition. The first issue is Christology, going to great pains to ensure that the church is confessing Christ as he was preached and revealed by the apostles. The details on Christ's identity as God and human being are defined with precision and passion in these seven ecumenical councils.

The second issue concerns the resolution of disputes. These disagreements cause problems from the very beginning, when the first council in Nicaea refutes Arius and defines Christ as true God and true human. The council did not eliminate Arian teachings, as evidenced by Arian appeals to the emperor to punish Athanasius. Egyptian rejection of the definition of the Council of Chalcedon is our most glaring problem because it has never been completely resolved, despite numerous attempts to reach a common understanding, from the decades following the council up until the present day.

Orthodoxy's affirmation of the ecumenical councils and devotion to continuing the anathemetizing of the heretics raises a sensitive question discussed mostly among historians and theologians in the academy. The church knows of the writings and teachings of these heretics almost exclusively through the lens of the church leaders who gathered at the councils. Most of the works of figures like Theodore of Mopsuestia, declared a heretic at the fifth ecumenical council, were destroyed. A handful of Theodore's works survived because they were translated into languages and preserved by communities outside of the Chalcedonian ones. To be fair, the majority of Orthodox people are probably unaware of these teachers and their writings. Nevertheless, the Church presents a view of people and their teachings without directly engaging their writings. In this sense, history from the perspective of Christian communities, including Orthodox, is written by the victors and is not critical.

The third issue concerns the motives underpinning the convocation of councils. We see a delicate evolution from the first to the seventh ecumenical councils within the exchanges of the emperor, the pope of Rome, the patriarch of Constantinople, and other religious actors. Imperial rulers convened the ecumenical councils, which took place in the East, near the imperial capital. Rulers were motivated by political designs to maintain stability and mitigate potential vulnerabilities among the people. Constantine essentially demands the convocation of the council in Nicaea because of the discord Arianism is creating among the populace. Diarmaid MacCulloch suggests that the empress Irene convened the seventh ecumenical council because she wanted to challenge the imperial and ecclesial establishment and set her own tone – not because of her own personal spiritual and theological convictions.[36] We see similar aspirations with Zeno's failed attempt to bridge the gap between Chalcedonians and miaphysites with the *henotikon* and the emperor Heraclius's and patriarch Sergius's attempt to use monothelitism as a means of reunification. State officials involved themselves in church affairs to achieve political objectives, including maintaining order, eliminating troublemakers, appeasing constituencies, protecting borders, and expanding them.

The conciliar proceedings bear witness to power struggles among the primary metropolises of the church. Constantinople's prestige grew because of its affiliation with the imperial court and its identity as the new Rome, receiving new privileges at the councils of Constantinople (381) and Chalcedon (451). The imperial capital's ascendancy threatened the primacy of Rome, which no longer enjoys an imperial apparatus to grant it support. Alexandria produced the theologians who took the lead in delivering arguments and writing definitions for the church, but when the emperor exiled Athanasius and used violence to end the protests at Chalcedon, the state minimized Alexandria, an important religious center in Orthodoxy, because it wasn't cooperating with the state's agenda. This seemingly small detail is important because, again, the Orthodox view of history depicts the Egyptians who rejected Chalcedon as being on the wrong side of history, but this version of the story does not consider the possibility that they were pawns in a larger geopolitical project.

Orthodoxy's loyal adherence to the declarations of the councils has complicated healthy administration of the church in the modern age. Imperial patronage was a two-edged sword, especially when emperors attempted to use coercion to achieve their objectives, but the imperial apparatus made the convocation of church-wide councils possible. The mere mentioning of the association of the church with the emperor and the imperial senate in canon 28 of the Council of Chalcedon manifests that church's relationship with the Roman Empire during the era of the councils.[37]

Two irreconcilable realities come together in Orthodoxy's veneration of the ecumenical councils as preserving the church's faith and unity. The Orthodox Church believes that the councils resolved the disputed issues when, in fact, many of them remained unresolved, especially the Council of Chalcedon. Orthodoxy's faithful adherence to the teachings of the ecumenical councils leads to the church's claim that they alone possess the truth and are therefore *the* one, holy, catholic, and apostolic church. The winners have the privilege of writing their version of history. In the case of those on the losing side of theological disputes, we have limited access to their history because much of it has been lost or destroyed. An honest reading of history beckons us to consider all sides of a story. In this instance, Orthodoxy's elevation to the first seven ecumenical councils to an exalted status reveals the community's sincere belief that they have inherited the repository of the truth about God from the fathers who gathered at these first seven ecumenical councils.

ORTHODOXY IN 900–1204: EVANGELIZATION, SCHISM, CONFLICT WITH ROME

Our examination of Orthodox history has focused on the regions of its original metropolises. We have seen how Christian communities grew in centers such as Antioch, Alexandria, and Rome, with some of the most famous apostles and theologians leaving their marks in these cities. We have also heard about the founders of church communities in other places.

The Orthodox Church teaches that the apostle and evangelist Mark founded the communities in Alexandria. In some instances, an existing Christian community appointed a bishop to found and organize church life elsewhere, as we saw with Athanasius's ordination of a bishop for Ethiopia. Christian communities in Armenia formed and expanded under the steady leadership of Gregory the Enlightener. He was ordained for ministry to the Armenians in Caesarea in Cappadocia, another important Christian center of late antiquity.[38] Christianity came to Georgia also in the fourth century, when the prophetess Nino went to Georgia from Jerusalem.[39]

Orthodox Christianity took an important step in expansion in the ninth century when Patriarch Photios sent two monks, Cyril and Methodius, to evangelize the khagan of the Khazars.[40] The Khazars did not accept Christianity, but Prince Rastislav of Moravia invited the two monks to evangelize his people.[41]

The people of Moravia were receptive to the preaching of Cyril and Methodius, and the two monks determined that the people should be able to practice their faith by hearing the preaching and praying the liturgy in their own native language. Cyril and Methodius essentially invented the Cyrillic alphabet, which became the core of the language for liturgy that neighboring Slavic peoples would adopt when they became Christian.[42]

Southern Slavic peoples began to take on Christianity. The Bulgarian tsar Boris became Christian but wanted the community of Christians under his rule to be autonomous and not subservient to Constantinople.[43] Boris approached Pope Nicholas I of Rome and exacerbated a rapidly brewing dispute between Rome and Constantinople, since Nicholas had not recognized Photios as the rightful patriarch of Constantinople and also desired greater authority over worldly church affairs.[44] Nicholas discouraged Boris from remaining within the Greek church, criticized its practices, and sent legates to the Bulgarian tsar. Boris, for his part, realized quickly that the pope would not grant his church an autonomous head, so he accepted Constantinopolitan jurisdiction at a council in the imperial city in 869–870.

The Slavs of Rus' and Serbia were among the converts to Orthodox Christianity who inherited the missionary legacy of the monks Cyril and Methodius. Orthodox missionary activity extended to Serbs that had settled in the Balkans in the ninth century. Church life developed and expanded among the Serbs during the rule of Stefan Nemanja in the twelfth century, with the dedication of churches and monasteries.[45] The creation of the Hilandar monastery created a connection between Byzantine and Serbian monasticism. Stefan's son, Sava, cofounded the monastery on Athos with Stefan, and Sava became the most beloved figure of Serbian church history, spending most of his life in Serbia, becoming its first autocephalous archbishop, and creating a collection of legislative texts that would contribute to the governance of medieval Serbian life.[46] Sava is an example of innovative Slavic adaptation of Orthodox Christianity and its application to church and state administration.

Constantinople encountered the peoples of Rus' in their commerce and wanted to establish a mission in Kyiv. The formal association with Constantinople begins with the baptism of the Kyivan Princess Olga in the imperial city in 955–956.[47] Bryn Geffert and Theofanis Stavrou suggest that Olga had political objectives, desiring to strengthen ties and increase trade opportunities with the empire.[48] The Orthodox Church had missionaries in Kyiv, but Olga's son Sviatoslav remained a pagan, as did her grandson, Yaropolk. Volodymyr, Olga's other son, arranged for the baptism of the people in Kyiv after his own baptism in Cherson in 988.[49]

The adoption of Orthodox Christianity by Kyivan Rus' illustrates a type of blueprint for the missionary activity created by the patriarchate of Constantinople in the ninth century. Constantinople made arrangements with the ruler of the people for their baptism and then sent missionaries into their land to initiate them into church life, primarily through the liturgy and the Orthodox spiritual practices of daily life. A monastery became the primary Christian center of Kyivan church life: the Kyiv Pechers'ka Lavra, established by the hermit monk Antony and further developed by Theodosius, who created a community from the monks living in cave cells.[50]

The missionary activity that established Orthodoxy in Rus' depended largely on the consistency of liturgical and monastic life. Sean Griffin writes that the ritual introduced to the people of Rus' in the tenth and eleventh centuries had been cultivated during ten centuries of "Christian myth-making."[51] The liturgy itself was able to narrate the unique history of Orthodoxy, from its origins, through the early christological controversies, and beyond the triumph of Orthodoxy with the restoration of icons. The role of iconography and chant is crucial here, given the passing on of textual traditions to the literate elite. Ordinary people learned about the fundamentals of their new religious tradition in the stories told by the Gospels and hymns sung in church and depicted for them in the iconography that had come to decorate the entire interior of the church in the middle of the ninth century.

The Slavs adopted Orthodox Christianity during a period of slow decline in the Roman Empire. Persian and Arab invasions had isolated many non-Chalcedonian Christian communities from Constantinople. The new Christians knew of them only through the eyes of the Greeks who had brought them Orthodoxy. New disputes and invasions would shape the Orthodox interpretation of history, beginning in the eleventh century. Despite the challenges confronting the empire, the church of Constantinople remained at the center of the orbit of Orthodox churches in the world because it had essentially planted the new churches in the Slavic lands.

THE FOURTH CRUSADE TO THE FALL OF CONSTANTINOPLE (1204–1453): NEW CENTERS

This survey of Orthodox history has already provided examples of episodes of tension between Rome and Constantinople. Rome objected to the new privileges given to Constantinople at the Council of Chalcedon, the city of Rome did not enjoy imperial security, and the schism between Pope Nicholas I and Patriarch Photios of Constantinople foreshadowed the full-blown crisis to come. Nicholas had not recognized Photios's legitimacy, and *Tsar* Boris of Bulgaria had manipulated the two prelates in an attempt to make his own church autonomous. Photios condemned the Church in Rome in 867 because of its introduction of the filioque clause into the Nicene-Constantinopolitan Creed, a practice that originated in sixth-century Spain and became more predominant in the ninth century.[52]

The position of the Church in Rome began to improve in the late eighth and early ninth century with the rise of Charlemagne and his Holy Roman Empire. Charlemagne's stabilizing efforts emboldened the Church of Rome, which resumed its practices of asserting its authority. Roman church officials attempted to Latinize parish communities in Southern Italy that had retained Byzantine Orthodox ritual practices. Patriarch Michael Cerularius objected to the Roman attempt to impose the use of unleavened bread in the liturgy and sent a letter condemning the practice to all the bishops in the West.[53] Pope Leo and his secretary, Cardinal Humbert, received the letter angrily and responded with a scathing letter of anathematization invoked upon Patriarch Michael and his assistants.[54] The patriarch of Constantinople and the synod responded with their own grievances of Roman abuses and anathematized Pope Leo, returning fire with fire.[55]

Almost all historical anthologies refer to the mutual excommunications of 1054 as the Great Schism. Those looking further into the event do not reach this conclusion. The church communities under the large umbrellas of Rome and Constantinople did not know that they had broken communion. The mutual edicts, however, not only entered into the historical annals of church discipline but were also never annulled or recanted by representatives of the two churches, at least until 1964. Furthermore, the letters of excommunication exchanged between Constantinople and Rome mentioned a number of abuses each church had allegedly committed, including the aforementioned disagreement on the kind of bread to be used for the liturgy – the Romans used unleavened bread, and the Orthodox leavened – to the filioque clause in the Creed. The anathemas magnified these issues, making some of them much more difficult to overcome than they might have been had the unpleasant affair not taken place.

This raises a reasonable question: what, then, sealed the division between the Roman and Orthodox Churches? It was the crusade of 1204 when crusaders sacked Constantinople and occupied it for fifty-seven years. The crusaders had arrived in Venice to be transported to Jerusalem, in a quest blessed by Pope Innocent III, to recapture the holy city. When the smaller number of troops was unable to meet the Venetians' price for the voyage, the exiled emperor Alexius IV offered to pay 8,000 soldiers to retake Constantinople and reinstall him as emperor. The imperial city refused to receive the exiled emperor, so the contingent laid siege to the city and viciously ransacked it.

The Western invaders looted Constantinople and installed both a Latin emperor and patriarch, an occupation that lasted until 1261 when imperial noblemen residing in Nicaea recaptured Constantinople.[56] The Roman Empire did not simply pick up where it had left off, however, given the number of decades that had elapsed during the Latin occupation. Mount Athos had become the new spiritual center of Orthodoxy, and the Slavic Orthodox Churches began to assert their autonomy.[57]

The Latin occupation of Constantinople was not permanent, but the memory of the event and its details entered into Orthodox historical memory, especially among the Greeks. Greeks held such a fierce grudge against the Latins for the violence of the Fourth Crusade that they have never forgiven them, even when Pope John Paul II attempted to apologize sincerely before the Greek people for the crime committed by others some 800 years earlier when he visited Athens in 2001.[58]

The alienation of Western and Eastern Christians, then, cannot be reduced to one single event. Misunderstandings originated because Greeks and Latins did not encounter one another often and did not speak the same language. The literal separation of the church communities occasionally caused confusion when they actually encountered one another, as we see with Rome's aversion to the use of leavened bread in the liturgy in Southern Italy. Heated disputes initially deepened both alienation and mistrust between them, and the use of violence broke the proverbial dam. The seeds of mistrust and enmity had been planted and would prevent efforts for reunion in subsequent centuries.

INTERLUDE: FAILED UNION, THE COUNCIL OF FLORENCE-FERRARA (1438–1439), AND UNIATISM

In the early fifteenth century, the Roman Empire was shrinking in the shadow of the rise of the Ottomans. Constantinople remained the nominal center of the Eastern Orthodox Christian world, but its liturgical traditions had faded and were maintained in Thessalonika. Mount Athos had become the primary spiritual cell of

Eastern Orthodoxy. In a last-ditch effort to preserve the empire and thwart the advancing Ottomans, the emperor sought reunion with the church of Rome, along with military assistance from the West. Assistance in the effort to defend Constantinople from the Ottomans was unlikely, given the humiliating defeat a large army of Westerners had suffered at the hands of the Turks in 1396.[59] Nevertheless, political and religious leaders of the West realized that they, too, were vulnerable to an Ottoman advancement.

A council convened in Ferrara in 1438 and consisted of an impressive number of representatives, with over 700 from Constantinople alone.[60] Readers should note that the council began in 1431 in Basel, consisting only of delegates of the Western church.[61] The council moved from Ferrara to Florence in 1439 because of a severe plague outbreak.[62] The churches of Rome and Constantinople agreed to union in 1439 in Florence, claiming that they had resolved all of their disputes.[63] The council addressed the filioque issue by reviewing the claims of both the Latins and the Greeks and formally adopted the filioque clause for the whole, newly reunited church.[64] The council also upheld the doctrine of purgatory, permitted the use of both unleavened and leavened bread for the Eucharist, and defined the pope as holding universal jurisdiction over the entire church.[65] The Orthodox delegation agreed to these declarations, a complicated state of affairs since Patriarch Joseph of Constantinople died while the council was in session.[66]

Almost all of the Orthodox delegates signed the agreement with the Latins in Florence. Bishop Mark of Ephesus refused to sign and allegedly claimed that the Latin position was heretical, in disagreement with many of his fellow Orthodox delegates.[67] The Council of Florence-Ferrara has a complicated legacy. The political backdrop to the council is not surprising. The ecumenical councils of the past were often convened to resolve theological disputes that had caused problems. Leaders of the delegations of East and West hoped that reunion could prove mutually beneficial in marshaling military resources to repeal Ottoman attacks. The military aspirations of both East and West fell through.[68] The imperial remnant in Constantinople was inconsistent in its reception of the Florentine council. The rest of the Orthodox world did not receive it, with the expulsion of Metropolitan Isidore of Moscow in 1441 the most notorious incident of the public's apparent rejection of the union.[69]

In terms of church reunion, the council failed to achieve a lasting reunion of the Catholic and Orthodox Churches. The terms of the council strongly favored the Roman Catholic position, especially the declaration of the pope's universal jurisdiction over the global church. Constantinople attempted to maintain the union with the Roman church in fits and starts, but it never held in Orthodoxy, though a form of union returned late in the sixteenth century. The deep lack of trust embedded in Orthodox historical memory prevented Orthodox, for their part, from accepting the union. Aversion to entering into dialogue with Catholics on the possibility of reunion remains in force for the majority of Orthodox today, largely because of Orthodoxy's version of the sequence of events that transpired from the Great Schism until the fall of Constantinople in 1453.

ORTHODOXY IN THE RUM MILLET

The fall of Constantinople brought many of the world's Orthodox Christians under the direct rule of the sultan, the head of the Ottoman Empire. Islam respected Christians as people of the book and permitted them to gather and worship, with certain prohibitions, such as not proselytizing Muslims. The Ottomans viewed their new Greek subjects as "Rum millet," the people of the Roman nation.

The patriarch of Constantinople took on a new role during the long period of the Rum millet. His duties expanded to include directly ruling over the people, tax collection, and adjudication on behalf of the sultan, so patriarchal clothing actually came to resemble the emperor's official vestments.[70] The patriarch had jurisdiction over all Christians within the Ottoman realm. This non-territorial arrangement meant that at some points, the patriarch of Constantinople ruled over the Greek Orthodox community that had belonged to the patriarchate, along with Serbs, Bulgarians, Albanians, Romanians, Moldovans, and even Coptic Christians.[71] Patriarchs used their new authority to populate their administrative apparatuses with their own people. Practically speaking, the patriarch of Constantinople was overseeing a broad expanse of Christians of multiple nations and regions. The tendency for the patriarch to favor Greeks and Hellenize other ethnic groups displeased people of other communities, including Bulgarians.[72]

Greece became independent in 1825, and the new government initiated a plan to create an independent Greek national church.[73] The ruling government was averse to the notion of having a majority church under the jurisdiction of a patriarch who was also a civil servant of the Ottoman Empire.[74] The new Greek republic was also in the difficult process of writing a meta-narrative that would bring together the legacies of ancient Greece and aspects of the Byzantine period. Depending on the Byzantine legacy and the memory of Constantinople alone would not serve the people's needs in the environment of nation-states and increased economic competition.

Greece was not the only new country to seek its own autocephalous church. The Bulgarians began to request greater autonomy in their church toward the end of the nineteenth century. The synod of the patriarchate of Constantinople issued a statement declaring *ethnophyletism* a heresy in 1872, in direct response to Bulgarian attempts to make their church community autonomous within the Ottoman millet system.[75] The declaration on ethnophyletism is essentially a disavowal of the kind of nationalism that favors one ethnic group over any other, a teaching that enables Orthodox Christians of any background to belong to a parish community.

Rapid geopolitical developments necessitated action on the part of the church. The decline and eventual collapse of the Ottoman, Austro-Hungarian, and Russian empires led to a reconfiguration of republics. In the initial phase, Greece and Serbia became independent, and the patriarch of Constantinople granted autocephaly to their churches in 1850 (Greece) and 1831 (Serbia). Constantinople also granted autocephaly to the small Orthodox Church in Albania (1937), Bulgaria (1945), and Poland (1924). The creation of these new churches coincided with the establishment of nation-states, though the process of granting autocephaly was often elongated.

If this development seems confusing, it is due to rapidly changing conditions caused by imperial collapse and war. Constantinople had exercised jurisdiction over many of these churches within the Rum millet system, and leaders of nations and churches that had just extricated themselves from the Ottoman Empire did not want to be subordinate to a church leader in Istanbul, as the Greeks initially indicated in 1830. The recognition of Greek and Serbian autocephaly, canonized by a *tomos* from the Patriarchate of Constantinople, normalized the existence of an autocephalous church within the borders of a sovereign nation-state republic.[76] Greece became something of a blueprint and case study for the creation of an autocephalous church within the borders of a national republic. Constantinople began to use this blueprint for the ensuing autocephalies.

A self-governing church of a national republic could gravitate toward nationalism, especially if church leaders and pastors use the church as a platform for expressing national identity. McGuckin astutely notes that minority church communities millet expressed their national identity in part because of the tendency for the patriarchate to impose hellenization on these communities.[77] John McGuckin criticizes both the Russian and Constantinopolitan churches for doing little to "preserve the indigenous rights" of the Orthodox peoples of different national and ethnic identities.[78]

In conclusion, the Rum millet religious system gave more power and authority to the patriarch of Constantinople. Orthodox communities had limited freedom for worship within the system and began to seek independence in conjunction with the creation of national republics as the Ottoman Empire declined. Two new precedents were set with the decline and fall of the Ottoman Empire. First, the patriarch of Constantinople was the one who granted autocephaly to the new churches. Second, Orthodox communities were defined by their new national borders, a development that contributed to a fusion of the Orthodox Church with national identity.

THE KYIV METROPOLIA AND THE RISE OF THE MOSCOW PATRIARCHATE

The church of Constantinople had established a church in Kyiv that ascended to the status of a metropolia. A game of thrones encompassed the principalities of Rus' in the eleventh through the thirteenth centuries, as Vladimir in northeast Rus' began to grow more powerful. Kyiv retained its status as the primary church center in Rus' until the Mongols invaded and ruined the city in 1240 CE. The metropolitan of Kyiv moved to Vladimir in 1299 and eventually to Moscow by 1326 while retaining the title of metropolitan of Kyiv. Metropolitan Philip's (d. 1326) administration of the church from Moscow, his burial in the Kremlin cathedral, and the story of his holiness contributed to Moscow as the new home of the metropolitan, who still carried the title of "metropolitan of Kyiv."[79] Yuri, the grand prince of Halych, successfully petitioned Constantinople to create a separate metropolitanate in Halych in 1303.[80] This move maintained some separation between the Orthodox people in the regions of Galicia and Volhynia and the principality of Vladimir to the northeast.

Moscow superseded Vladimir as the primary center in the northeast in the fifteenth century, while Kyiv became part of the Polish-Lithuanian Commonwealth in the fourteenth century. Orthodox Christians found themselves in two different environments. Orthodox in the Polish-Lithuanian Commonwealth had rights but were religious minorities in a Catholic-dominated society. Moscow's influence in the northeast continued to grow, and the city became the cell of an emerging empire. The Metropolitanate of Moscow asserted its autonomy in 1448 when it declared itself to be an autocephalous church, an act that rejected the continued attempts to retain the Florentine union in Constantinople.

While the Orthodox Church did not sustain the universal authority claimed by the Church of Rome, they did honor the rest of the order of ranks the Council of Florence had declared. This order listed Constantinople, Alexandria, Antioch, and Jerusalem as the other patriarchates. In other words, the Council of Florence declared a *pentarchy* – five patriarchal churches listed in order of their dignity – an order the Orthodox had already observed and respected since the Council of Chalcedon. Moscow was not included in this list, but its assertion of itself as an autocephalous church was an act of protest that foreshadowed its eventual demand for a patriarchate. Constantinople restored the Kyiv metropolitan for the large Orthodox minority in the Polish-Lithuanian Commonwealth in 1458, thereby maintaining the distinction between the Kyivan and Muscovite churches.

Political developments in the sixteenth and seventeenth centuries altered the fates of the churches of Kyiv and Moscow. Moscow continued to ascend in power, superseding Vladimir as the primary regional center of northeastern Rus' into the fourteenth century, and eventually defeating the Mongols in the famous battle of Kulikovo in 1380. Having declared its independence from Constantinople in 1448, Moscow became the capital of the Russian empire in the sixteenth century. Metropolitan Zosima of Moscow was among the first to describe Moscow as the "new Constantinople," and a new myth emerged, describing Moscow as the successor to the fallen Byzantine Empire, and also the new Jerusalem.[81] The monk Filofei of Pskov made this statement famous in the sixteenth century.[82] The tsars wanted to formalize Russia's ascension by elevating the church to patriarchal status, which would make it nominally equal to the ancient churches of the pentarchy. The tsar initially requested patriarchal status for the Russian church from Patriarch Joachim V of Antioch during his visit in 1586, and the patriarch promised to confer with his fellow patriarchs of Constantinople and Alexandria to render a decision.[83]

In 1588, Patriarch Jeremiah of Constantinople journeyed to Moscow with the hope of securing support for the church of Constantinople, now under the rule of the Ottomans. The tsar and his legates hosted the patriarch and, disgruntled by the absence of a decision on Moscow's request for patriarchal status, kept the Constantinopolitan patriarch in isolation for several days. Jeremiah agreed to elevate the church to the status of patriarchate, with Metropolitan Iov of Moscow becoming the first patriarch in its history in 1589. The Russian imperial officials used statecraft to achieve their objective, as Jeremiah never saw or met Iov until the liturgy of his elevation.[84] The Moscow Patriarchate joined the ranks of ancient churches that held the distinction of patriarchate. An interesting footnote accompanied this milestone event in the history of the Russian church. The elevation to patriarchal status never included an official act on the part of Constantinople or any of the other patriarchates in recognizing the autocephaly of the Russian church.

Meanwhile, the bishops of the Kyiv Metropolia agreed to a new union with the Roman church at a unification council in Brest in 1596. The Polish crown had placed immense pressure on the Orthodox bishops to accept the union, to which they all agreed.[85] A majority of Orthodox parishes, clergy, and laity remained Orthodox and refused to accept the new union. Brotherhoods consisting of laity sustained parish life through education and music. Prince Konstantin Ostrozsky was one of the patrons of the movement that promoted Orthodoxy, even before the union, founding an academy in Ostrih that educated candidates for the clergy and laypeople. Orthodox communities resisted the union until 1620, when Patriarch Theophilus of Jerusalem, traveling through Kyiv on a return trip from Moscow, consecrated new bishops for the Metropolia.

In 1632, the Kyiv Metropolia elected a new metropolitan, Petro Mohyla.[86] Mohyla oversaw a reform of the Metropolia, updating the education of clergy and liturgical practices. Students preparing for ministry studied Latin and occasionally performed religious dramas, both practices based on Jesuit models the Orthodox had learned from their Catholic neighbors.

Nikon became patriarch of Moscow in 1652 and served in this capacity until 1666. Nikon initiated a reform program on the basis of inconsistencies of Russian liturgical books with those of the Greek tradition.[87] Fierce opposition to Nikon's reforms erupted, especially in the person of the Archpriest Avvakum. This group was known as the "Old Believers" for retaining their traditions and was divided into two groups – those with priests and the priestless.

Nikon's struggle against the Old Believers caused serious problems for Tsar Alexis and the royal court. The creation of the Moscow Patriarchate had elevated the stature of the Russian church within Orthodoxy, but it had also increased the authority of the office of patriarch. Patriarch Michael (Romanov), one of Nikon's predecessors, was the father of the first Romanov tsar and used the title "Great Sovereign" while ruling Russia de facto instead of his son.[88] This kind of power dynamic in the person of the patriarch came into play with Nikon, who used a strong hand to attempt to impose reform on the church. The fierce resistance to these reforms placed immense pressure on the tsar, and Nikon was eventually censured by a local council that included the participation of the patriarchs of Antioch and Alexandria, even though he had retired to a monastery.[89]

The assertion of patriarchal authority in Russia came to a crashing halt in the early eighteenth century. Patriarch Adrian laid bold claim to an authority that would rival the tsar's in his opening encyclical after his enthronement, and after his death in 1700, there was no election and installment of another patriarch of Moscow until 1917.[90] Tsar Peter (the Great) initiated and eventually implemented a new system of church governance that positioned the church within the imperial administrative apparatus. A synod of bishops would govern the church with an appointed lay representative overseeing (oberprocurator) church administration and reporting directly to the tsar. A document titled "Spiritual Regulations" defined this new system, which became official in 1721.

The model of church governance in England, where the monarch was the head of the church and the chief archbishop clearly subordinate to the monarch, was one of the systems that influenced the Spiritual Regulation. The inauguration of this new system of church governance mitigated any attempts by church prelates to overstep their authority by removing the office of patriarchate. For Russia, the introduction of the Spiritual Regulation essentially annulled the creation of the patriarchate in the late sixteenth century. The Spiritual Regulation essentially illustrates the dynamic nature of Orthodox Church administration. The degree of power exercised by any given head of church is inexorably connected with the political and cultural environment of the time. Tsar Peter I was modernizing Russia to strengthen the imperial state and keep it more competitive, and his policies of modernization contributed to a reshaping of church administration. The reformation of Russian church governance in the eighteenth century revealed Orthodoxy's agility – an ability to adapt to circumstances and revise its forms of church administration while remaining Orthodox.

MOSCOW'S ABSORPTION OF THE KYIVAN METROPOLIA

In 1648, the Ukrainian Hetmanate won a significant battle over the Polish kingdom in an attempt to assert their rights as an autonomous people. Six years later (1654), Ukrainian emissaries made a treaty with the tsar's representatives in Pereiaslav, an event that essentially integrated Ukraine into the Russian empire. The Treaty of Pereiaslav is a contested historical event, with some Ukrainians interpreting it as a military treaty and Russians depicting it as the reunification of a significant portion of southwestern Rus' with the larger Russian empire.

One fact about Pereiaslav holds true – the treaty bound Ukraine's fate with imperial Russia. Russian imperial officials began to court Constantinople yet again, wanting to absorb the Kyiv Metropolia into the Moscow Patriarchate. Many of the clergy and bishops of the Kyiv Metropolia opposed this proposal, fearing that their native traditions would be replaced by Russian practices. In 1686, Patriarch Dionysius IV of Constantinople issued a series of canonical documents that changed the relationship between the Kyivan church, Constantinople, and Moscow.[91] Constantinople's address to the patriarch of Moscow stated that the patriarch of Moscow would ordain the metropolitan of Kyiv and function as his elder, but that the Kyiv metropolitan would commemorate the patriarch of Constantinople at the liturgy. In 1686, neither the patriarch of Constantinople nor the metropolitan of Kyiv had the power to resist complete absorption of the metropolia into the Moscow Patriarchate. Moscow did not stop at simply making the Kyivan church and its communities part of its apparatus, but the patriarchate imposed new traditions on the Kyivan church, including Great Russian pronunciation of the Church Slavonic language at liturgy and instruction in Russian instead of Ukrainian in seminaries and theological academies.

SYNODAL ORTHODOXY AND SPIRITUAL GEMS

Historians and theologians tend to hold a negative view of the so-called synodal period of Russian church history. Some are harshly critical of Tsar Peter I for abandoning the Byzantine model Russia claimed to have inherited and adopting a Protestant one instead. Recent scholarship challenges the assumption that Peter simply adopted the Anglican model and imposed it upon the church. Gregory Freeze argues that Peter's Spiritual Regulation did not transform the Russian church into a state organ but attempted to reform it by making it more collegial and creating an environment for an episcopal elite and parish clergy as a distinct social order.[92] Freeze argues that the church functioned differently from similar state organs and rose to the occasion to assert its rights and those of the clergy. Freeze notes that the synodal system the church used – an adaptation of the spiritual regulation – set the stage for a dynamic process that vaulted the church into the public square during the revolutionary period, with theologians functioning as crucial religious actors in discussions on the political and social orders and the need for reform.[93] John Mack asserts that the tsar's creation of the spiritual regulation was not an attempt to Westernize the Russian church but to purify it from the chaos into which it had descended, using the prerogative of the tsar as the people's "father" figure.[94]

Russia's encounter with the enlightenment challenged the political and religious status quo. Russia attempted to sustain its monarchy during the age of imperial collapse and national revolutions. Tsar

Nicholas I used the defeat of Napoleon to embark on a plan to strengthen the inner unity of the empire through Russian nationalism. Sergei Uvarov, his education minister, created a slogan of autocracy, Orthodoxy, and nationality as pillars of imperial unity.[95] Clergy and representatives of the church involved themselves in difficult political issues. Several clergy expressed their solidarity with workers during the revolution of 1904–1905, especially Georgy Gapon. Gapon became the public clerical face of Russian solidarity with workers' rights because of his participation in the march to Winter Palace in St. Petersburg in January of 1905, the tragic event known as Bloody Sunday when imperial forces used violence to stop the march.[96] Russian church leaders were split on how to address the political crisis. Some went so far as to deny church burials to people killed in the riots in an attempt to calm revolutionary tendencies. Others believed that the church needed strong leadership to guide its people through difficult times and a serious self-examination to ascertain why people were leaving the church and what could be done to turn the tide.

Church leaders sought the convocation of a churchwide council to deliberate difficult issues and, most importantly, to revitalize the Russian church. Leaders persuaded Tsar Nicholas II to create a preconciliar commission that would begin the process of identifying the most important issues and set an agenda for the council. The process began in 1905 with a questionnaire sent to the bishops, and preparations for the All-Russian Orthodox Church Council coincided with the creation of a parliament (duma), a major political move toward a constitutional monarchy.[97] Imperial Russia's political crises led to persistent delays in convening the long-awaited council.

The synodal era was not limited to church participation in social activism. Russian Orthodoxy enjoyed a period of spiritual flourishing during the synodal period. The Optina monastery became a haven for spirituality and pilgrimage. Russian writers of the nineteenth century brought fictional characters like the elder Zossima of Dostoevsky's *Brothers Karamazov* to life, and the church itself produced saints such as Seraphim of Sarov, Xenia of St. Petersburg, and John of Kronstadt. Vera Shevzov has written extensively about the importance of icons in communal and domestic piety in everyday religious practice and observance. Lay men and women would petition the Holy Synod to permit veneration of miracle-working icons.[98] Ordinary people bore witness to the presence and activity of God and the saints in their daily lives. The synodal period was also a time of mentorship, where people sought guidance from spiritual masters in monasteries and parishes. People of diverse backgrounds wrote out their confessions to John of Kronstadt, believing that this form of confessing their sins would bring them to absolution.[99]

Orthodoxy in the synodal period of imperial Russia was consistent with most of Orthodox history. Tsar Peter's creation of the Spiritual Regulation removed the strong authoritarianism invested in the office of patriarch, but it did not minimize the significance of the church in the everyday lives of believers. There was also great diversity and division among leaders in the Russian church and strong disagreement on exactly what reforms the church should implement.

THE SOVIET PERIOD (1917–1991)

The Revolution of 1905 previewed the tumult that would overcome Orthodoxy during the revolutionary period. Forces for the Church's proactive participation on behalf of the people met opposition in the upper strata of church authority from 1907 to 1917, the period in between the two revolutions.[100] Some clergy who also functioned as social activists openly criticized imperial officials, and church administrators asserted control by censoring their writings in church publications.[101]

Tsar Nicholas II's abdication of the throne and the creation of a provisional government in Russia disrupted church administration because it had depended on the imperial apparatus. Hyacinthe Destivelle notes that the abdication generated an impulse that led the Church to convoke its long-planned council.

The Moscow Council of 1917–1918 was one of the most important events in modern Orthodox history for two reasons. First, the council restored the office of patriarch to the Russian church, a decision that was enormously consequential for all of Orthodoxy up until the present day. Second, the Moscow Council included lay participation and elevated all-church councils consisting of bishops, clergy, and laity to the highest levels of authority in the church. The Moscow Council not only established a blueprint for Orthodoxy that drew from the ecumenical councils but also updated them by deliberately including lay men and women in deliberations. The council considered numerous reforms, such as the restoration of the order of deaconess and the use of modern Russian and Ukrainian for the liturgy, but constant interruptions and severe persecution of the church and a lack of funds prevented the council from completing its more far-reaching aspirations.

Patriarch Tikhon (Bellavin) was elected and enthroned as the first patriarch of Moscow since 1700. He remained neutral during the war until he anathematized all of those who had been baptized and were assaulting the church in early 1918.[102] Tikhon was arrested and imprisoned in the spring of 1922 on the charge of collaborating with counterrevolutionary forces.[103] He endured persecution and imprisonment and died in 1924. The patriarchate was again interrupted during severe Bolshevik persecution. Metropolitan Sergius, who administered the church in the interim period, pledged allegiance to the Soviet state in 1927. This pledge did not stop the Bolshevik assault on the church.

The Bolsheviks adopted the Marxist view that capitalist states used religion as a tool to keep workers in captivity. Leon Trotsky devised and implemented the plan to destroy the Russian Orthodox Church. Renovationist figures in the Russian church attempted to persuade Tikhon to resign so they could convoke another council to implement wide-ranging reforms.[104] Tikhon attempted to maintain control over the church, but his appointees were unable to administer the church in his absence. The Bolsheviks eventually adopted a divide and conquer approach by supporting an organized group of renovationist clergy and laity, who held a council in 1923, elected their own metropolitan, and renamed their body the Living Church.[105]

Parallel events in Ukraine, Constantinople, and Poland help to fill out the storms of the twentieth century and also make sense of some of the chaos that reigns in world Orthodoxy in the twenty-first century. The revolutionary war made Ukrainian national independence possible, and a horrific civil war engulfed Ukraine from 1917 to 1920. Orthodox Ukrainians knew their history and remembered their subordination to the church in imperial Russia. Patriarch Tikhon blessed the Ukrainians to have their own council, and it took place in 1918, under extreme duress. The council adopted autonomy (and not autocephaly) and retained Church Slavonic (and not

Ukrainian) despite a pro-Ukrainian majority among the constituency, due in part to manipulation of voting by the Russian bishops leading the council. The angry pro-Ukrainian party established Ukrainian-language parishes beginning in 1919 and eventually convened another council in October 1921, creating the Ukrainian Autocephalous Orthodox Church (UAOC) without any bishops participating in the council or leading the ordinations. The original founders of the UAOC attempted to secure assistance from both Constantinople and Georgia but were unable to receive help because of the dangerous conditions caused by the war. The UAOC existed alongside the patriarchal church in Ukraine until the Soviet government dissolved it in Kharkiv in 1930. The creation of the new UAOC opened the doors for the pursuit of Ukrainian autocephaly in the future.

The Patriarchate of Constantinople found itself a tiny minority within the new republic of Turkey, as the majority of Orthodox people that had been within the Ottoman Empire found themselves in nation-states. The patriarchate convened an important pan-Orthodox council in 1923 that adopted a new calendar for the fixed feasts of the year and refused to recognize the Living church. In 1924, however, the patriarch of Constantinople recognized the Living church as legitimate, as the Bolshevik state defended him against an accusation made by the ruling Turkish government.[106] Minority Orthodox populations in Finland and Estonia ultimately turned to Constantinople for jurisdiction, not willing to subordinate their churches to a persecuted body in a nominally atheistic state.[107]

The newly-formed republic of Poland had a large Orthodox minority consisting mostly of Belorussians and Ukrainians. Poland's government viewed the vocal Orthodox minority as a political opportunity to neutralize Catholic influence and appease ethnic minorities. The Polish state persuaded Constantinople to grant their church autocephaly after the tiny Orthodox synod in Poland voted three to two in favor of independence, by the thinnest of margins. Poland received autocephaly from Constantinople in 1924.

The years 1921–1924 saw a Ukrainian rebellion against Russian tyranny in the church, Orthodox politicians and bishops attempting to isolate themselves from Bolshevism, and Constantinople irritating the Russian church by favoring the renovationists, appeasing Finland and Estonia, and granting autocephaly to Poland. Constantinople's actions during one of the fiercest periods of Bolshevik persecution of the church would become inscribed upon Russian historical memory and contribute to the deepening of divisions decades later.

The war, Bolshevik persecution, and Patriarch Tikhon's death in 1925 caused chaos in Russian Orthodoxy. Clergy and laity who fled Russia during the war needed to carry out church life, and a synod of bishops was established outside of Russia in Karlovci, Serbia, under the leadership of Metropolitan Antony (Khrapovitsky). The primary group of this church eventually became the Russian Orthodox Church Outside of Russia (ROCOR). The creation of this synod was not seamless. Disputes on seniority and the relationships of the Russian synod with other Orthodox churches created a fine mess in Orthodoxy. An eparchy of Russian parishes formed in Western Europe under the jurisdiction of Constantinople. ROCOR eventually became a church body diffused over several countries. An Orthodox diaspora, consisting of parishes of specific ethnic backgrounds, grew in the decades following the revolution when people made the journey on steamers to new lands. The events of the 1920s expanded Orthodox identity, with ROCOR taking the lead in disavowing Moscow's declaration of loyalty to the Soviet state, and the other churches attempting to distance themselves from a church whose leadership was clearly compromised.

Orthodoxy maintained a slight pulse in the Soviet Union from 1927 to 1943. Daniela Kalkandijeva writes that only 100 parishes were open and functioning in the entire Soviet Union by 1939, mostly in big cities.[108] Over 200 bishops and thousands of priests had been killed by the Bolsheviks. Despite this catastrophe, Stalin permitted the church to appoint bishops to oversee church life in territories newly annexed by the Soviet Union in the Molotov-Ribbentrop agreement.[109]

Stalin permitted the renewal of the Orthodox Church to draw upon a familiar theme – the Orthodox identity of the people, fused with their national identity. Bishops used the pulpit to call upon the people to defend the fatherland, and Stalin permitted the church to reopen parishes and conduct some theological education.

The Soviet state revised its approach to the church, having found it useful in its geopolitical scheme. The Allied powers agreed to annex Western Ukraine to the Soviet Union after the war in 1945, which made millions of Ukrainian Greek Catholic people Soviet citizens. Stalin acted quickly by convening a Council of the Ukrainian Greek Catholic Church (UGCC) on false pretenses in L'viv in 1946.[110] The council dissolved the UGCC at the direction of the Soviet authorities, and the Moscow Patriarchate (MP) absorbed the communities into its apparatus. Stalin's policies also empowered the Moscow Patriarchate to exercise influence through participation in the World Council of Churches (in 1961) and to challenge the Ecumenical Patriarchate of Constantinople for power and prestige within the Orthodox world. The MP attempted to exercise this authority by granting autocephaly to churches in countries that were in the Soviet orbit or had a historical connection to Russian Orthodoxy. The MP granted autocephaly to the tiny church in Czechoslovakia in 1951 and to the American "Metropolia" in 1970. The Church in Poland was the most interesting political case. This church annulled the autocephaly it received from Constantinople in 1924 and received a new version of it from Moscow in 1948.[111] Church leaders justified the move by referring to historical connections and canonical territory, but the actual motive was clearly political: to make these small churches cells of influence for the Soviet state through the church.

The Soviet state's use of the MP to maximize its influence did not stop the state from repressing religious practices. Nikita Khrushchev's tenure as leader of the Soviet Union was particularly oppressive. Khrushchev did not use the kind of violent, terroristic tactics employed by the Bolsheviks in the 1920s, but he promoted a formidable ideological assault on the church by publishing debates between scientists and theologians in journals and magazines, placing severe restrictions on the number of open parishes, and limiting clerical activity. An authentic opening of religious freedom began only near the end of the Soviet period, on the eve of the celebration of the millennial anniversary of the baptism of Rus', which happened to coincide with the seventieth anniversary of the revolution. The Soviet state hosted a limited millennium celebration in Moscow in 1988, reopened a portion of the famous Kyiv Pechers'ka Lavra monastery, and, perhaps most significantly, restored the legal status of the UGCC and UAOC in Ukraine.

The Soviet Union's decision to legalize the UGCC and UAOC completely changed the religious status quo by undermining the absolute dominance of the MP. Over 1,000 parishes immediately abandoned the MP and returned to the UGCC and UAOC, especially in Western Ukraine, the region annexed to the Soviet Union in 1945. The UAOC convoked a council in 1990 and enthroned Metropolitan Mstyslav as its first patriarch in Kyiv in November 1990.

The Soviet period began with the restoration of the patriarchate in Moscow and the regime's attempt to destroy the church. Orthodoxy was already experiencing considerable readjustment with the decline and collapse of the Ottoman Empire, the isolation of the Patriarchate of Constantinople, and the creation of autocephalous churches in sovereign nation-states. The Bolshevik revolution catalyzed waves of immigration, with communities forming around ethnic identity and the church carrying the banner of overthrowing an atheistic state. Constantinople's response to appeals from Baltic and Polish communities reopened old wounds with the Moscow Patriarchate.

RAPID REVIVALS AND SHARP DECLINES (1991–2024)

The fall of the Soviet Union posed enormous challenges to Orthodox Church leaders. Once again, Church officials accustomed to working within a particular system found themselves in a new environment. The transition from severe restrictions to freedom brought both threats and opportunities. The MP suddenly enjoyed the freedom to resume the course established by the Moscow Council of 1917–1918. The immediate resurgence of Orthodox Ukrainians seeking to create their own canonically recognized autocephalous church threatened the MP's aspirations.

The Ukrainian Orthodox situation reached two important thresholds that would prove fateful for world Orthodoxy. The emergence of the UAOC posed a choice to the leaders of the Moscow Patriarchate in Ukraine: either become an autocephalous church in a sovereign Ukraine, a viable path with a precedent in Orthodox history, or remain a part of the Moscow Patriarchate, which could create tension with the government of an independent Ukraine. Filaret opted for the first choice by requesting autocephaly from the Moscow Patriarchate in 1991–1992. The Moscow Patriarchate's synod then had a choice – grant autocephaly to Ukraine and risk diminishing influence through the church, or use all possible means to minimize loss by retaining Ukraine. The Moscow Patriarchate opted for the second choice and ended up excommunicating Filaret when he refused to obey their directive that he retire. Filaret joined most of the UAOC in a council in 1992 that created the Ukrainian Orthodox Church-Kyivan Patriarchate (UOC-KP). Ukraine had three Orthodox Churches from 1992 to 2018 – the UOC-KP, the Ukrainian Orthodox Church under Moscow (UOC-MP), and the tiny remnant of the UAOC. The UOC-KP and UAOC had several unsuccessful attempts to unite but worked with Constantinople toward the eventual creation of an autocephalous church.[112]

In Russia, Metropolitan Kirill (Gundaev) succeeded Aleksy II as patriarch of Moscow in 2009 following Aleksy's death. Kirill had been a reformer with extensive international experience, and many clergy hoped his patriarchal tenure would inaugurate a period of genuine reform, equipping the church for the challenges of the twenty-first century.

Russia eventually adopted a nationalistic platform and political agenda during Boris Yeltsin's presidency, and especially after Vladimir Putin became president in 2000. Putin privileged a conservative ideological course following serious public challenges to his leadership in the elections of 2011 and made an alliance with the MP. The MP became one of the main vehicles for the public proclamation of the Russian World initiative.[113] The Russian World ideology retrieved conservative values from the imperial period and identified Russia as a defender of Christianity from all enemies. Kirill began to promote the idea of a Russian World as early as 2008.

Inter-Orthodox Church relations were already tense, especially with Constantinople's advocacy for Estonia in 1995 and for Orthodox Ukrainians in Canada and the United States in 1990 and 1995. Constantinople had been working steadily for decades toward the convocation of another pan-Orthodox council to resolve outstanding issues. These included fasting, marriage, and relations with other Christians, but the processes and mechanisms for the granting of autocephaly were the top priority. The preconciliar commission presented a proposal that required the consensus of all the Orthodox Churches for autocephaly, with the ecumenical patriarch granting the tomos to the new church.[114] The proposal checked many of the boxes for the MP, but they objected to the role of the patriarch granting the tomos, so autocephaly was removed from the list.

Constantinople scheduled the council for 2016 on the island of Crete. Three churches refused to attend – Antioch, Georgia, and Bulgaria. The MP withdrew their delegation at the last minute in an attempt to delegitimize the council. The council did indeed take place and issued numerous statements, but Moscow's last-minute withdrawal seemed to irritate Constantinople.

In 2018, Constantinople initiated the process of uniting the churches in Ukraine to establish one autocephalous church, according to the model of a church in a sovereign nation-state. Constantinople completed the process in January 2019, despite fierce resistance from the MP.[115]

Moscow initiated a series of responses to the creation of the Orthodox Church of Ukraine (OCU) and its subsequent recognition by the churches of Greece, Alexandria, and Cyprus. The Russian church broke communion with the bishops and clergy of these churches that recognized the OCU. The MP also created its own exarchate in Africa, further embittering relations with the patriarch of Alexandria. The Moscow Patriarchate's most consequential action was the decision of Patriarch Kirill to bless and justify Russia's invasion of Ukraine in 2022. Kirill used his position to communicate Russian propaganda that Ukraine had a neo-Nazi regime requiring a special military operation.

Constantinople refused to change its position in response to the Moscow Patriarchate's decisions. The other Orthodox churches attempted to find creative ways to conduct their affairs in the midst of the crisis of dispute. The Macedonian Orthodox Church, which had been out of communion with Orthodoxy for decades, reached an agreement with the Serbian church for autocephaly.[116] Their ability to find a way to resolve problems in the midst of a seemingly irreconcilable dispute between Moscow and Constantinople, the two most powerful churches, appeared to be extraordinary.

THE DIASPORA

From the beginning of this study, we have emphasized Orthodoxy's preferred feature as a local church. Orthodoxy spread beyond its original confines in the Middle East and Southern Europe into Central and Eastern Europe via missionary activity. The establishment of a church community via mission does not infer a diaspora, because the notion of a diaspora is that the people who have settled in a place will eventually return to their native homeland. It was natural for Russians to view their lives in Southern and Western Europe as temporary since they hoped a defeat of the Bolsheviks would permit them to return home.

Many people who left their homeland, moved somewhere else, and developed church life constitute the Orthodox diaspora. The diaspora includes regions such as North and South America, Western Europe, and Australia, among other places.

Technically, missionaries brought Orthodoxy to North America when Saint Innocent (later metropolitan of Moscow) went to Alaska to plant a mission in the nineteenth century. An Orthodox community grew in Alaska and honored the people's indigenous traditions by translating the liturgy into their native languages and Christianizing many of their traditions through inculturation.

Immigration is the second phenomenon that led to the creation of an Orthodox diaspora. Greeks in search of stable employment settled in the lands of the diaspora and constituted a large community. Many other groups migrated in search of work. Thousands of people of Carpatho-Rusyn descent settled in North America for employment in the nineteenth century, and many of these communities were Greek Catholic. Some of these communities became Orthodox after the Latin Rite Catholic bishops rejected the legitimacy of priests who were or had been married, with Alexis Toth, who served in Minneapolis and Wilkes-Barre, being the best-known example. Waves of immigration sustained church life even over multiple generations, though the viability of some parish communities has been compromised by socioeconomic developments.

Conversion to Orthodoxy is the third contributor to the diaspora community. Many conversions occurred through marriage, where the non-Orthodox spouse became Orthodox for the sake of the family unit. Studies by Dellas Herbel and Amy Slagle revealed complexities in conversion to Orthodoxy in the diaspora. Herbel's study shows that many of the Greek Catholics who became Orthodox via conversion returned to their native Greek Catholic Churches.[117] Slagle's anthropological study of conversions in the United States showed that people used a variety of sources for formation in learning how to be Orthodox and that converts often had different attitudes about the church than natives.[118] A group of Christians active in the Campus Crusade for Christ became Orthodox by joining the Antiochian Archdiocese of North America in 1987.[119] Recent studies on conversion suggest that more than half of the people in the Orthodox Church in America are converts and that the percentage of men becoming Orthodox is increasing.[120] Sarah Riccardi-Swartz's study of Orthodox converts suggests that political ideologies catalyze conversion to Orthodoxy, especially in ROCOR.[121]

Canonical jurisdiction of Orthodox in the diaspora is a contested issue. The aforementioned canon twenty-eight of the council in Chalcedon included a provision granting Constantinople jurisdiction over three dependent regions. Constantinople has argued consistently that the Orthodox diaspora should remain within its jurisdiction. The autocephaly granted by the patriarchate of Moscow to the OCA in 1970 was designed to remove the diaspora designation from North America, at least in part. The OCA created ethnic dioceses – Romanian, Albanian, and Bulgarian – to accommodate parishes that wished to retain their ethnic identity while the church gradually became American. The other Orthodox Churches in America did not join the OCA, so the model of a previously diaspora church growing into an autocephalous body has not formed, at least in America.

CONCLUSIONS

Our survey of the history of the Orthodox Church illuminates a number of pivotal events and turning points that guided the Church's direction. These turning points include the convocation of the first ecumenical council in Nicaea, the Fourth Crusade of 1204, the Fall of Constantinople in 1453, and the Bolshevik Revolution in 1917. These historical episodes did not determine the course of Orthodoxy, but each one of them reveals patterns that help us understand Orthodoxy and its identity. In each case, the Church found itself in an environment that required pastoral and theological responses and adjustments. While no two responses were identical, events often elicited theological activity that came to define Orthodox identity. Orthodoxy's tendency to seek stability led to the permanence of many theological teachings – especially in Christology.

NOTES

1 John McGuckin, *The Eastern Orthodox Church: A New History* (New Haven, CT: Yale University Press, 2020), 102.
2 Norman P. Tanner, ed., *Decrees of the Ecumenical Councils*, vol. 1: *Nicaea I to Lateran V* (Washington, DC: Sheed and Ward and Georgetown University Press, 1990), 32–33 (canon 3).
3 Tanner, *Decrees*, 31 (canon 1).
4 McGuckin, *The Eastern Orthodox* Church, 116.
5 See Tanner, *Decrees*, 43.
6 Lois Farag, "The Early Christian Period (42–642): The Spread and Defense of the Christian Faith under Roman Rule," in *The Coptic Christian Heritage: History, Faith, and Culture*, ed. Lois Farag (London: Routledge, 2014), 29.
7 Farag, "The Early Christian Period," 32–33.
8 Farag, "The Early Christian Period," 32–33.
9 Farag, "The Early Christian Period," 33.
10 Farag, "The Early Christian Period," 34.
11 See Tanner, *Decrees*, 83–84.
12 Tanner, *Decrees*, 83–84.
13 Tanner, *Decrees*, 91, 95.
14 Tanner, *Decrees*, 100.
15 See Farag, "The Early Christian Period," 34–35.
16 Farag, "The Early Christian Period," 35.
17 Farag, "The Early Christian Period," 35.
18 Robert W. Thomson, "Armenian Christianity," in *The Blackwell Dictionary of Eastern Christianity*, ed. Parry et al. (Malden, MA: Blackwell, 2001), 55.
19 Farag, "The Early Christian Period," 35.
20 Farag, "The Early Christian Period," 35.
21 Clive Foss, "The Empress Theodora," *Byzantion* 72 (2002), 143–144.
22 Thomson, "Armenian Christianity," 55.
23 "Jacobite" derives from Jacob Baradeaeus, bishop of Edessa in 543–78. J.F. Coakley, "Jacobite," in *The Blackwell Dictionary of Eastern Christianity*, eds. Ken Parry et al. (Malden, MA: Blackwell, 2001), 262.
24 Sebastian Brock, "Syrian Christianity," in *The Blackwell Dictionary of Eastern Christianity*, eds. Ken Parry et al. (Malden, MA: Blackwell, 2001), 468.
25 2010 Pew Research Center survey, "Ethiopia is an outlier in the Orthodox Christian world," https://www.pewresearch.org/short-reads/2017/11/28/ethiopia-is-an-outlier-in-the-orthodox-christian-world/ (accessed July 8, 2024).
26 Manfred Kropp, "Ethiopian Orthodox Church," in *The Blackwell Dictionary of Eastern Christianity*, ed. Ken Parry et al. (Malden, MA: Blackwell, 2001), 185.

27 Manfred Kropp, "Ethiopian Orthodox Church," 186.
28 Tanner, *Decrees*, 107–115.
29 See Tanner's comments in *Decrees*, 105.
30 Diarmaid MacCulloch, *Christianity: The First Three Thousand Years* (London: Penguin, 2011), 441.
31 MacCulloch, *Christianity*, 442–443.
32 Leslie Brubaker, *Inventing Byzantine Iconoclasm*, Studies in Early Medieval History (London: Bloomsbury, 2012), 32–34.
33 Tanner, *Decrees*, 136.
34 "The honor paid to an image traverses it, reaching the model; and he who venerates the image, venerates the person represented in that image," in Tanner, *Decrees*, 136.
35 See MacCulloch, *Christianity*, 448.
36 MacCulloch, *Christianity*, 448–449.
37 Tanner, *Decrees*, 100.
38 Thomson, "Armenian Christianity," 54.
39 Konstantin Lerner, "Georgia, Christian history of," in *The Blackwell Dictionary of Eastern Christianity*, eds. Ken Parry et al. (Malden, MA: Blackwell, 2001), 210.
40 McGuckin, *Christianity*, 157.
41 McGuckin, *Christianity*, 157.
42 McGuckin, *Christianity*, 158.
43 Muriel Heppell, "Bulgaria," in *The Blackwell Dictionary of Eastern Christianity*, eds. Ken Parry et al. (Malden, MA: Blackwell, 2001), 94.
44 Bryn Geffert and Theofanis Stavrou, eds., *Eastern Orthodox Christianity: The Essential Texts* (New Haven, CT: Yale, 2016), 184–185. (The Essential Texts hereafter).
45 Ken Parry, "Serbian Christianity," in *The Blackwell Dictionary of Eastern Christianity*, eds. Ken Parry et al. (Malden, MA: Blackwell, 2001), 442.
46 Parry, "Serbian Christianity," 443.
47 McGuckin, *Christianity*, 159.
48 Geffert and Stavrou, *Eastern Orthodox Christianity*, 185.
49 McGuckin, *Christianity*, 159.
50 McGuckin, *Christianity*, 160.
51 Sean Griffin, *The Liturgical Past in Byzantium and Early Rus*, Cambridge Studies in Medieval life and thought 112 (Cambridge: Cambridge university Press, 2019), 82–83.
52 Geffert and Stavrou, *Eastern Orthodox Christianity*, 235–236.
53 Geffert and Stavrou, *Eastern Orthodox Christianity*, 243.
54 Geffert and Stavrou, *Eastern Orthodox Christianity*, 244–246.
55 , 246–248.
56 MacCulloch, Christianity, 476.

57 MacCulloch, Christianity, 493–494.
58 Address of John Paul II to His Beatitude Christodoulos, Archbishop of Athens and Primate of Greece, https://www.vatican.va/content/john-paul-ii/en/speeches/2001/may/documents/hf_jp-ii_spe_20010504_archbishop-athens.html (accessed August 16, 2024).
59 MacCulloch, *Christianity*, 492.
60 MacCulloch, Christianity, 492.
61 Tanner, *Decrees*, 453–454.
62 Tanner, *Decrees*, 523.
63 Tanner, *Decrees*, 524–525.
64 Tanner, *Decrees*, 525–526.
65 Tanner, *Decrees*, 528.
66 MacCulloch, *Christianity*, 493.
67 Geffert and Stavrou, *Eastern Orthodox Christianity*, 260–261.
68 MacCulloch, *Christianity*, 493–494.
69 Geffert and Stavrou, *Eastern Orthodox Christianity*, 262–263.
70 Geffert and Stavrou, *Eastern Orthodox Christianity*, 270.
71 See Karen Barkey and George Gavrilis, "The Ottoman Millet System: Non-Territorial Autonomy and its Contemporary Legacy," *Ethnopolitics* 15, no. 1 (2015), 28 (24–42).
72 McGuckin, *Christianity*, 196–197. Hellenization refers to attempting to make a community more Greek.
73 Victor Roudometof, "Invented Traditions, Symbolic Boundaries, and National Identity in Southeastern Europe: Greece and Serbia in Comparative Historical Perspective (1830–1880)," *East European Quarterly* 24, no. 1 (1999), 432. (429–468).
74 Roudometof, "Invented Traditions."
75 Cyril Hovorun, *Scaffolds of the Church: Towards Poststructural Theology* (Eugee, OR: Cascade Books, 2017), 116–120.
76 A tomos is literally a part of a book. It is an official canonical document defining the canonical terms for an autocephalous church that comes from the ecumenical patriarch of Constantinople.
77 McGuckin, *Christianity*, 206.
78 McGuckin, *Christianity*, 206.
79 Paul Bushkovitch, *A Concise History of Russia* (Cambridge: Cambridge University Press, 2012), 23.
80 Orest Subtelny, *Ukraine: A History*, 4th rev. ed (Toronto: University of Toronto Press, 2009), 64.
81 Serhii Plokhy, *Lost Kingdom: A History of Russian Nationalism from Ivan the Great to Vladimir Putin* (New York: Penguin, 2017), 23–24.
82 Plokhy, *Lost Kingdom*, 24.
83 Plokhy, *Lost Kingdom*, 19–20.

84 Plokhy, *Lost Kingdom*, 25.
85 See Subtelny, *Ukraine: A History*, 92–102.
86 Subtelny, *Ukraine: A History*, 120–121.
87 Dimitry Pospielovsky, *The Orthodox Church in the History of Russia* (Crestwood: St. Vladimir' Seminary Press, 1998), 71–74.
88 Pospielovsky, *The Orthodox Church*, 69.
89 Pospielovsky, *The Orthodox Church*, 75.
90 Pospielovsky, *The Orthodox Church*, 105–106.
91 Ecumenical Patriarchate, "The Documents Speak: Ecumenical Throne and the Church of Ukraine." https://www.ecupatria.org/2018/10/04/the-ecumenical-patriarchate-and-the-church-of-ukraine-the-documents-speak/ (accessed August 17, 2024).
92 Gregory Freeze, "Handmaiden of the State? The Church in Imperial Russia Reconsidered," *Journal of Ecclesiastical History* 36, no. 1 (1985), 84 (82–102).
93 Freeze, "Handmaiden of the State?"
94 John Mack, "Peter the Great and the Ecclesiastical Regulation: Secularization or Reformation?" *St. Vladimir's Theological Quarterly* 49, no. 3 (2005), 243–269.
95 Bushkovitch, *Concise History of Russia*, 159–160.
96 Jennifer Hedda, *His Kingdom Come: Orthodox Pastorship and Social Activism in Revolutionary Russia* (DeKalb, IL: Northern Illinois University Press, 2008), 144–145.
97 Hyacinthe Destivelle, *The Moscow Council (1917–1918): The Creation of the Conciliar Institution of the Russian Orthodox Church*, trans. Jerry Ryan, ed. Michael Plekon and Vitaly Permiakov (Notre Dame, IN: University of Notre Dame Press, 2016), 31–32.
98 Vera Shevzov, "Petitions to the Holy Synod Regarding Miracle-Working Icons," in *Orthodox Christianity in Imperial Russia: A Source Book on Lived Religion*, ed. Heather Coleman (Bloomington: Indiana University Press, 2014), 229–230.
99 Nadieszda Kizenko, "Written Confessions to Father John of Kronstadt, 1898–1908," in *Orthodox Christianity in Imperial Russia*, ed. Heather Coleman (Bloomington: Indiana University Press, 2014), 152–153.
100 Hedda, *His Kingdom Come*, 176–177.
101 Hedda, *His Kingdom Come*, 183. Note that urban clergy who tended to support workers and were social activities came to be known as *renovationists* within the Russian Orthodox world.
102 Pospielovsky, *The Orthodox Church*, 209.
103 Daniela Kalkandijeva, *The Russian Orthodox Church, 1917–1948: From Decline to Resurrection* (London: Routledge, 2015), 17.
104 Kalkandijeva, *The Russian Orthodox Church*.

105 Kalkandijeva, *The Russian Orthodox Church*, 19.
106 Kalkandijeva, *The Russian Orthodox Church*, 21.
107 Kalkandijeva, *The Russian Orthodox Church*, 24–26.
108 Kalkandijeva, *The Russian Orthodox Church*, 65.
109 Kalkandijeva, *The Russian Orthodox Church*, 65. The Molotov-Ribbentrop agreement was a nonaggression pact between Nazi Germany and the Soviet Union to divide Eastern Europe between the two competing powers. Western Ukraine was ceded to the Soviet Union as part of the pact.
110 See the complete study by Bohdan Bociurkiw, *The Ukrainian Greek Catholic Church and the Soviet State (1939–1950)* (Edmonton: Canadian Institute of Ukrainian Studies, 1996).
111 For details on the political maneuverings in the Polish case, see Kalkandijeva, *The Russian Orthodox Church*, 226–231.
112 For details, see Nicholas Denysenko, *The Orthodox Church in Ukraine: A Century of Separation* (DeKalb: Northern Illinois University Press, 2018).
113 For background, see Elizaveta Gaufman, "Come all ye Faithful to the Russian World: Governmental and Grass-Roots Spiritual Discourse in the Battle over Ukraine," in *Religion during the Russian-Ukrainian Conflict*, eds. Elizabeth A. Clark and Dmytro Vovk (New York: Routledge, 2020), 55–63 (54–68).
114 See the translation of the 1993 text by John Erickson in Alexander Bogolepov, *Toward an American Orthodox Church*, foreword John H. Erickson (Crestwood, NY: St. Vladimir's Seminary Press, 2001), xvi–xix. The draft text is titled "Autocephaly and the Way it is to be Proclaimed."
115 "Exploring Ukrainian Autocephaly: Politics, History, Ecclesiology, and the Future." *Canadian Slavonic Papers* 62, nos. 3–4 (2020): 426–442.
116 Emil Saggau, "Checkmate: Serbian Orthodox Diplomacy in the Shadow of the Ukrainian War," https://publicorthodoxy.org/2022/09/21/serbian-orthodox-diplomacy-ukrainian-war/ (accessed August 17, 2024).
117 Dellas Oliver Herbel, *Turning to Tradition: Converts and the Making of an American Orthodox Church* (Oxford: Oxford University Press, 2014), 25–60.
118 Amy Slagle, *The Eastern Church in the Spiritual Marketplace: American Conversions to Orthodox Christianity* (DeKalb, IL: Northern Illinois University Press, 2007).
119 Herbel, *Turning to Tradition*, 105.
120 Matthew Namee et al., *Converts to Orthodoxy: Statistics and Trends from the Last Decade* (Orthodox Studies Institute: 2024).
121 Sarah Riccardi-Swartz, *Between Heaven and Russia: Religious Conversion and Political Apostasy in Appalachia* (New York: Fordham University Press, 2022).

ORTHODOX THEOLOGY
Christology, Pneumatology, Life and Death

The Orthodox Church has a reputation for retaining and sustaining features of traditional theology. Orthodox people knowledgeable about their faith tend to burst with pride about the traditional features of their theology. What makes this theological tradition "Orthodox"? Is there anything truly special about Orthodox theology, given its similarities with the beliefs and confessions of the Roman Catholic and many Protestant churches? This section begins with a brief examination of the main sources for Orthodox theology.

WHO IS GOD?

The Orthodox Church confesses faith in God, the God of Abraham, Isaac, and Jacob, and the Father of Jesus Christ. Orthodoxy believes that the Father is the same God as Yahweh of the Old Testament, the God who created the universe, created a covenant with Abraham, and liberated the Hebrew people from slavery to Egypt (Ex. 15). This is the same God who sent the prophets Isaiah, Jeremiah, and Ezekiel to the people of Judah and Israel, calling upon them to repent and return to the covenant. Orthodoxy worships the God who appeared to Moses in a burning bush, led the Israelites with a pillar of fire, appeared to Elijah with a still, small voice, and revealed himself to Daniel as the Ancient of Days (Dan. 7:9).

The Orthodox Church believes that the same God who kept his covenant to Israel has fulfilled it by sending his son Jesus

DOI: 10.4324/9781003433217-4

Christ into the world. This God is almighty, superior to all other gods, and unapproachable by humans, who cannot withstand the divine nature. Orthodox systematic theology speaks of God in both kataphatic and apophatic terms. Kataphatic theology uses language to express who God is with reference to examples and metaphors. For example, Orthodoxy retains the description of God in the biblical canticles, like the song of Moses' reference to God as a warrior who defeats his enemies with his mighty right hand.

Apophatic theology respects the unapproachable quality of God's nature. There is no way any human can understand God because God is beyond the capacity for humans to experience him. This category of theology prefers an apophatic approach, to speak of God with language referring to what God is not. Orthodoxy resists attempts to anthropomorphize God, to humanize God, because God is unlike humanity, though there are some exceptions to this principle. Technically, God does not have a gender since this belongs to creation, though the Orthodox Church regards God as Father to honor the witness of his son, Jesus Christ. God cannot be portrayed in an image because he is invisible and unseen.

For Orthodox, the two most important attributes of God are communion and love. God shares his divine nature with the Son and the Holy Spirit. Theologians refer to the three divine persons of the Godhead as dwelling in *perichoresis*, something like a dance where the three persons all look at one another.[1] The two attributes of God come together in the image of a divine dance – love, as the three are oriented toward the others (and not themselves), and communion, since life is shared together.

Divine communion and love extend to humankind and creation. Orthodoxy receives the first creation story of Adam and Eve in Paradise as ideal: the two humans live with God in Paradise. They can hear God walking in the garden. The humans, creatures, and God form a community. God creates Eve so that Adam and Eve can form a community. God creates a covenant with Abraham and all of his descendants, and God becomes the king of a nation and people so that God and the people form a community that transcends the chasm separating heaven from earth.

GOD IS LOVE

God's relationship with the people is anchored in communion and love. God's purpose for creating humankind was to share love, to be with one another and with God. Orthodoxy believes that the divine design for humanity was for all to become like God, fellow lovers of humankind. God always wants the people to remain in covenant with him. Orthodoxy interprets the love of God by drawing from Jesus' teachings. The parable of the prodigal son depicts God as the father who restores his lost son, running out to meet him with joy because he has found his way home (Lk. 15:11–32). God is like the shepherd who leaves the ninety-nine sheep in order to find the one that was lost, to bring it home (Mt. 18:12). God is the true shepherd in Ezekiel's prophecy, ruling directly over his people following the moral failings of the appointed shepherds (Ez. 34). God is the model for Jesus' commandment that his disciples forgive seventy times seven (Mt. 18:22). God wrote a new covenant on the hearts of the people, despite their betrayal of the covenant they forged with God (Jer. 31:33). The whole purpose of God's inviting people into his covenant is to be with them, to love them, and to restore them to life forever, with God and one another.

St. Symeon the New Theologian, a monk of the Monastery of St. Mamas in Constantinople in the eleventh century, was among the Orthodox theologians reflecting on the profundity of God's love.[2] Symeon expresses the Orthodox view on divine love for humankind in his ethical discourses. In his eighth discourse, Symeon describes divine love through the metaphor of a pearl. God sends down his love for humankind by allowing it to fall from heaven and penetrate each human heart. Discovering the priceless pearl in one's heart is transformative. One will do anything to preserve this love, and Symeon pairs this description with the kind of love God expressed toward humankind in being willing to dwell in human flesh and endure suffering.

Symeon frames the reception of divine love in terms of a paradox. He reflects on the finite quality of human gestures – our fasting, prayer, and self-control cannot save the world. The most faithful Christian remains a sinner in spite of their ascetical efforts. None of this changes God's pursuit of the human – God still sends love to dwell in the human heart, to make each person of God and of dwelling in God's presence. Symeon marvels at the relentlessness with which God loves each and every person, even to the point of capacitating the recipient of God's love to respond with thanksgiving and faith.

A number of theologians believe that God's love knows no limits and has been passed on into humanity. Orthodox monk and theologian Lev Gillet describes this attribute of divine love as "love without limits," a love so abundant that it spills over.[3] Divine love is the source that motivates humans toward belonging, to find community, and to partner with another. Gillet notes that even distortions of divine love are not completely bereft of the godly spark of connecting for communion, like a prostitute with a client.

PARTAKING OF THE DIVINE NATURE

While Orthodoxy claims that no one can behold the presence of God, Orthodox theology claims boldly that believers can partake of the divine nature. Theologians have developed this line of thinking in the teaching of St. Gregory Palamas, a monk of Mount Athos in the thirteenth century.[4] Palamas practiced and further developed the Orthodox tradition of interior prayer of the heart, focusing on a simple prayer to Jesus that brings one into union with God. Palamas defended the traditional Orthodox understanding of divine nature, stating that the "essence of God transcends" the senses and that God is superior to and beyond anything one might dare to say about God.[5] In his attempt to explain the light seen by the saints as the practice of interior prayer, Palamas states that the light comes from the grace of God impressed on the mind of the person praying.[6] This grace is not the essence of God, which is unknowable, but is divine energy poured out from God, which the human mind can comprehend by God's assistance.

Palamas's teaching was not without controversy – he was mired in a debate with the Latin theologians of his time, especially Barlaam, who lived in Constantinople. His claims are paradoxical – the unknowable God, beyond all comprehension and apprehension, can be known and seen by the mind through prayer – only by the grace of God. Orthodoxy holds this paradox as a sign of the beauty of God's love.

In summary, Orthodoxy confesses its faith in Yahweh, the God of Israel, and Jesus Christ. God is far beyond anything humans can experience and cannot be described, but God is love and calls all of humankind into an eternal community of love. When humans stray from God, err, and sin, God pursues them relentlessly, with neither pause nor end, to restore them to the covenant of love in and with him.

CHRIST IN THE ECUMENICAL COUNCILS

Orthodox theology begins and ends with Jesus Christ. This statement is consistent with titles given by the author of the book of Revelation to Jesus – Jesus is the alpha and the omega, the beginning and the end of everything for Christians (Rev. 22:13). For Orthodox, "end" does not refer to the conclusion of the earthly life or of a period of time, but end is actually a transition. It is more useful to think of "end" as the beginning of entering into eternity, the fulfillment of humankind's purpose. The content of eternity – life without end – is to dwell with Jesus himself and with the Father and the Holy Spirit through Jesus.

Where did such lofty notions of life without end in Jesus Christ originate? The previous chapter highlighted the significance of the ecumenical councils for the Orthodox Church. Ecumenical councils were convoked from necessity. Christians did not agree on Jesus' identity, and these disputes created division among people. Constantine was the first emperor to convene a council to push Christian leaders to arrive at a consensus that expresses their beliefs.[7] The declarations of these councils are important because Orthodoxy views ecumenical councils as the highest authority of the Church's expression of its beliefs. The declarations of ecumenical councils also contain passages that express Orthodox theology with the most clarity.

For Orthodox, the most important of these passages is the Nicene-Constantinopolitan Creed. The last chapter stated that the Creed bears this title because the delegates to the first council in Nicaea drafted the first version of this creed, followed by revisions and the final version of the text at the Council of Constantinople in 381 CE.

The Creed's statements about Christ are our first primary sources of Orthodox theology. It is a primary source for a second reason. An ecumenical council composed the Creed as an expression of the belief of the entire Church. The ecumenical council represents the belief of the entire church everywhere, in all places. Second, pastors instructed people preparing for Baptism by having them memorize the Creed. In other words, candidates for Baptism had to master the church's statement of faith in order to formally join the church community. Teaching the illiterate masses a complex statement of faith was no easy task and reveals the premium the Orthodox Church placed on believing and confessing faith in Christ correctly.

What exactly did the Church say about Jesus Christ? Here is the first section of the Creed[8]:

> We believe in God, the Father Almighty, Creator of heaven and earth and of all things visible and invisible. And in one Lord Jesus Christ, the son of God, the only-begotten, begotten of the Father before all ages.

The first part of the Creed reveals Orthodoxy's belief that Jesus Christ and God the Father are two distinct beings. Jesus has an origin – he did not appear out of nowhere – he came from God the Father. This teaching is fundamental to Orthodoxy – Jesus' origins are divine and are from the Father. The Creed has no prehistory of the Father – the Father and Jesus are one package, Jesus being God's only-begotten son. Jesus is not only God's only son – he is Lord, *kyrios*, the immortal one. The opening lines of the Creed link Jesus to his family of divine origin – to God himself.[9]

> Light of light; true God of true God; begotten, not made, of one essence with the Father, through whom all things were made.

This next section of the Creed brings us to the difficult passages. The Nicene Council deliberated on Jesus' divine nature passionately, finally settling on the teaching that Christ and the Father are of the same essence or substance (homoousian).[10] This section refers to one of the Orthodox Church's core values – Jesus is just as divine as God. They share the same substance without confusion. Orthodoxy does not teach that there is one God who appears in different modes – sometimes Father and sometimes Son – but always the same God. Orthodoxy teaches that Jesus and his father share the same divine nature – they are equal in their godhood.

Historically, the teaching of the Council of Nicaea placed a new emphasis on Christ as God. The Creed attempts to seal the fullness of Christ's divine nature (or godhood) by insisting that Christ was not a creature. Christ is light because God is light. There is no deficiency in Christ's divine nature – he is just as much God as God is. Therefore, God did not create Christ – this makes Christ unlike all other creatures. Furthermore, Christ was with God from the beginning, before time.

Humans cannot conceive of existing without time because time governs our existence. Time establishes the rhythms that govern our lives, our seasons, our joys, and our sorrows. Everything takes place within time. Sometimes, major life (or death) events feel like they suspend time. It feels like time stops when someone dear to us dies. It can also feel like time stops in moments of pure joy, as during a moment of intimacy shared on a date. The Creed claims that God and Christ existed and dwelt together before time.

The Creed asserts several central points. This teaching shows that the Father and Son are subordinate to no one nor anything. Every living creature, everything, is subject to God – the Father and the Son cannot be contained or constrained or limited in any way. Second, it is one thing to make this claim about the Father and another thing to describe the Son in this way. The Son is together with God before time to establish their inseparability and also the fullness of divine nature in the Son.

Third is the fundamental point about impossibility. How can something or someone exist before time? How is this possible? It can be possible only for an almighty divine power. The teaching is designed to remind Christians that it is inappropriate and inaccurate to ascribe human qualities, features, and characteristics to God. God is beyond humanity, totally other, and God's nature is incomprehensible to humans. And yet, despite the distance and gaps separating humankind from God, God grants us access to him – intimate, loving access – through the Son.[11]

> Who for us men and for our salvation came down from heaven, was incarnate of the Holy Spirit and the virgin Mary, and became man. And he was crucified for us under Pontius Pilate, and suffered, and was buried. And the third day he rose again, according to the Scriptures, and ascended into heaven, and sits at the right

hand of the Father; and he shall come again with glory to judge the living and the dead; whose kingdom shall have no end.

This section of the Creed briefly retells the story of salvation history. If the previous section emphasizes Christ's divine nature, these sentences establish the fullness of Jesus' humanity. Jesus came into the world from heaven and had the same human experience everyone else endures. He was born, suffered, and died, a full participant in the human experience. The Creed mentions Jesus as a historical person – his crucifixion took place under the governance of Pontius Pilate. The Creed establishes the fullness of Jesus' human nature. His birth was like everyone else's in that he had a mother; it was unlike everyone else's because he had no human father.

Including the record of Jesus' death under Pontius Pilate is a way of arguing against groups that denied the fullness of Jesus' human nature. We previously mentioned the docetists, who argued that Jesus had appeared to be human. The New Testament itself mentions bystanders who warned the Roman authorities that Jesus' disciples might steal his body (Mt. 27:64). The Nicene-Constantinopolitan Creed insists that Jesus died – he was not spared from death, like the prophet Elijah (2 Kings 2:11).

This section of the Creed ends with Jesus' resurrection and ascension. Orthodoxy confesses the real bodily resurrection of Jesus. The resurrection does not stand alone – it is fused with his ascension into heaven and seating at the right hand of the Father. Jesus' ascension into heaven is a crucial component of the paschal mystery. Jesus was with God before time and returns to God after his resurrection. This part of the paschal mystery expressed by the Creed implies a hopeful promise in Orthodoxy – Jesus, who endured the entire human experience, lives forever with the Father. A human being sits at the right hand of the Father. Orthodoxy understands Jesus' ascension into heaven as an eternal session – as the high priest, Jesus is the mediator for all of humankind with God (Heb. 8:6). He has also blazed the path for the rest of humankind – their destiny is like his, to dwell with the Father forever. Orthodoxy views Christ as the forerunner for all humans. Their ultimate destiny is to be with God for eternity.

The next part of the Nicene Creed iterates the promise of Christ's second coming. He will come again to judge the living and the dead.

The inclusion of this passage during the time of the composition of the Creed represents the expectation of the apostles themselves. Christian communities as minorities within the Roman Empire believed that Christ was coming again, and soon. The imminence of Christ's second coming inspired the Apostle Paul to declare that the present world is passing away (1 Cor. 7:29).

THE HYPOSTATIC UNION – LIKE US IN EVERY WAY EXCEPT FOR SIN

Does the Nicene-Constantinopolitan Creed express everything Orthodoxy has to say about Christ? The Creed revealed the desire of the council's fathers to substantiate their claims that Christ is indeed God and that the God of Abraham, Isaac, and Jacob is the Father with whom Christ was before the creation of time and the world. The emphasis on Jesus' godhood and the identification of Christ with the Word of God from John's Gospel raised new questions about the person Jesus and Christ. What kind of a person is both God and human? Did the Word of God descend into Jesus the carpenter from Nazareth, with two people coming together in one body? How could one explain that there was one Jesus who was both God and human? These kinds of questions are not foreign to inquirers of the twenty-first century who are familiar with meta-human comic book characters possessing powers obtained from diverse sources.

The next major council after Constantinople took place in Ephesus in 431. This council addressed the teachings of Nestorius, archbishop of Constantinople. In his attempt to make sense of Jesus as both God and human, Nestorius sought to maintain the distinction of the human and divine natures of Christ.[12] A cult of Mary, Jesus' mother, had begun to emerge among virgins and women in Constantinople, and Nestorius began to refer to Mary as Anthropotokos – the mother of a human. The Council of Ephesus defined Mary as Theotokos – the mother of God – to protect, again, the fullness of the divine nature of Jesus Christ, who received his human nature from Mary.[13] This teaching clarified the totality of Jesus' godhood. There was no deficiency in his divine nature because Mary was the mother of God.

The Council of Ephesus' definition of Mary as Theotokos introduced another term into Christian liturgy and piety. Communities began to dedicate their temples to Mary at this point in time, with particular feasts ascribed to events in Mary's life.[14] This book discusses the significance of Marian piety in the chapter on liturgy, but there is one point of theological emphasis worth mentioning here. The continued Christian emphasis on Christ as God widened the gap separating ordinary Christian believers from Jesus. Mary's new title, Theotokos, put the spotlight on Mary, and Christian faithful found her to be an accessible intercessor. Christ's divinity created an opportunity for Mary to become the primary mediator for ordinary Christians, who could relate to her humanity.

The Council of Chalcedon's (451) definition of the hypostatic union of divinity and humanity in Christ was supposed to resolve the debates raging among Christians. The Orthodox Church joins the Roman and most Protestant communions in confirming the Chalcedonian definition of Christ. Jesus is perfectly divine and human, two natures united by one person without commixture.[15]

The churches that continue to deny the Chalcedonian confession while believing that Christ is both divine and human in one nature essentially share the same belief. The Eastern Orthodox community of churches adheres to the Chalcedonian definition known as "diaphysite" (two natures) among theologians, whereas the Oriental Orthodox churches confess faith in Christ, whose nature is both divine and human. The one nature is miaphysite, and the Oriental churches faithfully confess the Christology of Cyril of Alexandria that shaped the Council of Ephesus, defended and developed by significant teachers such as Ephrem the Syrian (fourth century) and Severus of Antioch (sixth century).[16]

SYRIAN THEOLOGIANS: EPHREM THE SYRIAN AND SEVERUS OF ANTIOCH

Christian theologians celebrate Ephrem because of the eloquence of his poetry. Ephrem was born around 309 CE in Nisibis and served faithfully for many years as a deacon of his Syriac-language church.[17] He moved to Edessa toward the end of his life and participated in the distribution of grain to the hungry and poor during a famine that took his own life in 373.[18] Ephrem composed hymns for the church in the early stages of its Christological controversies, in between the councils of Nicaea and Constantinople. Ephrem's writings are reputed for their artistic prose, as he employed skilled technical devices that express Orthodoxy's core beliefs in Syriac idioms.[19] The homily "On Our Lord" expresses theological ideas featured by the Syriac-speaking communities of the fourth century. In this writing, Ephrem marveled at the incarnation of Christ, praising God for liberating those who were held captive in Sheol – a reference to Christ's paschal victory over death. Ephrem wrote, "and he journeyed from Sheol and resided in the kingdom, to tread a path from Sheol, which cheats everyone, to the kingdom, which rewards everyone."[20] Ephrem brings together the events of salvation history in this homily – Christ's birth, coming, and death – with rare poetic eloquence.

Severus was an anti-Chalcedonian patriarch of Antioch from 512 to 518.[21] While the Eastern Orthodox condemned Severus as a heretic, the Oriental churches regard him as a saint.[22] Severus's tenure as patriarch of Antioch is valuable to us because his writings express both an intentional sense of anti-Chalcedonian thought and the strong fidelity to miaphysite Christology retained by the Oriental churches. In one of his hymns, Severus attributes a drought to the sins committed by his flock and not because of their refusal to adopt the Chalcedonian definition of faith.[23] Severus refers to the Chalcedonians as "followers of the error of two natures" and declares "there is one nature in the incarnate word" to be the authentic orthodox faith.[24] In another hymn, Severus praises the birth of Christ as the fulfillment of Isaiah's prophecy, affirms Mary's ever-virginity, defines Christ as both "terrestrial and celestial," and exhorts the faithful to praise him as God and also "friend of humanity."[25] Severus serves as an important example of a creative and prodigious theologian of a miaphysite community who sustains the theological legacy of Cyril of Alexandria while resisting political pressure to adopt the Chalcedonian definition of faith.

The examples taken from Ephrem and Severus testify to expressions of Orthodox theology outside of the mainstream Greek fathers who shaped the ecumenical councils. Ephrem wrote and served with grace and eloquence in Nisibis and Edessa, in Syriac. Severus was a productive and vocal leader of the miaphysite community in the sixth century. These theological witnesses demonstrate the breadth of Orthodox theology and the contributions of teachers beloved to the Oriental Orthodox community from the patristic age.

SIXTH AND SEVENTH ECUMENICAL COUNCILS

The sixth and seventh ecumenical councils were important for Orthodox Christology. The sixth council (in Constantinople, 681) insisted that Christ had two wills, one divine and one human, consistent with the Chalcedonian definition. Christ submitted his human will to the divine will in this framework. The seventh council held in Nicaea in 787 endorsed the legitimacy of the veneration of the icons. The chapters on liturgy and spirituality will explore the minutiae of Orthodox icon veneration in church and domestic settings.

Theologically, Orthodox Christology essentially legitimized all icon veneration. The Christian doctrine of incarnation, the word of God becoming flesh, dwelling among us, and enduring the human experience made it possible to depict and worship his image. It is ironic that the first and most noteworthy period of Christian iconoclasm took place in the Byzantine East, because the victory of icon veneration had epic consequences. The interior decoration of churches changed permanently, and icons increased in their importance for presenting Jesus Christ to the faithful. In this sense, the seventh ecumenical council was just as significant for its endorsement of Orthodox Christology as the councils of Nicaea, Constantinople, and Chalcedon, a testimony that confirms icon veneration as a true triumph of Orthodoxy.

ST. ATHANASIUS'S ON THE INCARNATION: A FOUNDATION FOR ORTHODOX CHRISTOLOGY

St. Athanasius of Alexandria was the main ideologue of the Council of Nicaea in 325.[26] A deacon at the time of the council, he was the brilliant thinker who crafted the language that established the fullness of Jesus' godhood. Athanasius was consecrated bishop in 328 CE. He was exiled five times during his episcopate, for a total of fourteen years, a testimony to the turbulence in the Christian world of the fourth century. St. Athanasius expressed his thinking to refute the assertions circulated by Arius and his disciples. Arius taught that Jesus was superior to humanity, that God had raised him from the dead because of his righteousness, and that he was the son of God. Arius attempted to maintain the distinction between Jesus and his Father and taught that Christ was created and inferior to the Father.

We have encountered the legacy of Athanasius' insistence on the fullness of Jesus' godhood in our examination of the Creed. St. Athanasius develops Orthodox Christology with greater depth in his famous theological treatise, *On the Incarnation of Christ*.

Athanasius develops several assertions about Christ in his treatise that form the core of mainstream Orthodox Christology. He forms his thesis by posing a question framed around the notion of the "divine dilemma." The dilemma is what to do about humankind. Humankind has gone astray and is acting in a way alien to God's purpose in creating us.[27] Athanasius reviews possible acts of God to address this issue, including destroying humankind and repentance.

In the end, Athanasius says that there is only one way forward: to renew the image of God in humankind through the incarnation of Christ. Christ renews the divine image in all of humankind by becoming human himself.[28] His saving act is manifold. Christ offers himself as a sacrifice that settles humanity's debt of sin. His death is voluntary because of love. His saving death is final – it settles the account with sin once and for all, and there is no need to revisit the issue.[29] Christ alone performs this act on behalf of all humankind, which is why it is a saving act.

Athanasius emphasizes three points that are central to Orthodox Christian Christology. First, Jesus' death was necessary. Athanasius says repeatedly that there was no other way for God to save humankind, that Jesus' death was the only way to redeem a humankind that had become so corrupt. Second, Christ's voluntary death destroyed and annulled death itself because Christ's divine and immortal nature overcame death by filling it with the life of God. Athanasius insists on the immortality of the Word of God – the divine nature of Christ cannot die – and that the presence of the immortal Word of God destroys the power of death over humanity forever.[30]

Athanasius explains that Christ's incarnation and resurrection have transformed the human experience of dying. This teaching is important for Orthodox Christianity because the Orthodox Church does not deny the reality of death. Death itself is transformed into a transitory state of expectation of rising to new, glorified, and embodied life. Athanasius explains the hope of the resurrection for humankind by reassuring hearers that bodily mortality means only that "we are dissolved for the time which God has set for each," like seeds sown into the ground.[31] Athanasius follows the teaching of the apostle Paul in his first letter to the Corinthians in setting forth this section on the promise of the resurrection. He anchors his teaching in the testimony of Christians who no longer fear death but embrace it because of their own devotion to Christ and steadfast faith in the resurrection from the dead.[32]

Athanasius's Christology formed the core for Orthodox Christianity, which explains why his treatise remains a classic text, translated into numerous languages, to this day. Here is a brief summary of Athanasius's main points:

- The Incarnation of Christ, or the indwelling of the Word of God, was the only solution worthy of God's goodness and love to the dilemma of humankind's corruption.
- Christ took a human body from the virgin Mary in order to die.
- The indwelling of the Word of God in a human body restores the divine image given to each human being, like a resetting of human nature.
- Death was necessary because one person had to die to settle the account with death and annul humanity's transgressions.
- The death of Christ is a paradox: his death destroyed death forever, because the Word of God is immortal and cannot die.
- The destruction of death removes the power the devil held over humanity in death, and capacitates all of humankind to rise to new, eternal, embodied life.

CHRISTOLOGY IN THE LITURGY

How do Orthodox Christians learn about Christ? The liturgical tradition of Orthodoxy is its primary public expression of Christology. The Divine Liturgy and a handful of important holidays are the primary sources of Christology for the vast majority of Orthodox Christians. This section reviews the "Only-begotten Son" hymn appended to the second antiphon and the anaphora, or Eucharistic Prayer.

The "Only-begotten son" hymn sung as the hymn-refrain on the second antiphon is well-known to Orthodox Christians. Composed by Emperor Justinian in the sixth century, the hymn expresses Orthodox Christology concisely. I think of the Only-begotten hymn as a mini-creed in the Divine Liturgy, one occasionally sung and heard somewhat casually since it is so familiar to the people. Here is a translation of the Only-begotten Son hymn[33]:

> Only-begotten Son and immortal word of God, who for our salvation willed to be incarnate of the holy Theotokos and every-virgin Mary,
> Who without change became man and were crucified,
> O Christ our God, trampling down death by death
> being one of the Holy Trinity, glorified with the Father and the Holy Spirit: save us!

The hymn draws from the Creed to express Orthodox Christology. The divine and human natures of the Son of God are expressed by adjectives ascribed to God. Christ is immortal, incarnate of the Theotokos, and did not experience change when he took on humanity. The Trinitarian clause echoes the creed, and the hymn ends with a paschal petition – the one who has defeated death can save the faithful. The use of language from the creed and from the councils is also noteworthy. The outcome of the Only-begotten Son hymn is the same as the Great Doxology. The people relearn and confess the core fundamentals of the Orthodox Church when they sing and hear this hymn.

The anaphora, or Eucharistic prayer, expresses the quintessential high Christology characterizing Orthodoxy. Currently, the Orthodox Church uses three Divine Liturgies ascribed to St. John Chrysostom, St. Basil the Great (of Caesarea), and St. James of Jerusalem, along with the liturgy of Presanctified Gifts in Lent. The Eucharistic prayers of the Divine Liturgies express Orthodox Christology.

The language of the anaphoras is dialogical, with the Church addressing God the Father. The anaphoras recall Christ's paschal mystery. The anaphora of St. John Chrysostom is quite brief. The text praises God and uses words that embellish aspects of the divine nature that humans can neither experience nor comprehend[34]:

> For you are God: ineffable, inconceivable, invisible, incomprehensible, ever-existing and eternally the same, You and your only-begotten son and your Holy Spirit.

Orthodoxy expresses its reverence for God with these adjectives, which the text then assigns to the persons of the Son and the Holy Spirit. The heart of the Eucharistic prayer is the remembrance of Christ's paschal mystery. The church remembers the paschal mystery as Christ's saving acts done "for us" and iterates specifically the cross, burial in the tomb, resurrection, ascension, session, and second coming.[35] The paschal mystery functions as the catalyst for thanksgiving and petition. Pascha is not an isolated moment of the past but the crux of the present – remembrance of Christ's glorified humanity is what makes Orthodox Christology relevant in the present.

The Orthodox Church uses the Eucharistic prayer of St. Basil less frequently. One section of this prayer is a powerful narrative of Orthodox Christology at its best, a reflection on the New Testament narrative of Jesus Christ.[36] The liturgical text retells the story of Jesus Christ's salvation of the world in simple, prayerful language. The liturgy of St. Basil claims that God spoke to the world through the Son, who became human and saved the world by condemning "sin in the flesh."[37] The text explains how Jesus Christ saved humankind in ways that do not appear in the Creed. For example, the anaphora of St. Basil claims that God adopted the Christian people and identifies them as a "peculiar people, a royal priesthood, a holy nation."[38] St. Basil's Eucharistic prayer also mentions a dimension of Jesus' death and resurrection that appears neither in the Creed nor in the liturgy of St. John Chrysostom but is a staple of Orthodox Christology: Jesus' descent into Hades. This version of Jesus' salvation is similar to that of St. Athanasius: Jesus paid the debt owed through his death, a payment that freed the rest of humankind from death.[39]

Jesus' conquering of Hades ended humanity's destiny of separation from God. St. Basil's prayer envisions Jesus as a human trailblazer – by conquering death and rising in the flesh, he has enabled all humans to follow in his path and find eternal life – in the body – with God. It is essential to note that ordinary Orthodox Christians do not encounter this central teaching on how Jesus saves humankind and gives people hope for eternal life in the Creed or other shorter, memorable texts. St. Basil's prayer makes this claim, but it is confined to a select number of Sundays of the liturgical year, which means that people do not hear it recited very often. In fact, this portion of the prayer is customarily read silently so that the people do not hear it at all. The people's lack of awareness of this rich source of theology is lamentable, but it still remains one of the most important expressions of Orthodox Christology.

In conclusion, Orthodox Christology depends on the assertions of the ecumenical councils, especially the first four (Nicaea, Constantinople, Ephesus, and Chalcedon). While Orthodoxy confesses the fullness of Christ's divine and human natures, the church seems to emphasize the divine nature of Christ in its outward expression. Treatises like the one of Athanasius address questions about Christ that caused trouble in the early church. Athanasius, like Ignatius before him, goes to great lengths to argue that Christ was truly human and did not simply appear to be human. Athanasius demonstrates Christ's humanity by confirming he lived an ordinary human life, eating, drinking, and experiencing pain and anguish. He also argues that Christ's voluntary death was not the same as suicide – he accepted God's plan for him to die because this death offered on behalf of all for all was necessary. The ecumenical councils addressed some of these issues as well. For example, the sixth ecumenical council upholds the fullness of Christ's humanity by confirming the existence of a complete human will in Christ.

THEOLOGY OF THE HOLY SPIRIT (PNEUMATOLOGY)

The Orthodox Church is consistent in its theology of the Holy Spirit. The primary source for this theology is the repository of the ecumenical councils, along with reliance on the teachings of certain church fathers. This section introduces the term pneumatology – Orthodox belief on the Holy Spirit.

At the official level, Orthodox pneumatology is similar to Catholic and Protestant approaches. The Orthodox, Catholic, and Protestant churches believe that the Holy Spirit is one of the three persons of the Holy Trinity, foretold by the prophets, fully divine, and distinct from both the Father and the Son. There are two areas of difference. The first is doctrinal. Christian churches of the West added a clause to the Nicene-Constantinopolitan Creed, first at the Council of Toledo (589) and then more formally during the reign of Emperor Charlemagne in the ninth century. The line "And I believe in the Holy Spirit, the Lord and Creator of Life, who proceeds from the Father, and is worshipped together with the Father and the Son" changed to "proceeds from the Father and the Son," known as the filioque clause.

Orthodoxy's confession of the Holy Spirit as God originates from the apostolic age. Jesus instructs his disciples that he is sending the comforter to them, the Holy Spirit, even as he is preparing for his passion and death and, ultimately, his departure from the world (Jn 14). The book of Acts records that the Holy Spirit descends upon the disciples when they gather after Jesus' ascension into heaven. This is a crucial point in early Christian history – the apostles begin to establish communities centered around the retelling of the story of Jesus' coming and salvation of the world.

Fourth-century Christians grappled with precise definitions of the Holy Spirit even as they gradually developed language to describe Christ. The Council of Nicaea did not resolve questions about Christ definitively. Teachers like Appolinaris held that the soul of the Word of God replaced Jesus' human soul.[40] Disciples of disavowed teachers like Arius and Eunomius held diverging views on the person of the Holy Spirit. Some viewed the Spirit as created, others as angelic and ministering, but completely unlike the Father and the Son.[41] A group emerged that opposed the equality of the Holy Spirit as God. This group was known as the Pneumatomachians – fighters against the Spirit.[42]

Leo Davis writes that Athanasius, still the most prominent Orthodox theologian in between the councils of Nicaea and Constantinople, began to articulate a pneumatology claiming that the Spirit is consubstantial with the Father and the Son and therefore an equal member of the Holy Trinity.[43]

St. Basil of Caesarea, member of a prominent Christian family, ascetic, and author of numerous theological treatises, took the mantle of lead theologian after Athanasius' death in 373. Basil was the one who provided a more precise definition of the person of the Spirit and how the three persons of the Holy Trinity are differentiated. Davis notes that Basil was the theologian who cemented the use of the word hypostasis, which we usually translate as person, to show that Father, Son, and Holy Spirit are all distinct hypostases (persons). It is their essence or substance (ousia) that unites them. These distinctions are important. There are neither three Gods nor three modalities of one God, but three persons – Father, Son, and Holy Spirit – united by their shared godhood. Basil made another distinction among the three persons of the Trinity that would prove to be a central feature of Orthodox theology. The Father is the source of divine nature – it proceeds in the Son and is perfected in the Holy Spirit.[44] Basil's teaching contributed to the expansion of the Nicene Creed at the Council of Constantinople in 381. Here we will review the passage of the Creed pertaining to the Holy Spirit.

> [I believe in] The Holy Spirit, the giver of life, who proceeds from the Father, who with the Father and the Son is worshipped and glorified, who spoke by the prophets.

This short clause expresses the Orthodox belief in the Holy Spirit. The Holy Spirit proceeds from the Father. The use of the word "proceeds" distinguishes the Holy Spirit from the Son, who is begotten of the Father. In the first sentence, the Holy Spirit proceeds from the Father alone – there is no mention of the Son here. This sentence emphasizes the Father alone as the source of divine nature, a hallmark of Orthodox theology. The Holy Spirit's procession from the Father avoids any sense of the Spirit being inferior or subordinate to the Son. The final sentence emphasizes the divine nature of the Holy Spirit – the Spirit is worshipped together with the Father and the Son, an act that is appropriate only for God. The Orthodox Church uses this version of the Creed to this day – it has never added the filioque clause to the Creed. St. Basil himself testified to the Holy Spirit's godhood in his famous treatise "On the Holy Spirit," which includes an oft-cited passage of a prayer: "I render the glory due to God in both ways; namely, to the Father, with the Son together with the Holy Spirit, and to the Father, through the Son, in the Holy Spirit."[45]

It is necessary to turn now to the filioque clause, even though it interrupts some of the historical flow. The fact of the matter is that Orthodoxy has refused to adopt the filioque despite its sustained use in the Church of the West. The filioque emerged in the sixth century at the Third Council of Toledo (589) as the Western church continued to battle against Arianism.[46] Yves Congar states that the filioque was professed on multiple occasions in the subsequent centuries and never caused the Orthodox Church to break communion with the West.[47] Christians in the West believed that the filioque was part of the original Nicene-Constantinopolitan Creed and actually protested the absence of the filioque from the creed at the Second Council of Nicaea in 787.

As is often the case in church history, complaints about a theological issue and demands for the removal of a statement or the addition of a clause are noteworthy but do not necessarily warrant breaking communion. The Orthodox Church's rejection of the filioque clause stands on two fundamental points, theological and disciplinary. Theologically, Orthodoxy rejects the filioque because it appears to subordinate the Holy Spirit to the Father and the Son, and it also challenges the longstanding Orthodox position that the Father alone is the source of the divine nature. This was the position of Patriarch Photius of Constantinople already in the ninth century, before the Roman See invoked the filioque as one of its grievances in the bull of excommunication delivered to Hagia Sophia in Constantinople in 1054.[48]

The second issue for Orthodoxy is disciplinary. Orthodoxy is consistent in its adherence to the authority of ecumenical councils. Only an ecumenical council can revise a credal statement, and Orthodoxy insisted upon the originality and authority of the Creed of 381.[49] We reviewed a few of the thorny historical issues associated with the history of the creed in an earlier chapter, but in the mind and memory of the Orthodox Church as a community, the Creed hearkens back to its completion in 381.

THE HOLY SPIRIT AND THE SON OF GOD

The Orthodox Church believes that God the Father sent his only-begotten Son, Jesus Christ, into the world to save humankind. We have also seen that the Church believes that the Holy Spirit proceeds from the Father and is worshipped and glorified as God. What exactly does the Holy Spirit do, and where does the Orthodox Church identify the Holy Spirit's activity in salvation history?

The short answer to this question is that the Holy Spirit is active in creating, prophesying, and, most importantly, revealing God's presence and love in the world. Once again, it is the liturgical tradition of the Orthodox Church that serves as the primary source for its belief in the Holy Spirit. The following section presents examples from the liturgical tradition of the church to show how the Holy

Spirit is active in creation and making God present to the world. This analysis is limited in its scope to show how the Church's experience of the liturgy reveals its belief in the Holy Spirit.

THE HOLY SPIRIT IN THE EUCHARISTIC PRAYER

The Orthodox Church is clear in its belief about the true presence of Jesus Christ in the bread and cup used for Holy Communion. The bread and cup become the body and blood of Christ. This transformation takes place through the descent and activity of the Holy Spirit.

The Eucharistic prayers of the liturgies of St. Basil the Great and John Chrysostom reveal the activity of the Holy Spirit. The presider (bishop or priest) prays during the liturgy of St. Basil[50]:

> And having set forth the likenesses of the holy body and blood of your Christ, we pray and beseech you, o holy of holies, in the good pleasure of your bounty, that your all-Holy Spirit may come upon us and upon these gifts set forth, and bless them and sanctify and make […] this bread the precious body of our Lord and God and Savior Jesus Christ. And this cup the precious blood of our Lord and God and Savior Jesus Christ.

The text in the liturgy of St. John Chrysostom is slightly different[51]:

> We offer you also this reasonable and bloodless service, and we pray and beseech and entreat you, send down your Holy Spirit on us and on these gifts set forth, and make this bread the precious body of your Christ, [changing it by your Holy Spirit,] Amen; and that which is in this cup the precious blood of your Christ, changing it by your Holy Spirit.

These texts from the Divine Liturgy disclose the activity of the Holy Spirit that is most familiar to Orthodox people. The Holy Spirit acts by changing the bread and wine into the body and blood of Christ. The English translation of the texts uses a number of verbs to convey this transformation, usually with "make" and "change," and also the request that God would send down the Holy Spirit. The actual change is in the bread and wine in the cup – they become Jesus Christ's body and blood.

DOES ORTHODOXY HAVE A "MOMENT OF CONSECRATION?"

Many pastors and theologians of the Orthodox, Catholic, and Protestant churches have obsessed about the details about the transformation of bread and wine into Jesus' body and blood.[52] Some Orthodox and Catholic theologians engaged in a lively debate on exactly when and how this transformation takes place during the Divine Liturgy. The Church's desire to protect and defend correct doctrine – in this case, the true presence of Jesus Christ in the bread and the cup – motivated detailed reflections on the exact moment in the Divine Liturgy the transformation takes place. Catholic theologians identified the bishop or priest's recitation of Jesus' words – "take, eat, this is my body; drink of it, all of you, this is my blood" – as the moment of consecration.[53]

In response, some Orthodox theologians, especially the fourteenth-century mystagogue Nicholas Cabasilas, identified the descent of the Holy Spirit upon the bread and the cup as the moment of consecration.[54] Sometimes, theologians use the word "epiclesis" to define this moment. Epiclesis means "petition," and in the liturgy, epiclesis refers to the community's request that God would act. In most cases, theologians have the Holy Spirit in mind when God acts. The transformation of the bread and wine of Holy Communion into Jesus Christ's body and blood is the result of an epiclesis. In the late medieval era, Catholics identified Jesus' words as the epiclesis, and the Orthodox viewed the request that God would "send down" the Holy Spirit as the epiclesis. In our time, there is wide agreement among liturgical theologians that both Jesus' words and the sending down of the Holy Spirit are epicleses.

All of this obsessive analysis about the changing of bread and wine into Jesus' body and blood fails to answer the most important questions. Why does this matter at all? Why is this moment in the Divine Liturgy so important?

For decades, maybe even centuries, it seemed like persuading the Christian masses that the bread and the wine had truly become Jesus' body and blood was the most important aspect of the discussion. It would be a mistake to dismiss the debate as a relic of the past. Expressing confidence that the God the Church worships is living, active, and still creating, especially on the church's behalf, was and remains important. This topic was a concern to Jesus himself, who knows that some of his followers are scandalized by his bread of life discourse in the Gospel of John (Jn 6). Some of his disciples abandoned him at that point. To be sure, Jesus' own words are challenging. He says, 'unless you eat the flesh of the Son of Man and drink his blood, you have no life in you' (Jn. 6:53). The Orthodox Church goes to great pains to argue that the bread and wine are truly his body and blood. The church believes it is observing the tradition it inherited over the course of many centuries. Is the church attempting to defend cannibalism? If not, then what is the point of the teaching, and what does the Holy Spirit have to do with it?

Orthodox Christians are committed to preserving two truths. The first is that God remains active. History did not end with Jesus' resurrection from the dead and ascension into heaven. The Orthodox Church believes that Christ is present and active among his followers every time they gather in his memory. This is why the Divine Liturgy contains numerous instances of the greeting, "Christ is in our midst!" "He is and ever shall be!" Orthodoxy also preserves its unique teaching that the Holy Spirit is the one who makes Christ present. We have already seen how the Eucharistic prayers express this sentiment.

Pastors and theologians have traditionally focused on the passages of texts where one can identify an invocation that leads to a consecration, especially when God sends the Spirit on something material that then becomes a symbol of Christ's presence, like bread and wine. The texts also express the other purpose of the Holy Spirit's activity – to create a space in which the people live with the living God. Immediately after asking God to change the bread and wine into Christ's body and blood in the liturgy of St. Basil, the church continues to pray by asking that God would unite everyone who receives Holy Communion into "fellowship with the one Holy Spirit."[55]

This particular passage shows that changing the bread and wine into Christ's body and blood is just one part of the Holy Spirit's activity. The Holy Spirit comes to host an event – a sacred meal where all of the guests become part of God's family. The point of Communion is not to witness the miracle of bread and wine becoming Jesus' body and blood. The Orthodox view is that the Father sends the Holy Spirit to make Jesus Christ present among his people and for all of them to renew their covenant with God and begin the process of dwelling in him for all of eternity. Fellowship is a powerful bond, one that is much stronger than rushing through a meal to fill one's belly without paying attention to the host and the others dining at the host's dinner.

The Orthodox liturgy expresses a profound pneumatology. The most important conclusion we offer here is that the community asks God to send the Holy Spirit upon them and the gifts they offer. God responds by sending the Holy Spirit, who makes Jesus Christ present to the gathered community. The people strengthen their bonds with both the visible and invisible communities – Father, Son, and Holy Spirit; the ranks of archangels and angels; and the people of God in heaven and on earth – at these events.

The Orthodox liturgy frequently confirms the traditional interpretation of the relationship of the Spirit to the Father and to the Son. The Church addresses God the Father and asks him to send the Spirit to make the Son present among his people. The purpose of the descent of the Spirit on the Church is to make the Son present. All three persons of the Holy Trinity are active – the Father sending the Spirit, the Spirit making the Son present, and the people of the Church encountering the Father because they are united with the Son through Baptism, anointing, and communion.

GOD'S PLAN FOR HUMANKIND

The Orthodox Church follows St. Paul's teaching that Adam and Eve, the first human beings, lived with God in Paradise until they disobeyed God's command to abstain from eating the fruit from the tree of the knowledge of good and evil. God's expulsion of Adam and Eve from Paradise to earth subjected them to corruption and death. We reviewed St. Athanasius's teaching that humanity's separation from God kept humans in a vicious cycle of sin and corruption, marked by awful deeds and acts in the worst cases. St. Athanasius taught that the Incarnation changed human nature and enabled humans to become like God. This teaching is known as theosis – the process of becoming like God. Orthodoxy endorses theosis is God's plan for humanity, a most optimistic view of humankind's destiny.

A number of church fathers express the main themes of Orthodoxy's view on the human being. This section presents a selection of teachings from St. Basil of Caesarea, Gregory of Nyssa, and Maximus

Confessor that contributed to the shaping of the Orthodox view of God's plan for humanity.[56]

God created humanity to have dominion over all other living things. Humanity ruled over the other creatures by God's ordinance. This appointment to an august life requires temperance of spirit, so the humans understand that they remain subject and accountable to God, who alone governs the universe. Basil emphasizes the capacity for humans to maintain control over their inner lives. He acknowledges humanity's rule over even winged creatures and emphasizes that governing others requires strict rule over their own passions and thoughts. Humans desiring to exercise dominion over the other creatures will be unable to do so effectively if they cannot maintain control over their personal lives and private affairs.[57] Basil taught that the earthly origin of humanity serves as a necessary reminder of a humble disposition. God made humanity from the dust of the earth. Humanity has humble origins that have been elevated because of God, who endowed humanity with a soul.[58]

Humans are prone to indulge passions because of their unique composition as material creatures who are also made in God's image and likeness. Both Basil and Gregory of Nyssa (Basil's younger brother) note the distinguishing features of humans. Humans stand on two feet and are upright so that their inclination is oriented toward the heavens and not the earth. Basil describes God's purpose for sheep as dwelling in pasture to enjoy the pleasure of filling their stomachs. God's purpose for humans is to look to the sky because that is their destiny – heavenly citizenship.[59] Gregory makes a similar point, arguing that the upright form of the human is a mark of "sovereignty," with the purpose of exercising dominion over creatures who are oriented downwards, to the earth.[60] Gregory adds that human hands are special instruments expressing the rational gift of communication in writing. God gave humans rational nature, described by Gregory as partaking of reason and "ordered by intellect."[61]

Maximus Confessor, in *Ambiguum 42* (written 628–630), asserts that God gives each human being a soul from a divinely willed vital inbreathing.[62] The entire human being, soul and body, is created at the same time. Maximus states that this is the first of three births for each Christian person, with Baptism as the second birth and the resurrection from the dead the third.[63] Maximus takes on the problem of post-baptismal sin, an issue that continues to challenge theologians to this day. If Baptism recreates the divine image in human nature, why do Christians sin afterwards? Maximus describes the baptismal birth as twofold: the first is God's adoption of the Christian, endowing the recipient with the potency of grace, and the second is a birth into God's likeness, which orients the one born of God toward God.[64] Maximus explains that the second birth endows human will to seek God – to make the human will willing to be with God, as it were, or, as Maximus says, to seek deification (theosis).[65]

Basil, Gregory of Nyssa, and Maximus epitomize an Orthodox view of the human person. God has endowed humanity with properties that drive each human toward their ultimate purpose – to be with God for eternity. Human reason and intelligence, a robust spiritual life, and receiving the gift of the Spirit to enable one's will to seek God are the main aspects of God's will. The central point is the destiny of humankind – to return to Paradise and dwell with God there, in an exalted, glorified human life that differs from the one lived in the world. Gregory of Nyssa attempts to describe this life as a return to Paradise, which did not include procreation in the beginning.[66] Paradise is the end of the human journey – humankind possesses special gifts received from God that provide a compass to arrive safely at their divine destination.

HEAVEN, HELL, AND PURGATORY

The Orthodox Church's teaching on the salvation of humankind envisions a specific final destination for both humans and creation. Orthodox theologians tend to refer to this destination as a telos, or end. Theologians use the word eschatology to describe this topic – the theology of what happens at the end, in the last times or period of time before God judges humankind.

Orthodox thought on eschatology and the final destiny of humankind is diverse. Most mainstream Orthodox accept the two-judgment paradigm.[67] Each human being has one life – Orthodoxy rejects reincarnation. At some point soon after death, each human being continues to live as a soul. The human soul dwells for a short-time in an intermediate space, not yet ascending to God for judgment, until the body has been buried.[68] Soon afterwards, the soul ascends to meet God for the first judgment. When God judges a soul as righteous, that soul dwells in a state of happiness in the presence of God while awaiting Christ's second coming for the resurrection of the dead, reception of a new body, and the second and final judgment.[69] The Church expresses confidence that God will affirm the righteousness of the souls that have lived in his presence in the intermediate state. This teaching is not systematized – it is based on a synthesis of thought and the theology of prayers for the departed.[70] The two-judgment paradigm excludes the experience of purgatory, the aspect of judgment professed by the Roman church where all souls are completely purified of their sins before ascending to dwell in the presence of God for eternity.[71]

A minority of Orthodox theologians confess an alternate view on judgment, one that includes purgatory. This teaching is called *apokatastasis*, the recapitulation of all humankind and creation, sometimes known as universal salvation.[72] This teaching draws upon strands of the theology of the Apostle Paul, was initially developed by Origen, and was professed by Orthodox theologians including St. Gregory of Nyssa, St. Isaac the Syrian, Russian émigré theologian Sergius Bulgakov, and contemporary Orthodox theologian David Bentley Hart.

The core principle of universal salvation is the uncontainable power of God's love. Adherents of universal salvation believe that God will receive all of his creatures into his bosom, even outside of time. Gregory of Nyssa and Isaac of Nineveh imagined that even the devil himself would eventually reconcile with God. Bulgakov believed that every human soul would have to come to terms with the entirety of their life – including their sins and trespasses – and that the experience of resurrection prepared them to receive the gift of God's love.[73] Universal salvation differs from the mainstream two-judgment paradigm in its belief and hope that all would be saved at the end, because God's love demanded that all would be reconciled. This school of thought also allows for a type of purgatory.

The theological discourse on salvation raises questions on the fate of the wicked – are they bound to hell for eternity? And if this is the case, what is hell? Hell is customarily confused with Hades. Hades, Sheol in Hebrew, is the underworld location where the dead dwell, separated and isolated from God and all living things. Orthodoxy believes that Jesus destroyed Hades when he descended into hell, releasing the souls who had been held prisoner there. Jean-Claude

Larchet explains that Hades became a place reserved for the suffering of unrepentant sinners following Christ's victory over death.[74]

Orthodox opinions on what constitutes hell vary. Some mainstream thinkers depict hell in traditional terms, as a place of punishment holding the wicked who rejected God.[75] Kallistos Ware urged caution in speculating too much on what happens after death, referring to it as a great mystery.[76] Some thinkers view heaven and hell as the same thing or the same state experienced by both the righteous and the wicked.[77] This school of thought envisions that all humans and creation are in the presence of God for eternity after death. The presence of God is a state of bliss and joy for those who love him; it is eternal suffering and punishment for those who reject God.[78]

Orthodox thinking on the dynamic of time in judgment and eternity is underdeveloped. Many mainstream Orthodox believe that the first judgment occurs on the fortieth day after death. This opinion does not account for the absence of time in eternity – God is the author of time. The presumption of the immortality of the soul is also an issue for Orthodoxy. Orthodoxy has both inherited and embraced the Platonic notion of the superiority of the soul over the body, so that the soul survives death, while the body expires and decomposes. Roman Catholic theologians like Karl Rahner speculated that the final judgment and resurrection could take place immediately after death, since God and God's realm are outside of time.[79] Rahner also suggested that the human soul dies with the body at death, since the human person is unified and not fragmented into different parts. The gift of resurrection applies to both the body and the soul in this paradigm.

How does one make sense of all of these opinions and possibilities, granting that Orthodoxy prefers the two-judgment paradigm? Ware provides a hint when he asserts that death is a mystery and that God will reveal all when he fulfills his promise to save humankind.[80] The fact that so much about eschatology remains unknown is what permits speculation. Some Orthodox believe that conversion and repentance are possible after death and that the prayers offered by the faithful for their departed loved ones are efficacious.

A number of core beliefs are held by all schools of thought on eschatology. Orthodoxy believes without a shred of doubt that God desires the salvation of all humankind because of God's immeasurable love and mercy. The Church asserts that Christ will come into the world a second – and final – time to judge the living and the dead. The Church also believes that the righteous will live forever, embodied and immortal, living with God. Eternal life with God, in a raised body, is the fulfillment of God's promise of the resurrection.

Contemporary Orthodox thought has expanded its scope beyond humankind. This school of Orthodox thought is less anthropocentric (human-focused) and professes the salvation of all of creation with all of humankind. This theological viewpoint affirms the goodness of material things and of all of creation – including animal and plant life.[81] Discussions on the resurrection of beloved pets and whether or not one will see them in the next life are speculative because of Orthodoxy's affirmation that only humankind was created in God's image and likeness. It is the belief that God will redeem creation in some beautiful way that mitigates the anthropocentrism characterizing Orthodox eschatology for most of its history.

HERESY OR THEOLOGUMENA? ORTHODOX THEOLOGICAL CONTROVERSIES

Christians have disagreed on the core issues of Christian salvation from the very beginning. Many of Jesus' disciples abandoned him after his bread of life discourse in the Gospel of John (John 6). The author of the epistles of John complains about the number of anti-Christs who have come and betrayed the truth (1 Jn 2:16). We have briefly described some of the most troubling theological controversies that raged during the age of the ecumenical councils. The Orthodox Church has confronted other theological controversies that are worth mentioning as a conclusion to this chapter. These controversies are important because they reveal disputes about Orthodoxy's very core values, and they remain unresolved.

THE WISDOM OF GOD: SOPHIOLOGY

Sophiology has deep roots in the Christian tradition, hearkening back to its association with the neo-Platonic roots of early medieval Christianity. Orthodox theologian Marcus Plested reminds us that Sophiology developed along quite complex lines, with a number of intersections.[82] One cannot simply refer to one or two past thinkers and claim that Sophiology developed there. Plested's excellent survey shows us that a sense of an all-unifying wisdom lying in between the divine and the worldly influenced particular thinkers in both the Greek East and Latin West.[83] Plested shows how modern Russian Slavophiles developed complex cosmic viewpoints of unity between God and the world and acquisition of knowledge through participation in some kind of higher reality.[84] The primary theologians who developed this sophiology were Vladimir Soloviev and Pavel Florensky, but Sergius Bulgakov was the one who developed it into a profound theological idea. Bulgakov's theology was controversial, and both Metropolitan Sergius of Moscow and the Russian Orthodox Church Outside of Russia condemned it. Plested summarizes Bulgakov's sophiology as "denoting the divine life, the unity of the triune deity."[85] Wisdom itself is "God's self-revelation both in and outside of himself, a single principle existing in both uncreated and created forms."[86]

Perhaps the most difficult aspect of Bulgakov's concept of Sophia is hypostization. Plested notes that wisdom is not a hypostasis in Bulgakov's framework but is a principle capable of hypostacizing "in God, Christ, in Mary, and in the creation."[87] The association of Wisdom with a hypostasis seemed to suggest that Bulgakov was making Wisdom into one of the divine beings, along with Father, Son, and Spirit. This was not Bulgakov's intent – he was expressing God's use of divine power for self-revelation in the world, to humankind, and in creation.[88] Plested depicts Bulgakov as taking up the mantle that belongs to theologians to continue articulating unresolved points. Bulgakov went far beyond the claims of the ecumenical councils, going into areas they could not.[89]

Both the Moscow Patriarchate and ROCOR condemned Bulgakov for his promotion of Sophiology in 1935.[90] Plested notes that the Moscow Patriarchate fell short of declaring Bulgakov's teaching as heretical, whereas ROCOR adopted that route.[91] Three important Orthodox theologians adopted a negative view of Bulgakov's work that continues to carry weight in Orthodoxy up until this day – Vladimir Lossky, Georges Florovsky, and John Meyendorff.[92] Orthodoxy's tendency to prioritize teachings proclaimed by ecumenical councils or confirmed by the church's liturgy confines Sophiology to discussions among academic elites.

NEW DEVELOPMENTS IN ORTHODOX THEOLOGY

Among the most noteworthy developments in Orthodox theology of the twentieth and twenty-first centuries are the emergence of women theologians and the leadership exercised by Orthodox theologians in new fields. Women began to have an impact on Orthodox theology in traditional fields, such as early theology, patristics, and church history. Maria Skobtsova, later canonized as St. Maria of Paris by the Ecumenical Patriarchate of Constantinople, is among the first trailblazers for Orthodox women theologians. St. Maria participated in the lively dialogue among Russian émigré theologians and philosophers frequently captured by the journal Put'.[93] Her vision for renewed Orthodoxy in the world and a new kind of monasticism was both original and inspiring.[94]

Elizabeth Behr-Sigel is perhaps the most important Orthodox woman theologian, as a prodigious thinker who provided deep insights into the life and possible futures of the church.[95] Behr-Sigel influenced multiple generations of theologians who adopted her view of tradition as dynamic and open to possibilities through the intercession of the Holy Spirit and not a static museum piece of the past.

The twentieth and twenty-first centuries produced dozens of women who provided precious insight into modern church history. Vera Shevzov has written excellent histories of pre-revolutionary Orthodoxy in Russia and has also opened new windows on the significance of icon veneration among members of the laity in Russia. Nadieszda Kizenko's work includes an intellectual biography of St. John of Kronstadt, several important articles on the role of women in the church, and, most recently, a monograph on the mystery of repentance. Lois Farag is a leading historian and theologian of Coptic Christianity, especially in the early medieval period. Numerous women have made enormously important contributions to the liturgical history of the Orthodox churches, including Tatiana Afanasyeva's work on liturgical history in Slavonic manuscripts, Vassa Larin's study of the Orthodox hierarchical liturgy, Nina Glibetic's work on Slavonic manuscripts, and Gabriele Winkler's unparalleled scholarship on Armenian texts and the history of the Eucharistic prayer.

Orthodox women have emerged as strong leaders of theological associations and trailblazers in new areas of scholarship. Teva

Regule, a liturgical theologian, has most recently served as president of the Orthodox Theological Association of America. Inga Leonova founded a new journal of contemporary Orthodox theology, *The Wheel*.[96] Gayle Woloshchak has exercised leadership in both the church and the academy at numerous levels. Women in Orthodox theology played particularly important roles in providing a woman's perspective on the issues taken up by the Pan-Orthodox Council of Crete in 2016. Their publication of a book of reflections on the issue was a major feat, especially since women were not permitted to participate in the council.[97]

Perhaps the most significant contribution of women has been in diagnosing problems in hierarchical church structures and inviting the church to update its prayers for women at childbirth and its view on gender as a whole. Ashley Purpura's scholarship on hierarchy in Orthodoxy is challenging the church to consider the viability of its structures.[98] Carrie Frederick Frost's recent books on maternity and gender issues are challenging the church to consider its fidelity to gender essentialism and its interpretation of scriptural passages that appear to establish patriarchy.[99] The breakthrough of women into the mainstream of Orthodox theology in recent decades is a phenomenon destined to last.

Orthodox theology has also expanded to reach beyond its traditional pillars of liturgy, history, and patristics. Numerous theologians have appeared in the field of political theology, especially Aristotle Papanikolaou, Pantelis Kalaitzidis, and Cyril Hovorun. Kalaitzidis is associated with the Volos Academy of Theological Studies, an outpost of contemporary Orthodox intellectuals in Greece and a harbor of progressive theological thought.[100] Papanikolaou teamed with historian George Demacopoulos to oversee an Orthodox Studies program at Fordham University in New York. Hovorun, originally an expert in patristics, emerged as a public theologian during the years of Russian aggression in Ukraine. Finally, in 2018, Paul Gavrilyuk, a patristics scholar and philosopher, founded a groundbreaking organization – the International Orthodox Theological Association (IOTA). IOTA's mission is to transcend the issues that tend to polarize Orthodox theologians by bringing them into regular dialogue under the auspices of an independent and prestigious international theological academy.

Each of these scholars, among others, has delivered top-shelf contributions to their fields, frequently in dialogue with scholars and theologians of other religious communities and disciplines. The emergence of these three organizations represents Orthodoxy's continued existence in the liminal space between the past and the uncertain and unknown future. Older sources of Orthodox theology came from homilies, treatises, apologies, and hymns written primarily by monks and bishops. Orthodox seminaries and theological academies tended to produce theologians, represented by the likes of Sergius Bulgakov, Alexander Schmemann, and John Meyendorff – all presbyters. Fordham is perhaps the best example of a new direction in Orthodox theology. The Orthodox Christian Studies program is independent of church governance, given its existence within a Jesuit university. Fordham's program is intentionally dialogical and committed to addressing contentious issues, which often reach the public through their multilingual blog, Public Orthodoxy. Fordham's commitment to granting space to representatives of diverse positions tends to irritate some Orthodox people who prefer the previous system where ordained clergy tend to be the only public theologians. The emergence of these programs, associations, and especially the new people – both men and women – illustrates Orthodoxy's navigation of its liminal space of the patristic past and the uncertain future.

CONCLUSION

This chapter presents the fundamental aspects of Orthodox theology – its core values. Orthodoxy refers to the declarations of the first seven ecumenical councils as carrying the most authority in theology. The Council of Nicaea promulgated the Creed, and the Council of Constantinople completed it. The Nicene-Constantinopolitan Creed is the primary statement of faith defining Orthodoxy. This chapter has shown that Orthodox theology is dynamic and allows for minority opinions on important matters, such as life after death and the judgment of humankind. The business of theology is never finished in Orthodoxy – it is always moving, and no theological opinion can claim to be Orthodox until it has been received by the Church and enfleshed in its texts, rituals, and traditions.

NOTES

1. See, for example, Verna Harrison, "Perichoresis in the Greek Fathers," *St. Vladimir's Theological Quarterly* 35, no. 1 (1991), 53–65.
2. See St. Symeon the New Theologian, *On the Mystical Life: The Ethical Discourses, vol. 2: On Virtue and Christian Life*, trans. Alexander Golitzin (Crestwood, NY: St. Vladimir's Seminary Press, 1996), 103–110.
3. Gillet's collection of poems is published in English translation by the Orthodox Church in America, https://www.oca.org/reflections/archimandrite-lev-gillet (accessed July 25, 2024).
4. Numerous scholars have explored Palamas's theology and legacy, most recently Norman Russell and Tikhon Pino. See Norman Russell, *Gregory Palamas and the Making of Palamism in the Modern Age* (Oxford: Oxford University Press, 2019), and Tikhon Pino, *Essence and Energies: Being and Naming God in St. Gregory Palamas* (Abingdon: Routledge, 2023).
5. Bryn Geffert and Theofanis Stavrou, eds., *Eastern Orthodox Christianity: The Essential Texts* (New Haven, CT: Yale University Press, 2016), 216.
6. Geffert and Stavrou, *Eastern Orthodox Christianity*.
7. Leo Davis, *The First Seven Ecumenical Councils (325–787): Their History and Theology* (Collegeville, MN: Liturgical Press, 1983), 55–56.
8. Translation from the Orthodox Church in America, https://www.oca.org/orthodoxy/the-orthodox-faith/doctrine-scripture/the-symbol-of-faith/nicene-creed (accessed November 4, 2024).
9. https://www.oca.org/orthodoxy/the-orthodox-faith/doctrine-scripture/the-symbol-of-faith/nicene-creed (accessed November 4, 2024).
10. Davis, *The First Seven Ecumenical Councils*, 61–62.
11. https://www.oca.org/orthodoxy/the-orthodox-faith/doctrine-scripture/the-symbol-of-faith/nicene-creed (accessed November 4, 2024).
12. Diarmaid MacCulloch, *Christianity: The First Three Thousand Years* (New York: Viking, 2009), 225.
13. The council of Ephesus declared, "therefore, because the holy virgin bore in the flesh God who was united hypostatically with the flesh, for that reason we call her mother of God," Norman Tanner, ed. *Decrees of the Ecumenical Councils* (Washington, DC: Georgetown University Press, 1990), 58.
14. Hilda Graef, *Mary: A History of Doctrine and Devotion, vol. 1: From the Beginnings to the Eve of the Reformation* (New York: Sheed and Ward, 1963), 111–112.
15. Tanner, *Decrees*, 86.
16. St. Ephrem the Syrian, *Selected Prose Works*, trans. Edward G. Mathews, Jr., and Joseph P. Amar, ed. Kathleen McVey, Fathers of the Church 91 (Washington, DC: The Catholic University of America Press, 1994).

17 Syrian, *Selected Prose Works*, 25.
18 Syrian, *Selected Prose Works*, 36.
19 Syrian, *Selected Prose Works*, 270.
20 Syrian, *Selected Prose Works*, 274.
21 Pauline Allen and C.T.R. Hayward, *Severus of Antioch*, The Early Church Fathers Series (New York: Routledge, 2004), 4.
22 Allen and Hayward, *Severus of Antioch*, 32–33.
23 Text 33, Hymn 253 in Allen and Hayward, *Severus of Antioch*, 172.
24 Allen and Hayward, *Severus of Antioch*, 172.
25 Text 29 Hymn 8 in Allen and Hayward, *Severus of Antioch*, 169–170.
26 See the introduction and the text itself in Saint Athanasius, *On the Incarnation*, intro. C.S. Lewis, trans. John Behr, Popular Patristics Series (Yonkers, NY: St. Vladimir's Seminary Press, 2011).
27 Athanasius, *On the Incarnation*, 54–56.
28 See Athanasius, *On the Incarnation*, 57–60.
29 Athanasius, *On the Incarnation*, 70–71.
30 Athanasius, *On the Incarnation*, 71.
31 Athanasius, *On the Incarnation*, 71.
32 Athanasius, *On the Incarnation*, 80.
33 *Hieratikon, vol. 2: Liturgy Book for Priest and Deacon*, rev. ed., eds. Hieromonk Herman and Vitaly Permiakov (South Canaan, PA: St. Tikhon's Seminary Press, 2020), 95.
34 R.C.D. Jasper and G.J. Cuming, eds., *Prayers of the Eucharist: Early and Reformed*, 3d ed. (Collegeville, MN: Liturgical Press, 1990), 132.
35 Jasper and Cuming, *Prayers of the Eucharist*, 133.
36 Jasper and Cuming, *Prayers of the Eucharist*, 118–119.
37 Jasper and Cuming, *Prayers of the Eucharist*, 118–119.
38 Jasper and Cuming, *Prayers of the Eucharist*, 118–119.
39 Jasper and Cuming, *Prayers of the Eucharist*, 118–119.
40 Davis, *The First Seven Ecumenical Councils*, 105–106.
41 Davis, *The First Seven Ecumenical Councils*, 106–107.
42 Davis, *The First Seven Ecumenical Councils*, 107.
43 Davis, *The First Seven Ecumenical Councils*, 107.
44 Davis, *The First Seven Ecumenical Councils*, 114.
45 St. Basil of Caesarea, *On the Holy Spirit*, trans. and intro. Stephen Hildebrand, Popular Patristics Series 42 (Yonkers, NY: St. Vladimir's Seminary Press, 2011), 29.
46 Yves Congar, *I Believe in the Holy Spirit*, vol. 3: *The River of the Water of Life (Rev. 22:1) Flows in the East and the West* (New York: Crossroad Publishing, 2004), 52–54.
47 Congar, *I Believe in the Holy Spirit*, 54.

48 See Congar, *I Believe in the Holy Spirit*, 58, for Congar's explanation of Patriarch Photius's defense of the monarchical principle. See 54 for his brief discussion on the inclusion of the filioque in Cardinal Hambert's bull of excommunication.
49 See, for example, the response of Patriarch Michael Cerularius and the synod of Constantinople to the Roman See in *The Essential Texts*, ed. Geffert and Stavrou, 248.
50 Jasper and Cuming, *Prayers of the Eucharist*, 119–120.
51 Jasper and Cuming, *Prayers of the Eucharist*, 133.
52 See the summary in John H. McKenna, *Eucharist and Holy Spirit: The Eucharistic Epiclesis in 20th Century Theology*, Alcuin Club Collections no. 57 (Great Wakering: Mayhew-McRimmon, 1975), 71–78. Paul Bradshaw and Maxwell Johnson provide an updated analysis of the issue in *The Eucharistic Liturgies: Their Evolution and Interpretation* (Collegeville, MN: Liturgical Press, 2012), 179–189.
53 Bradshaw and Johnson, *The Eucharistic Liturgies*, 222–230.
54 Bradshaw and Johnson, *The Eucharistic Liturgies*, 182.
55 Jasper and Cuming, *Prayers*, 120.
56 For Basil's teaching, I am drawing from *On the Human Condition*, trans. Nonna Verna Harrison (Crestwood, NY: St. Vladimir's Seminary Press, 2005). This is a selection of homilies in which Basil comments on the human being. Readers should note that many scholars question the authenticity of Basil's authorship of the two central homilies. The other sources are John Behr, ed., *Gregory of Nyssa: On the Human Image of God*, Oxford Early Christian Texts (Oxford: Oxford University Press, 2023), and St. Maximus the Confessor, *On the Cosmic Mystery of Christ*, trans. Paul Blowers and Robert Louis Wilken, Popular Patristics Series (Crestwood, NY: St. Vladimir's Seminary Press, 2003).
57 Basil, *On the Human Condition*, 47 (from Basil's homily on the origin of humanity).
58 Basil, *On the Human Condition*, 58–59.
59 Basil, *On the Human Condition*, 61.
60 Behr, *Gregory of Nyssa*, 173.
61 Behr, *Gregory of Nyssa*, 175.
62 St. Maximus Confessor, *On the Cosmic Mystery* of Christ, trans. Paul Blowers and Robert Louis Wilken, Popular Patristics Series (Crestwood, NY: St. Vladimir's Seminary Press, 2003), 87.
63 Maximus Confessor, *On the Cosmic Mystery*, 89–90.
64 Maximus Confessor, *On the Cosmic Mystery*, 103, in *Ad Thassalanium* 6.
65 Maximus Confessor, *On the Cosmic Mystery*, 103–104.
66 Behr, *Gregory of Nyssa*, 232–235.

67. "Judgment," in https://azbyka.ru/otechnik/world/the-encyclopedia-of-eastern-orthodox-christianity/161 (accessed July 26, 2024).
68. For a more detailed explanation, see Jean-Claude Larchet, *Life After Death According to the Orthodox Tradition*, trans. G. John Champoux (Jordanville: The Printshop of St. Job of Pochaev, 2021), 23–26.
69. See Kallistos Ware, *The Inner Kingdom* (Crestwood, NY: St. Vladimir's Seminary Press, 2001), 37–40.
70. Ware, *The Inner Kingdom*, 34–36.
71. See Larchet's comparative analysis of Catholic and Orthodox positions on heaven, hell, and purgatory, in *Life after Death*, 68–79.
72. See Larchet, *Life after Death*, 198–205 for discussion of apokatastasis, especially in Origen.
73. Paul Gavrilyuk, "Universal Salvation in the Eschatology of Sergius Bulgakov," *Journal of Theological Studies* 57 (2006), 120–122 (110–132).
74. Larchet, *Life after Death*, 57.
75. The Sunday of the Last Judgment, one week before the beginning of Lent, contains numerous poetic hymns depicting the unfortunate fate of those who are judged as wicked. See, for example, the first stichera on the Praises which makes this claim: "those who have never repented shall weep and lament, departing to the outer fire," in *The Lenten Triodion*, trans. Kallistos Ware and Mother Mary (South Canaan, PA: St. Tikhon's Monastery Press, 2002), 164.
76. Ware, *The Inner Kingdom*, 33.
77. See Ware's brief description of Isaac of Nineveh's concept of hell in Ware, *The Inner Kingdom*, 207.
78. See Larchet, *Life after Death*, 78–79, for a description of God alone as the purifying fire leading to redemption.
79. See Karl Rahner, *Theological Investigations, vol. 17: Jesus, Man, and the Church*, trans. Margaret Kohl (New York: Crossroad, 1981), 114–126.
80. Ware, *The Inner Kingdom*, 40–41.
81. See, for example, Ecumenical Patriarchate, *For the Life of the World: Toward a Social Ethos of the Orthodox Church*, paragraph 68, https://www.goarch.org/social-ethos?fbclid=IwAR2RSPrgYRhPfAgT9p2iIQkd9wqtOYJ74Gtjnpmyq9xYdxshwqr6U1FJFiY# (accessed July 26, 2024).
82. Marcus Plested, *Wisdom in Christian Tradition: The Roots of Moder Russian Sophiology* (Oxford: Oxford University Press, 2022), 15.
83. Plested, *Wisdom in Christian Tradition*, 16.
84. Plested, *Wisdom in Christian Tradition*, 22.
85. Plested, *Wisdom in Christian Tradition*, 37.
86. Plested, *Wisdom in Christian Tradition*, 58.
87. Plested, *Wisdom in Christian Tradition*, 58.
88. See Bulgakov's exposition of sophianicity in *The Bride of the Lamb*, trans. Boris Jakim (Grand Rapids, MI: Eerdman's, 2002), 3–124.

89 Plested, *Wisdom in Christian Tradition*, 53.
90 Plested, *Wisdom in Christian Tradition*, 58.
91 Plested, *Wisdom in Christian Tradition*, 58.
92 Plested, *Wisdom in Christian Tradition*, 59.
93 See Antoine Arkjakovsky, *The Way: Religious Thinkers of the Russian Emigration in Paris and Their Journal, 1925–1940*, trans. Jerry Ryan, ed. John Jillions and Michael Plekon, foreword Rowan Williams (Notre Dame, IN: University of Notre Dame Press, 2013).
94 See the collected essays in Mother Maria Skobtsova, *Essential Writings*, trans. Richard Pevear and Larissa Volokhonsky, intro Jim Forest, Modern Spiritual Masters Series (Maryknoll, NY: Orbis, 2003).
95 Olga Lossky and Michael Plekon, *Toward the Endless Day: The Life of Elisabeth Behr-Sigel* (Notre Dame, IN: University of Notre Dame Press, 2010).
96 https://www.wheeljournal.com/ (accessed August 9, 2024).
97 Carrie Frederick Frost, ed., *The Reception of the Holy and Great Council: Reflections of Orthodox Christian Women*, Faith Matters Series (New York: Greek Orthodox Archdiocese of America, 2018).
98 Ashley M. Purpura, *God, Hierarchy and Power: Orthodox Theologies of Authority from Byzantium*, Orthodox Christianity and Contemporary Thought Series (New York: Fordham University Press, 2018).
99 Carrie Frederick Frost, *Maternal Body: A Theology of Incarnation from the Christian East* (New York: Paulist Press, 2019). Carrie Frederick Frost, *Church of our Granddaughters*, foreword by Vigen Guroian (Eugene, OR: Cascade Books, 2023).
100 Paul Ladouceur, *Modern Orthodox Theology: 'Behold, I Make All Things New'* (New York: Bloomsbury, 2019), 149.

CONCEPTUALIZING ORTHODOX SPIRITUALITY

Spirituality is the main public feature of Orthodox Christianity. People have come to embrace Orthodoxy because of its retention and cultivation of spiritual practices and traditions. The veneration of icons and the recitation of the Jesus Prayer are the best-known Orthodox spiritual practices, but four principles come together to form the engine that drives Orthodox spirituality. These principles are theosis, hesychasm, metanoia, and acquiring the Holy Spirit. The chapter begins by explaining the four principles and then examines spiritual practices, including some less-known rituals that are important for Orthodox people.

FOUR PRINCIPLES: THEOSIS, HESYCHASM, METANOIA, AND ACQUIRING THE HOLY SPIRIT

PRINCIPLE 1: THEOSIS

Theosis connotes the process of a Christian person becoming God.[1] This bold and stark assertion begs for clarification: didn't the chapter on theology emphasize God's complete otherness and state that ordinary people are unable to approach or connect with the divine nature? The chapter also suggested that laypeople can and do partake of God's divine nature and dwell in God, in a holy community consisting of God, the saints, and all of God's people and creation.

Theosis does not mean that human beings can become gods like God. Theosis is not a religious version of becoming metahuman or enhanced like a superhero from a comic book series. Theosis means that God has recreated each and every human being to become like Jesus Christ.

DOI: 10.4324/9781003433217-5

The teaching depends on the Orthodox dogma of the incarnation of Christ. The chapter on theology depicts St. Athanasius of Alexandria saying that God solved the divine dilemma by sending his only-begotten son to become human.[2] Athanasius claimed that the image of God constituting each and every human being had become distorted because of sin and corruption. Christ, who is the image of God, restores the image of God in each person. This restoration is more like a recreation – the image himself recreates human nature and capacitates humans to be like him.[3] This recreation was made possible in one way – by Christ becoming incarnate, human, and God dwelling together. Baptism is a crucial component of theosis. Each Christian receives the Holy Spirit at Baptism and is therefore anointed. Orthodox Christianity confirms the instruction of St. Cyril of Jerusalem on the meaning of this anointing. The word "christ" means "anointed one," so each person who is anointed becomes a "Christ," according to St. Cyril.[4]

The restoration and recreation of human nature, along with the anointing received at Baptism, permits one to become like Christ and therefore like God. Theosis comes about from a way of life, prayer, almsgiving, and genuine Christian living. There is no single practice that leads to theosis, and theosis is dynamic, a constant state of development. The ressourcement (return to the sources) movement in theology led to a renaissance in reflection on theosis. This tendency to see theosis as an end-all, be-all can be misleading, because the process of becoming like Christ has no conclusion in this life. Claiming that one has achieved theosis is alien to the spirit of Orthodoxy. Theosis is a core component of Orthodoxy's view on God's purpose for humankind (also known as theological anthropology). God sent Christ, appointed apostles, and called all to return to God so that humans could truly arrive at their destiny – to become like God.

PRINCIPLE 2: HESYCHASM

Hesychasm is a concrete spiritual habit of Orthodoxy.[5] The word *hesychia* means silence, and Orthodoxy has developed a number of practices to cultivate silence. Silence is similar to stillness, and Orthodoxy does not aspire to create external silence, as if the church could impose quiet on an entire metropolis. Orthodoxy aims for inner stillness, the quieting of the heart and soul, a skill that includes the unthinkable – learning how to silence one's thoughts.

Hesychia was a spiritual practice that drew from the monastic tradition and blossomed on Mount Athos. Athos produced a number of Hesychast theologians, including Gregory Palamas, mentioned earlier. Hesychasm is associated with the practice of reciting the Jesus Prayer.[6] One cannot learn how to cultivate inner silence through prayer alone, however. An entire way of life, constant vigilance, and dependence on God are necessary for the experience of hesychasm.

PRINCIPLE 3: METANOIA

When John the Baptist calls the Judeans to Baptism, it is for repentance – metanoia (Mk 1:4). Once again, metanoia is not only feeling sorry for one's sins. Metanoia means to turn around and change one's life in its entirety. Orthodoxy views repentance as a constant process, one requiring the changing of one's state of mind and a turning of one's heart to God.

Metanoia has been connected with confession of sins, and confession is certainly a core component of metanoia. Learning how to live without sin, practicing sinlessness, and committing to life in Christ – these all belong to the process of metanoia. Metanoia is repentance, and God does forgive sin through repentance, but repentance is lifelong. It is a process without end in this life, like theosis. Metanoia requires doing good and working for the common good, but it is not about behavior. Metanoia is about covenant. In Orthodoxy, metanoia means renouncing the evil one and turning to Christ. Metanoia is ultimately relational – creating a covenant with Christ and entering more fully into the covenant.

PRINCIPLE 4: ACQUIRING THE HOLY SPIRIT

Our final core principle is acquiring the Holy Spirit. This principle comes to us in two ways. First, as mentioned earlier, each and every Orthodox believer receives the Holy Spirit at Baptism and Chrismation. Orthodoxy confesses one Baptism – the gift of the Holy Spirit cannot be revoked, nor does it have an expiration date. It is permanently sealed on the faithful. Furthermore, the faithful deepen their fellowship with the Holy Spirit at each and every Divine Liturgy. Like theosis, acquiring the Holy Spirit is a process.

The acquisition of the Holy Spirit happens in the church's sacraments, but it is not limited to liturgical life. Orthodox believers continuously receive the Holy Spirit in their ordinary daily lives as well. The reception of the Holy Spirit is not a matter of rigid formalism, though the prayer to the Holy Spirit, "Heavenly King," belongs to the order of daily prayer for most of the liturgical year. Orthodox people believe they are in a process of acquiring the Holy Spirit by living as joyous people who love their neighbors and the world and receive all as images of Christ. The Russian St. Seraphim of Sarov inspired this teaching and practice, largely on the basis of the story of his life that circulated, especially a conversation he had with Motovilov on acquiring the Holy Spirit.[7] This notion of receiving the Spirit has become embedded in mainstream Orthodoxy.

DOMESTIC RITUALS

Local communities are the domain of Orthodox spirituality, and people bring the practices of the Church into their private homes. A tension between the official public liturgy of the Church and private devotions has always existed. The Roman church sought to revive the liturgy and reform the relationship between liturgy and devotion. It is not necessary to think of the tension as negative. It is probably most healthy for all Christians to cultivate both a Spirit-filled liturgical life and a vibrant private spiritual habit. The two spaces inhabited by the people can cross-pollinate one another.

This section examines practices observed by Orthodox Christians in their private spiritual lives. The relationship between the liturgy and domestic life is most evident in the people's observation of appointed fasts and feasts. We begin with the most intimate observance – the veneration of icons at home.

ICON VENERATION

The Orthodox Church has a powerful visual culture. Even the most modest Orthodox parish has icons. The chapter on Orthodox liturgy profiles the interior configuration of the typical Orthodox building. Icons became the primary visual features of the interior decoration of churches from the mid-ninth century onwards.

The seventh ecumenical council not only called for decorating churches with icons but also appealed for placing icons in public places and for people to venerate them in private.[8] The veneration of icons is the spiritual practice of intersection between the communal, domestic, and personal. Ordinary Christians have venerated icons in churches, homes, and hospitals and carry small icons with them during their travels.

Larger Orthodox Church communities with financial resources can commission icons by establishing a budget for an iconographic program and one or more master iconographers. Orthodox faithful inherited icons kept by their families for many generations. In many families, icon collections were modest and were often copies of archetypal icons. Some communities had no resources for painting icons and would paint their own by using water colors or inexpensive paint on paper outlines in frames. Some families create elaborate icon corners, or family altars, where they pray together. Others place icons as they wish in the rooms of their home. There is no predetermined rule or hierarchy for a family or personal icon collection – each person configures their own order for the collection. Many people own small icons or sets of two to three icons (known as diptychs or triptychs) that accompany them as they travel. Some people will recite their personal prayers in front of an icon or pray before and after meals.

Many Orthodox faithful will adopt an icon as a favorite. One such tradition concerns wonderworking (miraculous) icons that have their own holidays. Many faithful possess icons that are important to them for personal reasons.[9] Some Orthodox want an icon of their patron saint, and others might cherish an icon that belonged to a beloved family member. Orthodox people are fond of debating the quality of an icon, often referring to the reputation of the iconographer and the style they follow. Andriy Chirovsky argues that all icons are of equal value, even if an icon is merely a copy of a print or disfigured and distorted in some way.

Orthodoxy teaches that icons are windows into heaven and also mirrors. Venerating an icon brings one into contact with the person or people painted on the icon. The encounter is real. Angie Heo illustrates the broader experience of venerating an icon in her descriptions of an imaginary.[10] Heo explains that venerating an icon goes far beyond admiring the artistic mastery of the iconographer or even reflecting on the holiness of their life. It is a matter of sensory perception, like trying to imagine what it was like to endure a saint's particular experiences.[11] John Zizioulas states that the icon brings the person venerating the icon into the same space as the saint, an encounter of people with people.[12] Icons are windows in this sense. Icons are also mirrors. Every time an Orthodox Christian looks at an icon of Christ, they see who they are to become – like Christ. Orthodox people don't necessarily think of icons in this way. But most Orthodox people sense that there is a real encounter taking place and a real dialogue when they venerate icons in private prayer and devotion.

THE JESUS PRAYER

The spiritual practice of the Jesus Prayer enjoys the same degree of popularity among Orthodox Christians as icon veneration. The Jesus Prayer is the main prayer used in the spiritual habit of *hesychia*. The prayer has monastic origins, became popular on Mount Athos at the height of the hesychast movement, and circulated throughout the Orthodox monastic world. The prayer itself is quite short, consisting of the following petition: "Lord Jesus Christ, Son of God, have mercy on me, a sinner." The Jesus Prayer became quite popular among Orthodox laypeople, probably because of pilgrimages made to monasteries where laity learned the prayer from monks. The Jesus Prayer belongs to a larger body of monastic sayings concerning the prayer of the heart, and a famous collection of these sayings is held in a multi-volume set called the "Philokalia" – love of beautiful things.

Recitation of the Jesus Prayer is the domain of private prayer and devotion in Orthodoxy. The ideal setting is in a quiet place without distractions, where one can adopt a relaxed posture and say the prayer quietly, several times, though not necessarily in accordance with a rhythm or by a predetermined number. Some spiritual masters advise the one praying to orient themselves toward their chest, head pointed downwards, to direct attention to their heart. Others suggest reciting the prayer with a prayer rope. These bodily postures and rituals are often observed but are not strictly required. Furthermore, finding a quiet place is an ideal that cannot always be achieved.

The Jesus Prayer has become even more popular because of its centrality in spiritual literature. Contemporary writers like Lev Gillet, Kallistos Ware, and Frederica Mathews-Green wrote about the Jesus Prayer.[13] A spiritual classic from the Russian nineteenth century known as *The Way of the Pilgrim* chronicles the travels of a man hoping to reach Jerusalem in search of spiritual perfection – the tale is about his practice of the Jesus Prayer and his love for the spiritual sayings in the Philokalia.[14]

While a quiet place is ideal for the Jesus Prayer, it is appropriate to be said in any situation or context. Centering one's heart on Jesus and discovering stillness can happen anywhere – even in the most chaotic places. The objective is not to go to a quiet place but to discover the quiet in the interior of one's heart and soul.

FASTING

Fasting is no longer the exclusive domain of faith communities. Medical professionals, nutritionists, and food vendors have discovered the potential benefits of fasting. The public already had experience with the requirement for absolute fasting for certain blood tests. The obesity epidemic and a growing desire to promote healthy solutions for weight maintenance led to the emergence of the practices of intermittent fasting or the 18/6 diet.

The science of fasting to maximize physical health benefits and longevity continues to evolve. Valter Longo developed the "fast mimicking diet," a plan consisting of specific foods rich in certain nutrients that mimic an all-water fast while providing the body with sufficient energy.[15] Adopting this diet could improve the health of people suffering from obesity, cancer, and diabetes.[16]

Faith communities have appointed fasts for spiritual benefits. Jews fast on Yom Kippur in preparation for God's forgiveness. Muslims observe a rigorous fast during Ramadan in thanksgiving for the revelation of the Koran to the prophet Muhammad. Orthodox Christians observe fasting seasons and solemn fast days to repent of their sins and to prepare for the coming of God's kingdom. The fundamental source for the Orthodox observance of fasting is Jesus' instruction to fast humbly and quietly without calling attention to one's self (Mt 6:16–18).

The Orthodox schedule for fasting follows both fixed and mobile schedules. The fixed schedules include fasting every Wednesday and Friday, with a few exceptions to be explained below. The primary Orthodox fast takes place during Lent, also known as the "Great Forty Days."[17] Fasting continues at the end of Lent, through all of Holy Week, until the beginning of the celebration of Pascha (Easter). Lent is a mobile seasonal fast – the appointment of the date for the annual feast of Pascha dictates when Lent begins, always on a Monday.

The Orthodox Church also observes three other seasonal fasts, along with a handful of one-day fasts. The other seasonal fasts are the Christmas fast, beginning forty days before Christmas. Some Orthodox Christians know this fast as St. Philip's Fast. A shorter fast of fourteen days takes place on August 1, before the feast of the Dormition of the Theotokos. The final seasonal observance is the Apostles' Fast, one week before the annual feast of Saints Peter and Paul on June 29. These three fasts are unlike Lent because their dates are fixed. The Apostles' Fast is often shortened, however, when Orthodox Pascha takes place late. The later celebration of Pentecost – fifty days after Pascha – can eliminate the Apostles' fast altogether.

Orthodox observe a handful of strict one-day fasts before major feasts. These one-day fasts occur on Christmas Eve, the day before Theophany (January 5), the feast of the Exaltation of the Cross (September 14), and the Beheading of St. John the Baptist (August 29). The Christmas and Theophany fasts are connected to the high degree of solemnity assigned to the feast days, whereas the Exaltation and Beheading commemorations call for fasting to honor the martyrdom of Jesus and John, his forerunner.

One additional component of fasting must be mentioned. The Orthodox Church requires all clergy and faithful to fast before they receive Holy Communion. Some pastors urge those who are preparing for Baptism along with people in a state of repentance, to fast as well. The pre-communion fast is supposed to be absolute, requiring abstinence from eating, drinking, and sexual activity at midnight the day of Communion. It is essential to note that no pastors can actually enforce this rule, and many pastors allow exceptions. Many people need water and food before communion to accompany medications or for sufficient blood sugar. The requirement of fasting before Holy Communion can be difficult with the Liturgy of Presanctified Gifts, a service of Holy Communion appointed to evenings. Some pastors allow one morning meal with a longer daytime fast before the Liturgy. The requirement establishes an ideal, to abstain temporarily from eating and drinking before communion, while allowing for people to adapt the ideal to conform to their capacity for observance.

The ideal for pre-communion fasting is to observe an absolute fast. Absolute fasting means complete abstinence – no eating, drinking, or sex – and in some instances, no socializing, talking, or entertainment. Absolute fasting differs from the dietary fast, which calls for abstaining from meat, dairy, fish, olive oil, and alcohol. The following sections explain the meaning of both types of fasting, absolute and dietary.

One principle applies to both absolute and dietary fasting – to form the participant into depending solely upon God for everything. For Orthodox and most Christians that observe seasonal fasts, the absolute fast is an adaptation of Jesus' forty days in the wilderness. The New Testament states that Jesus went without food or drink while he was in the wilderness. Jesus also went into solitude, bereft of social interactions. Abstaining from food, drink, sex, and social activity is a way of sharpening one's faculties to focus exclusively on God. This abstinence is supposed to be temporary – it does not mean that Orthodoxy views food, drink, and sex negatively. Food and drink are essential for existence, but they need not be one's sole focus. The principle of absolute fasting calls upon one to recognize that they can indeed go without food and pleasant activities for an appointed time. The church would emphasize that it is good for one's body and soul to be free of the distraction of the next meal or fun activity and to direct one's self elsewhere.

Some Orthodox describe fasting as attending to the health of one's soul. Caring for the soul is a way of caring for the whole person. Occasionally, some Orthodox depict the soul as superior to the body, following the thought of the apostle Paul and other Christian thinkers influenced by Platonic thought. Some stories of saints and related monastic literature speak of the mortification of the flesh, punishing the body for the sake of purification of one's soul. A fine line separates cultivating the soil of one's soul, strengthening and purifying it through abstinence, from an inverse relationship asserting that punishing one's body strengthens the soul. Occasional abstinence is good for both the soul and the body. Orthodox people can embrace the new science of fasting that wards off disease and promotes health and pair it with the soul-strengthening aspects of fasting.

How, then, does fasting strengthen one's soul? A monastic principle can be helpful in explaining the soul-strengthening dimensions of fasting. Monastic life is supposed to run on a tight budget. The members of the community live and eat frugally. They purchase food to provide only what is needed to live. Many monasteries settle in the desert or wilderness and live off the land. Monks grow fruits and vegetables, gather fish and other foods, and use only enough to sustain their living. During fasting seasons, monks eliminate products like olive oil and wine. This practice is one of time. The monks occupy themselves with other activities, like prayer and almsgiving, instead of making olive oil and wine. They are free to eat olives and grapes – eating the whole fruit is a way of demonstrating dependence on God. The irony of eating natural fruits from trees in honor of God is not lost upon us (Adam, Eve, and the apple as forbidden fruit). The difference now is that natural fruits and vegetables are not forbidden – eating them in moderation during fasting seasons symbolizes humanity's dependence on God for sustenance.

Devoting less time to food selection, preparation, and actual meal time creates space for prayer and care for the less fortunate. Fasting is therefore connected organically to prayer and almsgiving. Creating space to care for another is an important way of caring for one's soul. The dietary fast is designed to literally enlighten the Christian. Free from the weight of savory meals and alcohol, one's senses are sharpened and they can become aware of the needy.

HOW ORTHODOX CHRISTIANS FAST

The preceding section describes the ideal Orthodox fast. Now we will describe the reality of fasting. The best way to describe the way Orthodox people fast is with reference to a pattern one can adapt to their situation. Not all Orthodox Christians observe the appointed fasts. A 2017 Pew research survey shows that 27% of Orthodox respondents fasted during Lent.[18] Orthodox who attend church regularly are more likely to observe fasting requirements to the best of their ability.

The core group that constitutes a typical parish – the regulars – will observe Lent, the Christmas Fast, the absolute fast before the Divine Liturgy, and fasts that involve community meals. Non-Orthodox visitors to Orthodox parishes will not find meat or dairy products at community meals or coffee hours during fasting seasons, and potluck gatherings typically adhere to the rules.

What happens in domestic settings can differ, however. Some Orthodox will fast from meat but continue to eat dairy products. Others will refrain from taking a meal on Sunday morning but will have coffee or tea. In many instances, there is festive fasting, with favorite Lenten foods on the menu, like pierogies without meat or dairy or fattoush salad and falafel cooked without olive oil. Orthodox parishes occasionally publish Lenten cookbooks. Some communal meals, such as the *sviata vechera* (holy supper) of Eastern Slavic households (described below), have special dishes designated for fast days. These festive occasions can appear to violate the spirit of fasting. Furthermore, zeal for adherence to the law of fasting can ruin the moment. Once again, moderation and simplicity are two of the three practical legs holding up the stool of fasting. The third is adaptation. People adopt the rule to the best of their ability. Some Orthodox people gather at local bars on Fridays for fish fries even though this violates the rules because it fits their purpose. The bottom line is that active Orthodox observe the fasts, even when they adapt them.

Orthodox people who are less observant or on the margins tend not to observe the fasts. This doesn't necessarily mean that Lent is not important to them, but some question the significance of fasting if it is simply a dietary change. Orthodoxy's preference for retaining traditions means that fasting rules have not been updated. The Pan-Orthodox Council of Crete of 2016 issued a declaration on fasting that calls for the people to adhere to the fasts while acknowledging the need for adaptation and the fact that many people ignore fasting.[19]

Perhaps the increased societal interest in fasting propelled by scientific investigations into the health benefits of fasting will revive Orthodox practices. An update on the larger picture of the purpose of fasting could encourage people to take it up again. For example, the relationship between fasting and care for the environment, by reducing the amount of beef and red meat consumed and eating responsibly, is one potential update. Permitting unlimited amounts of seafood while prohibiting fish is an example of a precept that needs updating, especially given the increased cost of temporarily transitioning to seafood during Lent. Finally, a holistic view of fasting would account for social engagement, especially with smartphones and digital media. Integrating intentional smartphone and digital media breaks into fasting seasons could be potentially meaningful. Orthodoxy is flexible enough to support principles for fasting that can accommodate multiple practices.

FEASTING

People of all religions mark holidays with feasts. Jews mark Passover with an appointed Seder meal, cooked in accordance with established traditions. Muslims prepare a lamb feast for Eid al-Fitr. Many Western Christians mark Easter with ham and chocolate. Orthodox Christians celebrate their feasts with special foods.

The celebration of the Eucharist is central to each feast. Dining at the table of the Lord, partaking of Holy Communion, and giving thanks for the bread and wine refer to the meal Jesus hosted with his disciples and continues to convene today. Theologically, the bread and wine taken at the Divine Liturgy break the absolute fast held beforehand. One of the main themes of Holy Week is the absolute fast Orthodox observe on Good Friday, in memory of the Lord's death. The first Liturgy celebrated on Pascha – usually sometime on Holy Saturday, in practice – breaks the fast. The feast of the Eucharist is just as much a matter of coming together with the Lord, in the fullness of his presence, as it is receiving the bread and wine in thanksgiving.

Orthodox households also host feasts on holidays, often in parallel with the theology of dining with the Lord Jesus. Faithful people prepare sumptuous foods in preparation for Christmas and Theophany. The parish temple feast is important for each community. Each parish community has patron saints or is named in honor of a feast of the Lord or Mary during the liturgical year. It is typical for the parish to organize a major event on their feast day, with the pastor inviting area parish communities to come and concelebrate or arranging for the bishop to visit. The annual temple feast day will often culminate in a post-liturgical dinner organized by the parish.

Easter is a major holiday for all Christians, but it is truly an experience for Orthodox because of the intensity of the fasting leading up to the feast. The domestic celebration of Pascha rivals the liturgical feast. All Eastern Orthodox boil and color eggs in anticipation of Pascha. The boiled egg symbolizes the resurrection of Jesus, and eggs are one of the dairy products restored on Pascha. Most Orthodox parishes will boil and color hundreds of red eggs and distribute them to the people at the end of the services. A playful tradition has emerged in some areas of Ukraine – the presider will toss eggs for anyone in the crowd to catch, like an Easter egg version of tossing the wedding bouquet.

The process of preparing food for the domestic Pascha is serious business, and traditions vary in accordance with ethnicity. Many Greek Orthodox parishes will prepare and serve a formal dinner featuring soup (magiritsa) after the services, even at 2:00 a.m.! Slavs have prepared baskets of their favorite foods and brought them to church for a special blessing for centuries. There is no single blueprint for a Pascha basket, but Orthodox natives are familiar with people bringing colored eggs, sausages, salt, ham, cheese, sweet and savory breads, and special desserts like "cheese paska."

The migration of Orthodox people to new places like North America led to the development of new traditions. It is common for people to place burgers, pizza, enchiladas, tamales, and cheesesteak sandwiches in their baskets. Bottles of beer, wine, and liquor are often stuffed into the baskets. The presider blesses the baskets at the end of the Paschal service. Some larger parish communities conduct multiple basket blessings to accommodate crowds. The popularity of basket blessings has created a pastoral dilemma. Some people come to church for the basket blessing only and do not participate in the paschal services. This development testifies to the longevity of the feast and the degree of its importance in people's private prayer lives. In other words, even people who forgo the church services want to observe the domestic feast. Some Orthodox pastors complain that pandering to the desires of the crowds when they don't even go to church cheapens Pascha in some way. The Pascha service itself requires the presider to read a sermon attributed to St. John Chrysostom of the fourth century.[20] St. John eloquently proclaims the triumph of life over death, but more importantly, he refuses to shame those who arrive for the feast at the last minute or even after most of the service is finished. The Lord's resurrection has vanquished death and ended the separation of God and humankind – all are now invited to the feast.

Some Orthodox faithful look forward to the domestic portion of Pascha more than any other. Faithful spend hours on their feet in kitchens, seasoning meat, carefully cutting sausage, boiling eggs, kneading dough, baking bread, and cleaning up. Many of these chefs are the same people preparing choir rehearsals, standing for long hours in church holding candles, and chanting verses. The process of preparing for the feast and then breaking bread with loved ones, the community, and yes, the family members difficult to bear, is a spiritual one. It is a veritable preview of the life to come, with God and all humankind. The famous scene from My Big Fat Greek Wedding captures the spirit of communal Pascha aptly. People greet one another with a holy kiss, play the egg-breaking game, and gather around a table laden with treats. In many communities, the first paschal meal is taken as a community after the midnight liturgy.

The initial picture from the communal and domestic celebrations of Pascha and other solemn holidays is one of joy. Many families create and sustain traditions of such celebrations. Orthodox people are like everyone else – they, too, experience brokenness and loneliness and live through the disputes and outbursts that occasionally occur in these settings. Orthodox people of all ages dread these holiday gatherings because of expectations, family tensions, and underlying trauma.

In summary, the central feature of every Orthodox feast is the gathering of the church community with the risen Christ for the celebration of the Eucharist. Partaking of Christ's body and blood in the context of a meal is the centerpiece of each feast. Orthodox communities prepare elaborate communal and domestic meals to celebrate each feast. The domestic celebrations are important, but they are neither equivalent to nor in place of the Eucharist.

OFFICIAL AND UNOFFICIAL VENERATION OF THE SAINTS

It is impossible to speak of Orthodoxy without landing on a discussion that mentions a saint in some way. The Orthodox Church commemorates saints on its calendar each and every day of the year. The Church remembers saints by celebrating a Divine Liturgy, permissible on every day of the year except for the weekdays of Great Lent and Great and Holy Friday.

Saints are woven into the fabric of official church identity. Ideally, every Orthodox Christian adopts the name of a saint when they are baptized or chrismated. Many churches are named after specific saints, often important to the identity of their national or regional identity. Every Orthodox Church contains some kind of relic of a saint.[21]

The church builds altar tables that include relics or, at minimum, have a special altar cloth called an antimension that has relics of a saint or saints sewn into it. The antimension testifies to the authority given by the local bishop for the parish community to gather for the Divine Liturgy. Some parishes have icons with small compartments containing saints' relics. Cathedrals and monastery churches throughout the world contain shrines, often complete with the grave of the saint, that attract people for veneration.

The translation of relics is an old practice that Orthodoxy has sustained. Relics are translated when a community that possesses the relics of a specific saint gives them to a representative of another church. The reception of the saint's relic is both a custom of church gift-giving and also a way for the receiving church to introduce the saint into their calendar. Reports of miracles occurring through the intercession of the saints are common in Orthodoxy, and the church often commodifies saints by scheduling mega events for the people to celebrate the life of the saint. Sometimes the Church will share stories of miracles to bring people into the church as a tool of evangelism. They will print multiple hand-sized copies of the saint's icon and distribute them to the people.

Orthodoxy has an unofficial tradition of venerating saints, arguably more formidable than the official, liturgical version. In this unofficial tradition, the people find inspiration in saints, collect their icons, and pray to them – often in their own words. Some people who describe themselves as not religious have shrines that speak to them because it reminds them of who shaped them, often a holy person. People will collect their own relics of people who are meaningful to them. Letters, cards, jewelry, clothing, and especially photos.

This kind of everyday hagiography is quite common and transcends religious boundaries. In Orthodoxy, an unofficial cult of holiness appears when a community begins to venerate a person as holy.

Orthodox churches have commissions that study claims to holiness and consider requests for official canonization. Fyodor Dostoevsky's fictional elder Zossima, a character he patterned after an elder of the Optina monastery in Russia, led to the popular notion that a person cannot be a saint unless their body has not decomposed.[22] The Orthodox Church does not require bodily incorruption to make someone into a saint at the official level.

The everyday practice of people remembering their loved ones' holiness is a reminder of the meaning of saint – a holy person. The essence of Orthodoxy is that each baptized member of the church is a saint, even if they have sinned voluntarily in this life. The ancient call to communion, "the holy things are for the holy" – intoned at the elevation of the holy bread at every Divine Liturgy – is a reminder that the people of the church are themselves the communion of saints.

The clergy, singers, servants, people in the pew, and those who are absent all belong to this communion of saints. The living saints intercede for those who ask for their prayers. This dialogue of asking for and receiving prayer plays out on a daily basis among Orthodox Christians, people communicating in person, over the phone, via text, email, and on social media apps requesting prayers from their fellow Christians in the church. Requests for prayers appear during livestreamed Divine Liturgies, people providing the names of the living and the dead who are near and dear to them. The audacity to post the names of one's loved ones on a livestreamed service demonstrates the people's confidence that someone from the community will pray for them. Or perhaps it is more accurate to say that the mere act of posting the names is a way of committing their loved ones to the living saints, who will then pray for them before God's throne.

The unofficial, everyday manner with which Orthodox people speak of and pray to the saints shows that the veneration of saints is not limited to the official liturgical gatherings of the church. Dependence on the intercessions of the saints, both heavenly and earthly, is central to the daily rhythm of Orthodox life and practice.

MOVEMENTS

Orthodoxy has had its share of movements throughout the centuries. The *kollyvades* movement originated in Greece and sought to revive lay participation in church life, beginning with frequent receiving of Holy Communion.[23] Syndesmos was an organization of youth created to build networks across borders. This section will survey a handful of the more recent movements that shaped contemporary Orthodox identity.

GREECE: THE ZOE BROTHERHOOD

Historically, the Zoe brotherhood of theologians was one of the first modern renaissance movements in Orthodoxy, emerging in the nineteenth century.[24] Paul Laudoceur explains that Zoe formed during the "difficult circumstances" of rebuilding church life in Greece following the collapse of the Ottoman Empire. Zoe's objective was to promote spiritual life and growth in modern Greece. The brotherhood, consisting of both clergy and laity, contributed to church life by publishing books and periodicals and striving to live in accordance with the high moral rigor of Orthodoxy.[25] Zoe's activity during difficult circumstances symbolizes Orthodox theology in the twentieth century. The Orthodox churches were persecuted, constantly adjusting to policy changes and economic tumult, ministering to impoverished and traumatized people, and calling upon a shrinking cadre of theologians to sustain the church's liturgical life and educate the church and the people with sparse funding available. Disagreement occurs among the proponents of movements like Zoe when conservatives want to lean into the established tradition of monasticism and spirituality and progressives look to push adaptation within the church so that its leaders are able to communicate effectively with the people when changes descend rapidly on society. Laudoceur observes that visitors to Greece both praised and criticized Zoe's people for their ideas in the middle of the twentieth century.[26]

THE NEO-PATRISTIC WAY

The neo-patristic way is more of a theological principle, and a broad one at that, than a mass movement.[27] The Orthodox version of the neo-patristic way originated with the ecumenical process of returning to the sources – learning about ancient Christianity by consulting, translating, editing, and interpreting sources like the writings of the apostolic fathers, liturgical texts, lives of the saints, and collections of sermons.

Orthodoxy's neo-patristic movement originated in an ecumenical context. Scholars of the eighteenth and nineteenth centuries adopted a scientific approach to theology, examining the books of the Bible, along with questions of age, dependence, and authorship. Theologians and historians applied their sciences to Church history and began to collect and edit manuscripts of antique and late-antique Christianity. The ressourcement movement – a desire to understand Christianity's origins and early development by closely examining its sources – is essentially the starting point for Orthodoxy's neo-patristic way.

Orthodox people use a variety of phrases to describe their understanding of the neo-patristic way. Some refer to the teaching and witness of the early church, while others speak of apostolic tradition. The most common phrase one hears in Orthodoxy is the teachings of the holy fathers. A blanket reference to the holy fathers sounds a bit vague – what do people have in mind?

Orthodox people express reverence for the holy fathers. They usually have specific theologians of the late antique period in mind. Informed Orthodox insiders possess some knowledge of fathers like Saints Basil the Great and John Chrysostom because of the liturgies that bear their names. People who participate in adult education or read independently might possess more expansive knowledge about teachers like Athanasius of Alexandria and Cyril of Jerusalem and fathers like John Climacus and Gregory Palamas, who have fixed dates on the liturgical calendar.

These figures represent a wide variety of places and times in the Orthodox world. It is inaccurate to speak of all theologians ranging from the second to the twenty-first centuries as one collection of "holy fathers." Each bishop, pastor, and theologian had his own voice. Christians have always attempted to point to a consensus, however, as we see with the review of the ecumenical councils. The councils made proclamations on behalf of the universal church that symbolize univocality – a unity of voices, or a harmony. When Orthodox refer to the teachings of the church fathers, they have this univocality in mind, like a stream running constantly and consistently through a forest filled with various plants, trees, and animals. The notion of a universal unity among the church fathers has ancient origins. It is attributed to a rather famous phrase of St. Vincent of Lerins in the fifth century, who spoke of teaching held by the fathers always and everywhere.[28]

The neo-patristic way draws upon the popular Orthodox belief in teachings held by the church fathers always and everywhere. The neo-patristic way, however, is more of a theological principle, or set of methods, than a single teaching. Emigre theologian Georges Florovsky popularized the notion of the neo-patristic way in his writings on the ways of Russian theology.[29] Florovsky bemoaned the Russian church's adoption of Western Christian categories of thinking and expressing theology.[30] Florovsky identified the seventeenth and eighteenth centuries as the periods of the migration of Western thought into Russia. Peter Mohyla, who was metropolitan of Kyiv from 1632 to 1647, was perhaps the most prominent Orthodox figure who adopted Western categories of thinking and even customs and rites in his works. Mohyla's reforms occurred in a context of Orthodox encounter with the West, and the Russian imperial recruitment of Ukrainian church leaders, musicians, and artists introduced this phenomenon to Russia.

Florovsky referred to the westernization of Russian theology as a Babylonian captivity, the adoption of a method alien to authentic Orthodoxy. Florovsky favored the retrieval of a patristic method to restore authentic Orthodoxy. Some theologians devoted thought and energy to recreating a patristic method for the renewal of Orthodox theology. This method shares some similarities with the Western ressourcement movement. For example, Catholic scholars believed they had discovered the authentic liturgical traditions of Rome from the early third century in their discovery and translation of liturgical texts attributed to Hippolytus.[31] The Catholic Church also retrieved elements of fourth-century instructions on the meaning of Baptism and anointing with chrism to reform their rites of Confirmation and Holy Communion.

Alexander Schmemann was another champion of the neo-patristic way. Schmemann criticizes Western and scholastic methods of theology in his writings, and he also complains about the captivity of the church.[32] Schmemann's primary contribution to theology is in his assertions on the place of liturgy. Schmemann claims consistently that liturgy itself, as a communal event convened by God, is the locus of primary theology. Schmemann frequently said "lex orandi est lex credendi," meaning that the law of prayer forms the law of belief. Schmemann proposed that the community's encounter with God is what enables them to theologize. The event itself, the appearance of God, and the events of being in God's presence are the primary sources for theology. In other words, theology begins with revelation and inspires the people to say something about God. Schmemann proposed that the Church needed to revive its liturgical tradition to capacitate it to rediscover Orthodox theology, and he identified liturgical theology as both superior to and the source of secondary and tertiary methods of theologies of the liturgy, which he often caricatured as textbook or scholastic theology. Schmemann was fluid in his references to sources, referring to the early church and the fathers in similar veins.

The neo-patristic way has a great deal of clout in contemporary Orthodoxy, though it may have reached its peak with the generation of twentieth- and early twenty-first-century theologians like Kallistos Ware. The new wave of public theologians continues to follow the lead of the Church fathers but does not hesitate to pursue interdisciplinary methods of theology.

SPIRITUAL CROSSROADS

The Orthodox Church is at a spiritual crossroads as of this writing. Two conflicting spiritual movements are circulating within the Church simultaneously. One movement is neo-conservative, seeking to recreate Orthodoxy in the image of a nostalgic past, often anchored in conservative moral values.[33] The chapter on cultural issues will examine this point with greater scrutiny, but the point here is to note a significant shift in social influence in Orthodoxy.[34] Orthodoxy now has a masculine component, one that revels in exclusivity, opposition to feminism and same-sex partnerships and marriage, and cooperation with other Christians and faith communities. Presently, social influencers of the neo-conservative Orthodox type have emerged on platforms like X (formerly known as Twitter), TikTok, Instagram, and YouTube. These figures can gather large followings, which points to inquirers becoming acquainted with Orthodoxy through social media instead of more traditional pathways.

A movement that originated with Christian socialism seeks to build community through ecumenical means and ministering to the world. Once again, the encounter with the world originated in an ecumenical context. Catholics supported workers' rights in the nineteenth and twentieth centuries, as expressed by the encyclical of Pope Leo XIII, *Rerum novarum*, and figures such as Dorothy Day and Virgil Michel.

Russian Orthodox clergy were also active in support of workers and the creation of democratic institutions, as demonstrated by the activity of Fr. Georgy Gapon and other clergy in the revolutionary period of 1905–1907.[35] Many Orthodox intellectuals retained and continued to cultivate social activism despite the church's attempt to stifle them, ultimately influencing prominent theologians such as Sergius Bulgakov, Nikolai Berdaev, and Maria Skobtsova.[36]

Skobtsova became a nun and exercised her ministry in a new and unconventional way.[37] St. Maria devoted her energy to meeting with people on the margins, venturing outside of her convent to meet with people who needed a companion during the strain of World War II in the city. St. Maria projected a vision for a new kind of monastic life that veered away from rigid devotion to rituals and toward service to all people of the world. She appealed to monastics to view the world itself as their monastery and emphasized each living human being as the real icon of God, bearing the divine image and therefore worthy of Orthodox love and companionship. St. Maria articulated her message in her writings and also demonstrated her teachings through her life. She issued baptismal certificates to save Jews and took the place of a Jewish woman who was to be executed in a gas chamber. St. Maria literally offered herself to save others, acting in accordance with her own teachings. Her witness reveals a strand of Orthodox spirituality that began to emerge in the nineteenth century and took on its form during the terrors of World War II. Her canonization to sainthood by the Ecumenical Patriarchate of Constantinople honored her legacy, and thousands of Orthodox honor her legacy through their activity in and for the world.

CONCLUSION

Orthodox Christians observe a vibrant spiritual life through diverse practices. These practices include the veneration of icons, prayer, fasting, feasting, and social action. Spiritual movements have appeared in Orthodoxy, including the neo-patristic way. The principles of theosis, hesychasm, metanoia, and acquiring the Holy Spirit catalyze Orthodox spirituality. Perhaps most important is the reality of vibrant spiritual life outside of the Church's official liturgical services. Orthodox people have maintained their practices through poverty, war, revolution, migration, economic depression, and persecution.

NOTES

1 The fundamental book that introduces theosis is Norman Russell, *Fellow Workers with God: Orthodox Thinking on Theosis* (Yonkers, NY: St. Vladimir's Seminary Press, 2009).
2 Saint Athanasius, *On the Incarnation*, trans. John Behr, preface C.S. Lewis, Popular Patristics series 44b (Yonkers, NY: St. Vladimir's Seminary Press, 2011), 56–58.
3 Athanasius, *On the Incarnation*, 63–64.
4 Saint Cyril of Jerusalem, *Lectures on the Christian Sacraments: the Procatechesis and the Five Mystagogical Catecheses Ascribed to St. Cyril of Jerusalem*, trans. Maxwell E. Johnson, Popular Patristics series 57 (Yonkers, NY: St. Vladimir's Seminary Press, 2017), 104–105.
5 Aristeides Papadakis, "Hesychasm," in *The Oxford Dictionary of Byzantium* (Oxford: Oxford University Press, 1991). https://www.oxfordreference.com/view/10.1093/acref/9780195046526.001.0001/acref-9780195046526-e-2276 (accessed September 30, 2024).
6 Columba Stewart, "Jesus Prayer," In *The Oxford Dictionary of Late Antiquity* (Oxford University Press, 2018). Retrieved September 5, 2024, from https://www.oxfordreference.com/view/10.1093/acref/9780198662778.001.0001/acref-9780198662778-e-2487 (accessed September 30, 2024).
7 Irina Goraïnoff and Serafim Sarovski, *SéRaphim de Sarov: Sa Vie*. (Paris, Bégrolles-en-Mauges: Les Editions du Cerf; Abbaye de Bellefontaine, 2019).
8 Norman Tanner, ed., Decrees of the Ecumenical Councils (Washington, DC: Georgetown University Press, 1990), 135–136.
9 See the discussion on this matter by Andriy Chirovsky, "Can I Pray with This Icon if it's Only a Print? Toward a Pastoral Interpretation of Orthodox Iconography," in *Icons and the Liturgy, East and West: History, Theology, and Culture*, ed. Nicholas Denysenko (Notre Dame, IN: University of Notre Dame Press, 2017), 170–175.
10 Angie Heo, "Imagining Holy Personhood: Anthropological Thresholds of the Icon," in *Praying with the Senses: Contemporary Orthodox Christian Spirituality in Practice*, ed. Sonja Luehrmann (Bloomington: Indiana University Press, 2018), 84–85.
11 Heo, "Imagining Holy Personhood," 85.
12 Metropolitan John Zizioulas, "Symbolism and Realism in Orthodox Worship," trans. Elizabeth Theokritoff, *Synaxis: An Anthology of the Most Significant Orthodox Theology in Greece Appearing in the Journal Synaxe*, vol. 1: *Anthropology, Environment, Creation*, trans. Peter Chamberas, ed. Liaidan Sherrard (Montreal: Alexander Press, 2006), 251–264.
13 Lev Gillet, *In Thy Presence* (Crestwood, NY: St. Vladimir's Seminary Press, 1998); Kallistos Ware, *The Jesus Prayer* (London: Catholic Church Society,

2014); Frederica Mathewes-Green, *Praying the Jesus Prayer* (Belmont, MA: Paraclete Press, 2011).

14 Olga Savin, trans., *The Way of a Pilgrim and the Pilgrim Continues His Way*, intro Thomas Hopko (Boston, MA: Shambhala, 2009). See St. Nikodemus of the Holy Mountain, St. Makarios of Corinth *The Philokalia,* 3 vols., trans. and eds. Phillip Sherrard and Kallistos Ware (New York: Farrar, Straus and Giroux, 1983). See also St. Nikodemus of the Holy Mountain, St. Makarios of Corinth *The Philokalia,* vol. 4, trans. and eds. Phillip Sherrard and Kallistos Ware (New York: Farrar, Straus and Giroux, 1998), and St. Nikodemus of the Holy Mountain, St. Makarios of Corinth *The Philokalia,* 3 vols., trans. and eds. Phillip Sherrard and Kallistos Ware (New York: Farrar, Straus and Giroux, 1983), and Anna Skouboulis, trans., *The Philokalia of the Holy Neptic Fathers,* vol. 5 (n.p.: Virgin Mary of Australia and Oceania, 2020).

15 "Fasting-like Diet Reduces Risk factors for Disease, Reduces Biological Age for humans," https://gero.usc.edu/2024/02/20/fasting-mimicking-diet-biological-age/#:~:text=The%20FMD%20is%20a%205,people%20to%20complete%20the%20fast (accessed September 30, 2024).

16 https://gero.usc.edu/2024/02/20/fasting-mimicking-diet-biological-age/#:~:text=The%20FMD%20is%20a%205,people%20to%20complete%20the%20fast (accessed September 30, 2024).

17 On the origins of Lent, see Nicholas Russo, "The Origins of Lent" (Ph.D. diss, University of Notre Dame, 2009), 126–149.

18 "Religious Belief and National Belonging in Central and Eastern Europe," Religious commitment and practices in central and eastern Europe | Pew Research Center (accessed September 11, 2024).

19 "The Importance of Fasting and Its Observance Today," https://www.holycouncil.org/fasting (Accessed September 9, 2024).

20 St. John Chrysostom, "The Paschal Sermon," The Paschal Sermon – Orthodox Church in America (oca.org) (accessed September 11, 2024).

21 A relic is a tangible material item connected to the saint, ranging from bones and body parts to clothing, books, or possessions of the saint.

22 Fyodor Dostoyevsky, Susan McReynolds Oddo, Constance Garnett, and Ralph E. Matlaw, *The Brothers Karamazov: A Revised Translation, Contexts, Criticism*. 2nd ed. (New York: W.W. Norton & Co., 2011).

23 Cyril Hovorun, "Kollyvadic Fathers," in *The Encyclopedia of Orthodox Christianity*, vol. 2, ed. John McGuckin (Chichester: Wiley-Blackwell Publications, 2011), 365.

24 Paul Laudoceur, *Modern Orthodox Theology: 'Behold, I Make All Things New'* (New York: T & T Clark, 2019), 129.

25 Laudoceur, *Modern Orthodox Theology*, 130–131.

26 Laudoceur, *Modern Orthodox Theology*, 132.

27 For an overview, see Ciprian Iulian Toroczkai, "The Orthodox Neo-Patristic Movements as a Renewal of Contemporary Orthodox Theology: An Overview" *Review of Ecumenical Studies* 7, no. 1 (2015), 94–115.
28 See Jaroslav Pelikan, *The Christian Tradition: A History of the Development of Doctrine, vol. 1: The Emergence of the Catholic Tradition (100–600)* (Chicago, IL: University of Chicago Press, 1971), 333.
29 Georges Florovsky, *Ways of Russian Theology* (Belmont, MA: Notable and Academic Books, 1987).
30 Paul Gavrilyuk, *Georges Florovsky and the Russian Religious Renaissance* (Oxford: Oxford University Press, 2014).
31 Paul Bradshaw and Maxwell E. Johnson, *The Eucharistic Liturgies: Their Evolution and Interpretation* (Collegeville, MN: Liturgical Press, 2012), 315–316.
32 Nicholas Denysenko, "Ressourcement or Aggiornamento? An Assessment of Modern Liturgical Reforms," *International Journal for the Study of Systematic Theology* 20, no. 2 (2018), 192–198.
33 See Paul Laudoceur, "Neo-Traditionalist Ecclesiology in Orthodoxy," *Scottish Journal of Theology* 72 (2019), 398–413.
34 See, for example, Sarah Riccardi-Swartz, "Orthodoxy and the E-Spirit of Radicalism," Sarah Riccardi-Swartz: Orthodoxy and the E-Spirit of Radicalism—Jacob's Well (jacobsmag.org) (accessed September 30, 2024).
35 Jennifer Hedda, *His Kingdom Come: Orthodox Pastorship and Social Activism in Revolutionary Russia* (DeKalb: Northern Illinois University Press, 2008), 126–187.
36 On this topic, see Michael Plekon, "Church, Society, Politics: Perspectives from the 'Paris School'," *Logos: A Journal of Eastern Christian Studies* 53, nos. 3–4 (2012), 198–219.
37 For a biographical profile, see Michael Plekon, *Living Icons: Persons of Faith in the Eastern Church,* foreword Lawrence Cunningham (Notre Dame, IL: University of Notre Dame Press, 2002), 19–80. See also: Incommunion St. Maria Skobtsova Resources – Incommunion (accessed September 30, 2024).

MYSTERIES IN ORTHODOXY

This chapter supplements the material in Chapter 6, which provides a macro-level explanation of liturgical life in Orthodoxy. Every Orthodox Christian begins their journey with Baptism, and ends its earthly portion with the rite of burial. Orthodoxy, like Catholic and Protestant communities, has liturgical rituals that mark these important threshold moments: life, love, sickness, ordination, and death.

The Orthodox Church has something of a classical text widely read and beloved by numerous global Christians that reflects on these mysteries – Alexander Schmemann's famous For the Life of the World.[1] Schmemann's text, reprinted multiple times, represents a different approach to explaining the mysteries. Schmemann doesn't describe the ritual and attempt to present the spiritual meaning of each component. Instead, Schmemann brought the rituals, at a macro-level, into dialogue with an Orthodox perspective on God's purpose and love for humankind, much more along the lines of a classical patristic text, like Athanasius' *On the Incarnation*, or the treatises on the sacraments ascribed to St. Cyril of Jerusalem.

This short chapter attempts to honor Schmemann's classical treatise on the sacraments by commenting on how the mysteries reveal the dynamic love of God for humankind. It is sensible to think of Orthodox sacraments as one mystery into which a community of people enters, and not a list of sacraments. The mystery is relational, a community responding to God's reaching out his divine hand in love, living together with God, Father, Son, and Holy Spirit. The people enter into and sustain this mystery through liturgical ritual practice and the personal rites of prayers and devotions practiced every day. The Orthodox mystery is not a list of sacramental rites from which one can select à la carte, as if it were a lunch menu. It

DOI: 10.4324/9781003433217-6

is one mystery of a covenantal relationship with the living God, and the people make and sustain loving contact with God through the liturgical rites described briefly in this chapter.

BAPTISM AND CHRISMATION

We begin by bringing Baptism and Chrismation together because there is no real separation of these mysteries in the Orthodox tradition. The commentary is timely because Orthodoxy is gradually becoming a church of converts, especially in Europe and North America. Baptism and Chrismation in Orthodoxy are deeply covenantal and serious, akin to standing on the edge of a cliff and making the most important personal commitment of one's life.

Orthodox Baptism retains a feature that the Western churches have diminished – exorcism. This is not the kind of exorcism dramatized in a horror series on streaming subscriptions, but an exorcism where the church asks an honest question of catechumens, along with parents and sponsors of infants and young children: do you truly renounce evil and the source of evil, satan? When the church instructs a candidate to renounce the devil, spit upon him, and then turn around, profess their belief in Christ as King and God, and bow down before Christ – the church is asking the candidate, parents, and sponsors to make a commitment. Rejecting satan cannot be translated into lip service while resuming one's usual way of life. Orthodoxy believes that rejecting satan is ending all interaction with him, dalliances, demonic practices, and the kinds of sins that people claim they commit as coping mechanisms. Rejecting satan is the end of a relationship to which one cannot ever return.

Committing to Jesus Christ begins a covenant that will remain permanent no matter what happens. The church hopes, prays, and, in its finest moments, supports people to remain committed to Christ throughout their lives. The church also teaches that Baptism means participation in the death and resurrection of Christ (Rom. 6:4). Entering into water is always dangerous, even if it seems fun, playful, and necessary. The church anoints candidates with oil to remind them to be vigilant, to equip them to navigate the storms of life, as if the oil were a potentially lifesaving vest.[2]

The baptismal waters wash away sin and function as a birth canal for the new Orthodox Christian. Birth canals are dangerous and require the watchful eyes and steady hands of nurses, doctors, and sometimes midwives. Becoming Orthodox via Baptism is by no means a guarantee of an easy life. The Orthodox way is the way of the cross, and God will provide crosses for everyone to bear at some point. Carrying the cross will be tiring and will tempt the person to question their commitment to Jesus Christ. Orthodoxy promises that Jesus Christ will be with the faithful member through the very worst of their experiences, including the most unjust and traumatic ones. Sometimes, the people of the church fail to live up to their commitment to support one another, but Christ is ever-present and loving. The anointing with Chrism completes, perfects, and finishes Baptism by giving the neophyte the spiritual capacity they require to become like God as they navigate life's challenges.[3]

The Orthodox Church also uses this special Chrism to mark the presence of Christ and the church's fervent commitment to him in the rite of the dedication of churches and for the reception of Christians into the church who have already been baptized.[4] One might view Chrismation used for the reception of converts, as a sealing into Orthodoxy's specific way of life to continue the process of becoming God's chosen people.[5]

From the church's perspective, God performs an act at Baptism and anointing. The neophytes and converts join the people of God, and they are also changed and transformed. The message of John the Baptist that opens the Gospel of Mark and appears in the early sections of the other gospels is one of repentance, of a change of life, of mind, and of heart. The person receiving Baptism is committing to turning away from sin and leading a righteous life. The prayer for the blessing of baptismal waters asks God to make the waters into a place of regeneration and remission of sins.[6] The person newly born from the church's birth canal is one who has experienced regeneration and has had their sins forgiven. The expectation for this person is that they will no longer sin from this point forward because they now have the capacity to lead a righteous life because of the gifts God has endowed them with.

One cannot claim that people are completely aware of these realities, of the dignity with which they are endowed when they are baptized and anointed. The Orthodox Church does not gather to consecrate Chrism – the fragrant oil used for Chrismation – very often. When these gatherings do occur, the church claims, in its prayers, that the Chrism will be used to make these people into God's priests, prophets, and kings by the descent of the Holy Spirit. The Orthodox Church sets a high bar for its people – they are to become holy priests, prophets, and kings. Sometimes, the church fails to communicate this ideal effectively and to offer people the support they need to maintain their commitment to Christ.

One constant in all of this is the promise of God's love. God will never abandon his people, even when they deny him, which happens in the worst-case scenarios. God receives them back into the fold if they have a change of heart and decide to return to the church after straying.

Orthodox don't always agree with one another about the fullness of Baptism in other churches. There were limited episodes of Orthodox rebaptizing faithful whose Baptism had come into question.[7] Most Orthodox churches today will honor the Baptism of someone who was baptized in water in the name of the Father, Son, and Holy Spirit. There are also some discrepancies in the way the church receives people baptized elsewhere into the church. Some Orthodox have received Catholics through confession and communion, without Chrismation, because Catholic Confirmation is based on the same principles as Orthodox Chrismation.

SPIRITUAL AND EARTHLY REALITIES: BAPTISM AND CHRISMATION

The brief presentation on Baptism and Chrismation above attempts to lay out the spiritual reality of what happens to a neophyte, as well as identify a small handful of problems that occur when the Orthodox Church is suspicious about the legitimacy of a Baptism that happened elsewhere. Here are two brief descriptions of what actually happens when people are either baptized or chrismated in Orthodoxy.

When families want to baptize their children, they contact the pastor. Ideally, the pastor will meet with the parents to ascertain their readiness to raise their child in the church and will prepare adults seeking Baptism (or Chrismation) through some program of catechesis. Many young adults coming into Orthodoxy are learning about the church via handpicked online outlets, ranging from YouTube posts by Orthodox influencers to a hodgepodge of readings and online posts. The content they're gleaning from handpicked sources might miss the mark of the reality of what it means to live as an Orthodox Christian by a wide margin. This means that many people who become Orthodox are learning about it as they go, in reality.

Baptism for both infants and adults follows the following ritual forms. Reception into the catechumenate, exorcisms, renunciation of satan, profession of faith in Jesus Christ, blessing of baptismal waters, adding oil to the water, prebaptismal anointing, Baptism in water via immersion or pouring (or both), vesting in baptismal garment, Chrismation, Holy Communion (if the Baptism occurs within Liturgy), removal of chrism, and tonsure (offering of hair).

For converts becoming Orthodox, there is no single, universal program of preparation for becoming Orthodox. Parishes customize programs, if they prepare people at all. The Orthodox Church does not have a catechetical program comparable to the Roman Catholic Rite for the Christian Initiation of Adults and its associated formation materials.[8] When the pastor determines they are ready and the bishop blesses them for reception, they can become Orthodox via Chrismation, and then participate fully in the life of the church. Orthodoxy never separates Chrismation from infant Baptism, because Orthodoxy views each human person as possessing the dignity of the divine image, even the youngest member of the church. Each human being has the spiritual capacity to entreat God, to love, and to receive love. Infants are chrismated and receive Holy Communion immediately.

THE EUCHARIST, BAPTISM, AND CHRISMATION

The Eucharist fulfills Baptism and Chrismation because the community gathers for the Eucharist to bear witness to the initiation of new people in God's community. Baptism and Chrismation can take place outside of the Divine Liturgy, and this is the usual process, but it is not ideal. The Orthodox Church has blueprints for the ideal setting for Baptism and Chrismation. A number of feasts on the liturgical calendar appoint the singing of "As many as have been baptized in Christ have put on Christ" (Gal. 3:26–27) instead of the Trisagion hymn at the Divine Liturgy. These feasts include Pascha (both liturgies), Pentecost, Christmas, Theophany, and Lazarus Saturday. The church sang "As Many" because Baptisms had taken place, and the neophytes were participating in their first Divine Liturgy after their Baptism.

The Paschal Vigil provides the best blueprint and ideal pattern for how these events took place. At Vespers, after Psalm 140 and the "Gladsome Light" entrance hymn, the patriarch baptized all approved candidates in the baptistry of Hagia Sophia in Constantinople while the appointed Old Testament readings were recited in the church. As soon as the Baptisms concluded and the patriarch was ready to lead the neophytes into the church, the pastoral assistants would alert the chanters to take the final reading (from the prophet Daniel). The neophytes would enter into the church and would join the rest of the assembly to hear the readings from the New Testament and participate fully in the Divine Liturgy.[9]

Joining the rest of the assembly is the key to understanding the principle of this liturgical sequence. The neophytes belonged to the people of God once they had been baptized and anointed with Chrism, and the chosen people of God assembled to offer the Divine Liturgy and receive the gift of God in Holy Communion. Baptism and Chrismation are deeply personal, creating relationships with God's community in heaven and also on earth, among the people of the church.

The Eucharistic Divine Liturgy initiates the process of Baptism. The church community that gathers for the liturgy is the host of the baptismal event, even when it is celebrated with only the presbyter, the person being baptized, and their family and sponsors. The same church community comes together to ask God to bless the oils for the anointing with Chrism. God initiates the mystery of covenantal love by calling people to join his chosen people. The chosen people, the church, host the event, welcome the people into the community, and invite them to join them for their regular encounters with God at the Divine Liturgy. This is how the Eucharist is the focal point of Baptism and Chrismation.

Some Protestant church communities have permitted a customizable reconfiguration of the ordering of this process of joining the church by allowing people to participate fully in the Eucharistic liturgy before they are baptized.[10] Proponents of this revised process state that the Eucharist is the covenantal community and the order can be reversed or revised, so Baptism after Eucharist is something along the lines of grace upon grace. It is likely that some people have received communion in an Orthodox parish before they were baptized if the ministers did not know them. This is the exception, though, and not the rule. For Orthodox, Baptism is the portal into the Eucharistic community. Experiencing the process of renouncing satan, committing to Christ, receiving a new birth through water, and receiving the Holy Spirit in Baptism and anointing is essential before joining the community.

PENANCE AND CONFESSION

Baptism and Chrismation recreate human nature so that the Christian can become like Christ and lead a righteous, sinless life. Orthodoxy holds up this ideal for each member of the people of God to become like Christ, to make turning away from sin and pursuing righteousness one's habit and way of life. What happens, then, when people sin after Baptism?

Post-baptismal sin became a serious issue in late antique Christianity. The stories of prominent adults who requested Baptism show that some of them waited until they were near death to be baptized, lest the temptation to sin overcome them. The emperor Constantine's story of postponing Baptism until he was near death is among the best-known instances.

Addressing postbaptismal sin became an issue in the earliest Christian communities, as St. Paul directs the Corinthian community to expel a man guilty of adultery (1 Cor. 5). Restoration to the community is possible for this person. Paul's instruction established an initial blueprint for the process of penance, which eventually becomes confession. Christians mired in sin have to amend their ways before they can return to the community. We might think of this as a spiritual process of unlearning and then relearning in our time.

Another problematic issue emerged during a period of persecution when some Christians offered sacrifices to the gods to avoid torture. Cyprian of Carthage taught that these Christians could return to the church after a period of penance upon the recommendation of a confessor, someone who had suffered from torture during the persecution.[11] Readmittance to the church included the laying on of hands by the bishop, who oversaw the process of penance. The laying on of hands for penance relates to Baptism and Eucharist in somewhat subtle ways. In the Western church, Chrismation (known today as Confirmation) always included the bishop laying his hands on the neophyte, a practice established by the apostles (Acts 8). The handlaying rite of restoring someone who had sinned (a penitent) to the community drew from the apostolic laying on of hands at Baptism and Chrismation. The laying on of hands at penance restored the penitent to the community of the Holy Spirit.

The Western and Eastern traditions of penance and confession have similarities and differences. From the very beginning, Eastern penance emphasized a therapeutic dimension, which often included a dialogue between a confessor and the penitent. The confessor would listen to the penitent, assess their situation, and provide them with guidance on how they might amend their way of life. This practice prioritizes care and love for the penitent, a desire to help them learn how to grow into the Christian life of the community. The adoption of the tariff system in the Western church of the medieval period depicted penance as transactional. Committing a sin and admitting it would result in a penalty or fine, which, when paid, would create a clean slate for the penitent.[12] The punitive emphasis of medieval Western penance facilitated a system of assigning lists of prayers and actions one could perform to receive forgiveness of sins and be reunited with the Eucharistic community. This does not mean that Western Christian pastors did not care about their people – it simply testifies to the different trajectory of the evolution of penitential practices.

People began to receive Holy Communion infrequently as early as the fourth century. The infrequent reception of communion influenced a type of liturgical piety that emphasized a sense of personal worthiness when receiving communion. Zealous preparation for communion included the need to repent immediately beforehand, so many Orthodox would make a confession the evening or morning prior to receiving communion at the Divine Liturgy. Perhaps the best-known version of this ritual sequence was the one that became anchored in the Russian imperial period. The combination of infrequent communion with the expectation of sinlessness led to a rigorous practice of reciting special prayers of repentance, intense fasting, and confession, often in a monastery.[13] This practice was known as govenie, and the pairing of rigorous preparation and confession with communion led to the popular belief that confession was required before one could receive communion. This convergence of events – generations of infrequent communion combined with an intense process of fasting and penance with confession – led to the notion that the faithful person was worthy of communion only after they had fasted and confessed their sins.

The contemporary Orthodox rite of confession is among the most flexible and customizable rites, one that can be quite lengthy or very short. The model used by most of the churches in the Slavic tradition is probably the one that is most recognizable. A layperson can approach their pastor to request confession. The pastor, or another assigned presbyter, will meet the layperson in church, recite some initial prayers, and invite the layperson to confess their sins. This segment of the rite of confession is absolutely crucial – the person shares their sins with the presbyter, who is bearing witness to the act of stating one's sins. Mustering up the courage to confess one's sins and committing to a process of turning away from them is why we call this rite confession.

The presbyter hears the confession and responds to the layperson with questions or advice. The burden of responsibility placed on the presbyter at this point is heavy and crucial. The presbyter might simply validate the sorrow and contrition of the penitent and gently guide them on how they might reconfigure their lives. He might provide concrete suggestions as a spiritual director to show the penitent a way to recommit themselves to Christ. The pastoral task becomes difficult and potentially dangerous when the presbyter notices something outside of his field of expertise, perhaps a sign of mental or emotional illness or abuse. Spiritual practice cannot replace the therapeutic methods that can lead to recovery, coping, and hopefully healing for people suffering from various forms of mental, emotional, and physical trauma. Many pastors are trained to guide the penitent to resources that can help them find their way to holistic healing. The rite concludes with one or more prayers of confession, with the presbyter absolving the penitent of their sins and restoring them to communion.

Orthodox practices of the rites of confession vary.[14] Many Orthodox faithful in the Middle East and Greece had not participated in confession because certain monasteries were the only ones authorized to hear confessions, which required a pilgrimage to a monastery. Monastic elders who were respected because of their humility and knowledge of spirituality tended to be popular confessors. Women monastics could also hear confessions. Any monastic who is not ordained but authorized to hear confessions must refer the penitent to a presbyter or bishop for absolution, the rite of handlaying that readmits the penitent to communion. In the Slavic tradition, it is customary for any ordained presbyter to hear confessions. In the Greek tradition, only some presbyters can hear confessions. Bishops can, of course, hear confessions, but deacons cannot.

The most important part of confession is the dynamic relationship between forgiveness of sins and the person's commitment to the covenant in Christ and the body of his church. This is why the actual act of confessing one's sins stands at the center of the rite. Confessing one's sins, committing to turning away from them, and doing so in the presence of a presbyter-witness requires courage. The act demonstrates acknowledgement of one's failure to live up to the covenant in Christ, at minimum. Confession has the capacity to move the penitent to have the courage to unlearn sinfulness, learn righteousness, and receive God's embrace of forgiveness, above all. The privilege of taking one's seat at God's holy table of Communion is the outcome of confession. It is simply the church's way of nourishing and sustaining people who truly desire to remain within the covenant, even if the performance of the ministry is all too often imperfect.

MARITAL LOVE

Marriage was a civil matter for much of the history of the Orthodox Church. Keeping in mind the vastly different social and cultural environment of arranged marriages for teenagers, couples were married in accordance with civil ordinances. Canons began to emerge in the late seventh century to regulate marriage and to prevent violations of the church's moral values. Orthodoxy adheres to Jesus Christ's ideal of one marriage between one man and one woman (Mt. 9). The church eventually permitted up to three marriages for laypeople but prohibited remarriage for clergy who were divorced or widowed, at least until recently.[15]

Rites for betrothal and crowning appear as early as the eighth century, and the Orthodox Church began to regulate marriage by the ninth century.[16] Many Orthodox scholars taught that the wedding was affixed to the Eucharistic liturgy because it begins with "*Blessed* is the kingdom," and the sharing of the common cup seems to be residual from Holy Communion. The opening exclamation, "blessed is the kingdom," was the formula used for all divine services at Hagia Sophia in Constantinople. Furthermore, the common cup is a non-Eucharistic ritual that seems to have evolved from something akin to the Jewish smashing of the cup. In our case, it seems that the cup migrated from a domestic ritual into the liturgy. There is no substantial extant evidence showing that the rite of marriage had been affixed to the Eucharistic liturgy. There is, however, evidence that couples received Holy Communion from the Presanctified Gifts during the rite of crowning.

In fact, the evidence suggests that the reception of Holy Communion by the bride and groom – from the Presanctified gifts – was a staple and stable feature of Orthodox marriages from the eighth through the fifteenth centuries. Michael Zheltov suggests that receiving Holy Communion was an important feature of the service and disappeared from the rite only because the collapse of the Byzantine Empire removed the need to include partaking of Holy Communion with the Greek Orthodox population now part of the Rum millet of the Ottoman Empire.[17] Zheltov notes that the section on Holy Communion was removed in the service books published in the fifteenth to sixteenth centuries.

The existence of the couple receiving the presanctified gifts during the rite of marriage shows, once again, the relationship between marriage and the covenant of communion in Christ and the body of his church. Contemporary discussion on marriage in Orthodoxy is dominated by polarized positions on same-sex marriage, pre- and extra-marital sexual activity, and the pandemic of divorce. The Orthodox Church remains unwavering in its adherence to Jesus' ideal of one marriage between one man and one woman. The church does not permit same-sex marriages or blessings of unions and considers all pre- and extra-marital sexual activity to be sinful.

Currently, Orthodox theologians have a robust discussion on the theological meaning of marriage. Alexander Schmemann compared marriage to the image of Christ in the church in one of his less-frequently quoted essays in *For the Life of the World*.[18] Schmemann used the evocative language of marriage as the sacrament of divine love, and he also suggested that marriage must transcend popular notions of the "Christian family" so that it has "cosmic and universal" dimensions.[19]

Orthodox theologians have attempted to depict marriage as sharing the calling of kenotic service that is the equal of both the monastic and celibate courses of life. Paul Evdokimov insisted that arguing for the superiority of one path over the other (monastic and marital) is futile because the "Gospel in its totality is addressed to each person; everyone in his own situation is called to the absolute of the Gospel."[20] Evdokimov proposed that the nuptial and monastic churches intersect and work together in service for Christ, without strict separation. He identified room for chastity within marriage, meaning that one "belongs totally to Christ."[21] Married couples give themselves completely to Christ within the context of their marriage, in their shared lives. Evdokimov suggested that marriage is even a type of monasticism because it requires both renunciation of certain parts of the past and a new birth.

Divine love grows within this nuptial microcosm of the church. The husband and wife practice a type of renunciation, a constant dying to one's self by giving to the other, rehearsed on a daily basis. Romanian theologian Ciprian Ioan Streza defines the carrying out of nuptial love eloquently[22]:

> The love between the spouses grows through the exercise of this mutual responsibility, and conversely, this responsibility grows through love. This very responsibility becomes visible in acts performed outside the family unit, within society, for the family cannot properly function well without also fulfilling certain obligations in society.

Streza arrives at the same conclusion as Evdokimov on the purpose of marriage – to become a true human person by "living the altruistic love of God and sharing it with his family and then with all the other Christians."[23] Streza's assertions are compatible with Evdokimov, Schmemann, and the statement on marriage of the Pan-Orthodox Council of Crete – marriage is a spiritual communion with cosmic dimensions because it is anchored in the love of Christ.[24]

The social ethos statement of the Ecumenical Patriarchate of Constantinople expresses this ideal of marital love with a similar eloquence[25]:

> It is a bond also that intertwines formerly separate individual spiritual efforts into a shared vocation to transfigure the fallen world, and to tread the path toward *theosis* in Christ.

Orthodox theology is optimistic about the potential of marriage to contribute to the life of the world. Schmemann, Evdokimov, Streza, and the documents of Crete and *For the Life of the World* (FLOW) emphasize the anchoring of Orthodox marriage in and upon Christ. The historical inclusion of partaking of the Presanctified Gifts during marriage confirms the direct relationship of marriage to the Eucharist. No additional prooftexting is needed to define marriage as a micro-level icon of the kingdom. Marriage is participation in the fellowship of the Holy Spirit.

The idealization of marriage and its potential for transfiguring the world must come into dialogue with the painful realities of broken marriage. Schmemann mentioned these realities when he said that marriage can become a "demonic distortion of love."[26] We see similar acknowledgements elsewhere. FLOW has an entire paragraph devoted to the breakdown of marriage and the need to acknowledge that "shattering kinds of mental, physical, sexual, and emotional abuse" occur in families.[27] The document states that divorce is sometimes necessary for the protection of the most vulnerable members of a family unit from abuse.

The typical experience for a couple getting married in the Orthodox Church entails meeting with the pastor, with the possibility of pre-marital counseling, and preparing for the wedding. Almost all Orthodox Church weddings are in a church building and take place on a Saturday or Sunday. Sunday weddings are the norm, and Saturdays take place with permission. The service itself has two parts – the first betrothal, with several prayers and the exchange of rings. The second part is crowning, with prayers, readings from Ephesians (5:22–33) and John (2:1–12), the actual crowning, sharing a common cup of wine, and the bonding of hands with a short procession. The service does not include a lighting of candles, and the rite does not hold space for the groom and bride to write their own vows. Grandiosity in parish weddings depends on the couple's participation in parish life. Some parish choirs charge a fee for wedding music, and pastoral staff might assign one or more singers to chant the responses in other instances.

The rite of marriage is like Baptism and Chrismation in that it takes place one time. Marriages encounter changes, major challenges, sickness, family disputes, and the matter of growing together over time. One or both partners in marriage occasionally fail, stray, or even walk away. The Orthodox principle that God is always present in Baptism and Chrismation applies here also – God remains faithful to the covenant of marriage if both partners are able and willing to anchor themselves in the cross and work out their problems. There are occasions when it is not safe for one partner to remain in marriage. For this reason and others, the church permits people divorce and remarriage.

For couples in marriages sustained over an adult lifetime, the covenant of love rehearsed on a daily basis with one another is anchored in love for God and also for all of humankind, including in large measure to people outside of one's family. Marriage can be a participation in and foretaste of eternal life to come if it does not exclude love for others. It is possible and even desirable for Orthodoxy to expand its sense of family outside of blood relations and traditional family units.

It is crucial to note that Orthodoxy has not addressed a significant demographic reality – the steady decrease in the number of people seeking marriage and the increase in single people who are not monastic.[28] It is possible for the single person to enjoy companionship with all people that is anchored in love and deep friendship. Christian tradition does not subordinate single people to the married – the authentic Christian single life is one of great dignity and honor, even if it is lived outside of the monastic community (1 Cor. 7:32). The pastoral approach to addressing singles is to work together with them to learn how to form relationships anchored in love and to recognize when desire, which is part of the human experience, becomes distorted into objectification. Another way of saying this – the single life is just as meaningful and purposeful as married life. The single life of the various forms of companionship is innately sacramental.

SICKNESS AND DEATH

For centuries, the Western and Eastern churches celebrated the anointing of the sick as a threshold rite for people on the verge of death – the last rites. The Western church undertook a reform of the anointing of the sick so that it would be used for sick people. Orthodoxy has a longstanding tradition of anointing the sick – in church, in people's homes, in hospitals, and in hospice centers. Anointing is not magic – it does not bolster chances for medical miracles or inexplicable physical improvement. Anointing asks God for physical and spiritual restoration. The church believes that healing is possible even in instances where a sick person will deteriorate, suffer, and eventually die. Anointing is medicinal in the healing of relationships – with God, spouses, children, family, and others. The portion of the prayer that asks God to forgive the sins of the sick person is not designed to cast some sin they committed as having caused the illness in divine retribution or punishment. The prayer asks for the restoration of the whole person – body, mind, heart, and soul – and this includes the continued turning away of the sick person from sin.[29]

Sickness, especially painful, terminal sickness, can traumatize the person bearing this heavy cross. Remaining faithful through a sickness that destroys the body is enormously challenging. The anointing of the sick brings the church to the sick person not only for prayer but also for fraternal support, for the church as a community to remain faithful to its covenant to love all of the people constituting the body of Christ.

The anointing of the sick is typically celebrated for someone with a serious illness, but anyone who is sick can request it. The gradual increase in mental health awareness and the devastation wrought by untreated trauma open the possibility for regular celebrations of the anointing of the sick in public, for the church to participate in the destigmatization of mental and emotional illnesses.

The full form of the anointing of the sick is not celebrated often, so when it is, the entire church comes together for a series of readings and prayers, with as many presbyters participating as possible. The epistle of James stands at the center of the blessing of the oils for anointing of the sick (James 5:14–15). Many parishes host communal anointing services on Wednesday of Holy Week to prepare people for Holy Communion.

The anointing of the sick reveals a central truth in Orthodoxy's view of humankind: God wants everyone to be whole and healthy, no matter the affliction. The rites of anointing the sick with prayers for the restoration of all forms of health illustrate the church's response to God's purpose for humanity. The people of the church want to be whole and healthy, so they gather to ask God to heal them and support one another through their illnesses.

DEATH AND BURIAL

The chapter on Orthodox doctrine discusses Orthodox beliefs on what happens when people die. This section mentions the popularity of the short requiem services, bearing multiple names and descriptions, such as Trisagion, Litiya, and *panikhida*. Orthodox people have diverse opinions on the afterlife, with a two-judgment process the most prevalent one. The soul, believed to be immortal, ascends to an initial judgment at some point after death and awaits reunification with their body and the resurrection of the dead promised by Jesus at the last judgment.

Using the prevailing belief as our starting point, the rites of burial are essentially the church's way of bidding the departed farewell and sending them to God. The community expresses grief, lament at death, love for the departed person, and above all, hope in the resurrection. The readings from 1 Thessalonians (4:13–17) and John (5:24–30) express the community's belief that God will fulfill his promise and raise the departed to new life. These readings are taken at the main service, the actual burial rite itself.

The number and sequence of liturgical gatherings vary in Orthodoxy. A typical sequence would include an initial memorial service at the funeral home, followed by the burial rite in the church, and concluding with the burial in a cemetery. People occasionally request additional memorial services or the rite of burial within a Divine Liturgy. Embalming is optional, and the casket can be either open or closed. The Orthodox Church prohibits cremation, although bishops sometimes permit exceptions by having the rite of burial before cremation.[30]

The burial service includes a poignant moment of farewell when the presbyter invites the people to come forward for the final goodbye with the departed, accompanied by the hymn, "come, let us give the last kiss."[31] The final goodbye is an acknowledgement of death, an act of sending, and an expression of trust in God, that God will receive and take care of the dead. Prayers for the dead continue without ceasing after the funeral and burial have concluded. Death has become a passage, and the departed person has gone through to God, remaining in the body of the church on the other side of the impassable chasm.

Orthodoxy does not grant burials to people who attend church but do not belong, by rule.[32] Strict adherence to this rule causes pastoral problems for Orthodox people who were married to a non-Orthodox spouse, especially if that person participated in community life. Pastors frequently permit both burial and memorial services for non-Orthodox family members as a token of love and respect for their families. The Orthodox Church has a special burial rite for infants but prohibits burial for people who die from suicide, again by strict adherence to the rule.[33] The Ecumenical Patriarchate and Orthodox Church in America allow the bishop to permit a church burial if mental health issues are involved in a suicide.[34]

CONCLUSION

Coming together with God and the people of God who rest in heaven stands at the core of the Orthodox mystery of communion. The liturgical life of the church is oriented toward responding to God's invitation to join this community of heaven and earth, making a commitment to adhere to the commandments of God's kingdom, learning how to love God and God's people, and sustaining the covenant through the trials and tribulations of this life. Orthodox people believe that they dwell in a space that intersects both this world and the realm of God's kingdom. Faithful service to God requires love for and service to the people of this world. The people of God often fall short and fail because they are always in a process of becoming like Christ and occasionally succumb to their weaknesses. God's love is limitless, which is why God remains faithful to the covenant, even when the people stray from their promise.

NOTES

1 Alexander Schmemann, *For the Life of the World: Sacraments and Orthodoxy*, rev. ed., foreword Edith Humphrey (Yonkers, NY: St. Vladimir's Seminary Press, 2018).
2 Paul Lazor, ed., *Baptism* (New York: Department of Religious Education, The Orthodox Church in America, 1972), 53–55.
3 Lazor, *Baptism*, 58–59.
4 For more on Chrismation, see Nicholas Denysenko, *Chrismation: A Primer for Catholics* (Collegeville, MN: Liturgical Press, 2012).
5 Denysenko, *Chrismation*, 65–76.
6 Lazor, *Baptism*, 49–53.
7 Denysenko, *Chrismation*, 42–44. See also Job Getcha, *The Euchologion Unveiled*, Orthodox Liturgy Series Book 4 (Yonkers, NY: St. Vladimir's Seminary Press, 2021), 40–42.
8 Here is the description for the RCIA: https://www.usccb.org/beliefs-and-teachings/who-we-teach/christian-initiation-of-adults (accessed July 29, 2024). See also *Rite of Christian Initiation of Adults* (Washington, DC: United States Conference of Catholics Bishops, 1988).
9 See, for example, the description of the Paschal Vigil in Constantinople in Juan Mateos, ed., *Le typicon de la grande église, vol. 2: Le cycle des fêtes mobiles*, Orientalia Christiana Analecta 166 (Rome: Pontifical Oriental Institute, 1963), 88–89.
10 For an analysis of the debate among Protestants, see Charles Hefling, "Who Is Communion for? The Debate over the Open Table," https://www.christiancentury.org/article/2012-11/who-communion (accessed July 29, 2024).
11 James Dallen, *The Reconciling Community: The Rite of Penance*, Studies in the Reformed Rites of the Catholic Church, vol. 3 (Collegeville, MN: Liturgical Press, 1991), 37–42.
12 Dallen, *The Reconciling Community*, 102–113.
13 For a description of govenie, see St. Theophan the Recluse, *The Path to Salvation: A Manual of Spiritual Transformation*, trans. Fr. Seraphim Rose and the St. Herman of Alaska Brotherhood (Platina, CA: St. Paisius Brotherhood, 1996), 274–279.
14 Additional resources for learning about Orthodoxy and confession include John Chryssavgis, *Confession and Repentance in the Orthodox Church* (Brookline, MA: Holy Cross Orthodox Press, 1990); Aristotle Papanikolaou, "Liberating Eros: Confession and Desire," *Journal of the Society for Christian Ethics* 26, no. 1 (2006), 115–136; Nadieszda Kizenko, *Good for the Souls: A History of Confession in the Russian Empire* (Oxford: Oxford University Press, 2021).

15 The Ecumenical Patriarchate of Constantinople will now consider requests for the remarriage for clergy on a case by case basis.
16 For the history of the rites of betrothal and crowning in the Byzantine rite, see Gabriel Radle, *Marriage in Byzantium: Christian Liturgical Rites from Betrothal to Consummation* (New York: Cambridge University Press, 2024).
17 Michael Zheltov, "Обзор истории чинов благословения брака в православной традиции," in *Православноеучение о церковных таинствах*, v. 3, *Православное учение о церковных таинствах* (Moscow: Synodal Biblical-Theological Commission, 2009), 123–126 (109–126).
18 Schmemann, *For the Life of the World*, 82.
19 Schmemann, *For the Life of the World*, 82.
20 Paul Evdokimov, *The Sacrament of Love: The Nuptial Mystery in the Light of the Orthodox Tradition* (Crestwood, NY: St. Vladimir's Seminary Press, 1985), 65.
21 Evdokimov (sp), *The Sacrament of Love*, 66.
22 Ciprian Ioan Streza, "The Mystery of Marriage: Mystery of Human Love Crowned in Glory and Honour. An Orthodox Perspective," *Review of Ecumenical Studies Sibiu* 10 (2018), 390.
23 Streza, "The Mystery of Marriage," 393.
24 "The Sacrament of Marriage and Its Impediments," holycouncil.org/marriage (accessed July 29, 2024).
25 Ecumenical Patriarchate, *For the Life of the World: Toward a Social Ethos of the Orthodox Church*, paragraph 68, https://www.goarch.org/social-ethos?fbclid=IwAR2RSPrgYRhPfAgT9p2iIQkd9wqtOYJ74Gtjnpmyq9xYdxshwqr6U1FJFiY# (accessed July 26, 2024). Hereafter FLOW, Paragraph 20.
26 Schmemann, *For the Life of the World*, 82.
27 FLOW, paragraph 22.
28 Daniel Cox, "The Societal Cost of Marriage Decline," The Societal Cost of the Marriage Decline | Institute for Family Studies (ifstudies.org) (accessed July 30, 2024).
29 See Paul Meyendorff, *The Anointing of the Sick*, Orthodox Liturgy Series, Book 1 (Crestwood, NY: St. Vladimir's Seminary Press, 2009), 77–78.
30 See Getcha, *The Euchologion Unveiled*, 189–190.
31 "Come, let us give the final kiss, brethren, to the dead, as we give thanks to God; because he/she has left his/her family and is hastening to the grave, he/she has no further care for things of no moment, affairs of the much-wearied flesh. Where now are his/her relatives and friends? Now as we are parted let us pray that the Lord will give him/her rest," translation by Archimandrite Ephrem Lash, anastasis/files/funeral.md at master · brianglass/anastasis · GitHub (accessed July 30, 2024).
32 Getcha, *The Euchologion Unveiled*, 190–191.

33 See, for example, the following rite of burial for infants and children published by the Greek Orthodox Archdiocese of North America, Funeral Service for Infants – Greek Orthodox Archdiocese of America – Greek Orthodox Archdiocese of America (goarch.org) (accessed July 30, 2024).
34 See, for example, FLOW no. 31, and Orthodox Church in America, "Guidelines for Clergy," 2023-OCA-Guidelines-for-Clergy.pdf (accessed October 2, 2024).

ORTHODOXY'S LITURGICAL HERITAGE

The best way to get to know the Orthodox Church is by participating in its liturgical life. The exterior features of Orthodox liturgy have long attracted admirers, converts, and seekers. Icons, candles, colorful vestments, incense, chants, and choreographed ritual movements create a picture of ancient worship. These exterior features are certainly meaningful, but they do not express the inner meaning of Orthodox liturgy on their own.

The offices of the Orthodox Church have been precious sources for exploring the history and theology of the church for scholars since the nineteenth century. Most scholars employ the method of comparative liturgy, a rigorous examination of texts that responds to questions of geographical location, date, authorship, influences, and dissemination and use.[1] Numerous scholars have blazed a trail for the current generation of theologians working on liturgical history. The current generation of scholars generally follows the methodology of comparative liturgy refined by the late Jesuit scholar of Byzantine liturgy, Robert Taft. Taft's multivolume history of the liturgy of St. John Chrysostom set the bar for historical scholarship on the liturgy of the Eastern churches.[2] Many of Taft's former students are enriching our understanding of Orthodox liturgy with their work on the history and theology of Orthodoxy's liturgy.[3]

Alexander Schmemann was probably the best-known Orthodox liturgical thinker.[4] Schmemann was trained in history and came to teach liturgy at St. Vladimir's Seminary in New York out of necessity. Schmemann was the father of a multi-generation period of liturgical renewal that came to define much of the Orthodox Church outside of the Soviet Union. Schmemann's fundamental

DOI: 10.4324/9781003433217-7

premise was somewhat simple: liturgy is the primary source for all of theology because it is the event where the people of God encounter God. Schmemann adopted a phrase attributed to Prosper of Aquitaine: lex orandi est lex credendi, the rule of prayer establishes the rule of faith.[5]

How can one learn and then say something about God? By participating in the liturgy, because God is present and reveals himself to the people when they gather for liturgy. This captures the spirit of Schmemann's prioritization of liturgy. Schmemann viewed the restoration of the people's full participation in the liturgy as the key to church renewal.[6] For centuries, liturgy had become something of an object, an ornate ritual admired from a distance. Baptisms were largely private events, with parents making arrangements for a fast service with a priest and one singer. Churches were empty on major feast days and Saturday evenings. People attended the Divine Liturgy on Sundays but often arrived quite late, with the presider preaching at the end of the service or not at all.

The most glaring mark of the people's detachment from the liturgy was their infrequent reception of Holy Communion.[7] The vast majority of the people received Communion once a year or on some other special occasion. People typically received Communion on one of the Sundays of Lent or on Pascha, soon after having made their annual confession.

Communion was so rare that small customs emerged around it to make sense of the service. I recall three distinct customs from my childhood parish where the people participated actively. The first entrance of the liturgy takes place with the clergy bringing the Gospel book from the altar into the front part of the nave, only to return to the altar where they place the book back on the table as the people sing the entrance hymn, "Come, let us worship" (Ps. 91). When a deacon celebrates with the priest, he holds the Gospel book out for the priest to kiss before intoning the entrance hymn and placing the book back on the holy table.

The other two customs took place around Holy Communion. First, it was customary for children to receive Communion at every Divine Liturgy, in a kind of reversal from the experience of contemporary Roman Catholics. Children received Communion at every liturgy until they began to participate in confession, usually around the age of eight or so. The children would form a line, joined by a parent or other adult monitoring them and any adults who happened to receive Communion. When the priest would show the chalice to the people after Communion before bringing it to the table of oblation in the sanctuary, he would first bring the chalice out to the people standing in the line to touch their heads with it.

Finally, it was customary for parishioners to congratulate people who had received Holy Communion with a hug or a handshake, noting that it was some special occasion. While these three examples represent the local practice of my childhood Ukrainian émigré parish and not necessarily all of Orthodoxy, they all point to one common thread: receiving Communion was rare and was therefore a special occasion warranting extra rituals.

Schmemann was the main Orthodox theologian who called for a restoration of the ideal of the Divine Liturgy: for the people to actually partake of Holy Communion.[8] Schmemann referred to the chief objective: the point of the liturgy is the transformation of the faithful into holy people and not a spectacle of witnessing the magical change of bread and wine into Christ's body and blood.

If Taft's scholarship has deeply enriched the church's knowledge of her own liturgical history, Schmemann's legacy has challenged pastors to celebrate the liturgy in such a way that people are engaged. Both legacies remain crucial for the Orthodox Church today. The rest of this chapter will explore the Orthodox liturgy as the people know and experience it.

ORTHODOX CHURCH ARCHITECTURE

The liturgical environment shapes the people's experience of liturgy. While every community has its own design features, there is something of a standard blueprint for every Orthodox Church. This pattern is sometimes known as the middle-Byzantine paradigm because its primary features were established around the ninth century, after the final victory of Orthodoxy over iconoclasm.[9]

The interior liturgical design of an Orthodox Church has three distinct spaces. The first is the *narthex*, which usually functions as a threshold space in between the main entrance and the primary liturgical space. The *nave* is the second space – it is the largest of the three, the main gathering space for the people, and the space where most of the liturgical rituals are performed. The *sanctuary* is the third space, containing the holy table (altar), the table of oblation, many of the liturgical vessels such as vestments, wine, and incense, and is the space where the bishops, presbyters, and deacons exercise their ministries, along with assistants.

The nave and sanctuary are not technically separated, though a large wall of icons called an iconostasis typically stands as a physical marker separating the two. A *solea* is a platform in front of the sanctuary where the deacon offers petitions and where some of the rituals are performed. Some Orthodox churches have an ambon, where the deacon or presbyter reads the Gospel. Orthodox people often conflate the ambon with the solea because church buildings with only a solea tend to arrange for readings to take place there. Spaces for singers vary widely. Many churches have spaces on one or both sides near the sanctuary for chanters or a choir. Some churches have the choir positioned in the back of the church or in a gallery on the second level

All Orthodox Church buildings have iconography. Some churches have more icons than others. The most ornate churches have icons covering every inch of space, often following a particular pattern. The most minimalist churches have a handful of icons. At a minimum, each church has at least two icons – one of the risen Christ, holding a Gospel book, and the other of the mother of God. Facing the sanctuary, the icon of the Mother of God is slightly to the left of the holy table, and the icon of Christ is slightly to the right. These two icons are fixtures in every iconostasis (Figure 6.1).

For churches with more expansive iconographic programs, there is typically an icon or fresco on the wall the assembly faces, usually known as the apse. An icon of the Mother of God is usually placed here. Many churches have installed icons of the mystical supper, where the risen Lord is distributing the bread and the cup to his disciples. Churches with the mystical supper icon on the wall of the apse are essentially communicating that receiving Holy Communion from Christ himself is the objective of the Divine Liturgy, since the apse is one of the main focal points. This fresco of the wedding at Cana of Galilee (Jn. 2) is another image of the Eucharist in the Orthodox iconographic tradition (Figure 6.2).

Another focal point of the church is the dome, which brings us to a brief consideration of the exterior. Orthodox churches typically have at least one dome, and sometimes many more, in a variety

Figure 6.1 Interior Orthodox Church Altar, Odessa, Ukraine.

Figure 6.2 Painting on the Wall of Hagia Sophia Church, Trabzon, Turkey.

of shapes and organizational patterns. A church with five domes is somewhat prototypical since the four smaller domes on the corners would represent the four evangelists. On the exterior, the dome provides a feature that invites people to come in, especially larger domes that are visible to the public from diverse vantage points.

Not all Orthodox communities are able to have domes for financial and legal reasons. A dome is a beloved but not essential feature of Orthodox architecture. It is possible to arrange the interior configuration so that the space the dome would normally occupy has an icon at the highest interior point. On the interior, it is traditional to place an icon of Christ the Pantocrator (creator of all things), though again, it is neither universal nor required.

Despite variances, when one walks into an Orthodox Church, they will enter a narthex area, then go into the nave where the laity gather. They will be facing the sanctuary and will see the iconostasis with a minimum of two icons. They will see the holy table with a cover, the Gospel book, and a number of other vessels, including a candelabra with seven candles. The presider – usually the parish presbyter, though sometimes the bishop – will stand at the front of the holy table during the services. If the parish has a deacon, he will stand at the presbyter's right and will intone the prayer from the center of the solea, so it looks like he is standing behind the presbyter.

One crucial feature of worship – everyone is facing the same direction, toward the east, or *ad orientem*. Some might suggest that the presider has his back to the people, but the actual spirit of the presider's posture is that the whole community faces the same direction. The purpose of facing east is one of direction and journey – everyone is looking toward their destiny, to be restored to life in paradise, with God, East of Eden.

There are no absolute requirements about the exterior design, despite the popularity of the dome. Most Orthodox churches have either a large Greek cross or the Slavic cross with three bars on the exterior, and some churches have icons that express Orthodox identity. Budget limitations and local municipal regulations contribute to the shaping of exterior design. Most Orthodox parishes have practical considerations in mind – parking, accessibility, and space for non-liturgical purposes, such as education and recreational activities. Many churches have bells, though contemporary sound systems permit parishes to use recordings instead of live bell-ringing.[10] Designating space for outdoor processions is desirable but not always possible, a consideration that depends again on budget and spatial parameters.

The interior space also must be conducive for liturgical music, since Orthodox liturgy is sung. Constantinople's Hagia Sophia used natural materials to generate sonorous sounds, so the experience would be like worshipping in heaven.[11] While contemporary churches do not have the resources of an imperial budget to maximize soundscapes, the interior must accommodate the requirements of both liturgical music and preaching.

LITURGICAL MUSIC

The most striking feature of Orthodox liturgy is the sheer volume of chanting and singing, in addition to icons. The vast majority of the Orthodox liturgy is chanted or sung in accordance with tradition, though instrumental accompaniment is not prohibited by rule. The core principle of liturgical music is that sound itself is theological. God acts and reveals himself in creation, and the voice of God appears in select passages of the Scriptures. Furthermore, in Orthodoxy, hymns have an exalted role. The liturgical tradition of the church features an impressive corpus of hymns that express and communicate the meaning of each day to the people. Some hymns are appointed for all the people to sing, and communal singing is a unifying act, where the people respond to petitions with one voice.

It is neither possible nor desirable to attempt to synthesize Orthodoxy's multifaceted tradition of regional chants.[12] The number of melodies that underpin chants is seemingly inexhaustible. Orthodoxy is somewhat unlike the Roman tradition and its Gregorian chant, which occasionally functions as a universal musical source. Regional chant traditions originated as local melodies composed and performed by trained soloists. Some of these melodies were written according to complex sign systems, and others remained unwritten and were passed down via oral tradition. Orthodox people tend to categorize their chants by calling them "Byzantine," "Carpathian," or "Znamenny," to name some of the most popular. But even these categories function as umbrellas, as there are dozens of melodies clustered within the larger "Znamenny" tradition, for example.

Some chant traditions were quite influential because of mission and evangelization and migration. Byzantine chants remain important in Iasi, Romania, because of monasteries that retained the original melodies and transposed them to new liturgical languages. Many of these chants have been adapted for English-language liturgies as migrant communities attempted to retain their legacies of liturgical music while worshiping in the local language.

Once again, the liturgical tradition of Hagia Sophia is archetypal for Orthodox chant, largely because of the prominence of the kontakion.[13] The kontakion, one of the hymns expressing the primary themes of the liturgical day or occasion, had as many as twenty-four stanzas. A trained soloist would chant the kontakion from the elevated ambon in Hagia Sophia. The performance of the kontakion, set to special music, functioned as a performed sermon. The musical element is essential, just as important as the eloquence of the text. This ideal from the legacy of Hagia Sophia sets the tone for all Orthodox liturgical music. The texts of the hymns are saturated with the theology of the fathers, but they do not stand alone. The chanting of the texts adds an essential element of expression. The music itself is multifunctional. It contributes to the clear communication of the text and is also composed to inspire the people, to invite them to sing along (when appointed), and most of all, to glorify God.

Most Orthodox churches of the world have retained some aspect of their medieval chant traditions, but liturgical music has also developed. Observers will note the preponderance of polyphonic choral music in Orthodoxy, with choirs assuming roles equal to, and in some cases surpassing, those of chanters.

Chanting and singing are assigned to everyone in the community. The bishops and presbyters typically chant the prayers assigned to them, even when they give the sign of peace to the people. The deacons chant the petitions, with the people also responding musically, a combination of "Lord, have mercy," "grant this, Lord," "to you, Lord," and Amen. Deacons and chanters lead responsorial psalmody, with either the choir or the choir and people singing the common refrains. "Alleluia" is the best example of a common refrain, sung at many liturgical offices and functioning as the appointed psalm refrain for the Gospel readings on all Sundays.[14] There are dozens of chant melodies set to "Alleluia." While the choir sings Alleluia, it is customary for the people to sing with the choir.

Much of Orthodoxy's adoption of polyphonic music depended on musical styles originating in Western European artistic centers like Italy.[15] Orthodox communities in Ukraine, Belarus, Russia, Serbia, and Bulgaria (among others) embraced Western polyphony wholesale, and their native chant traditions faded into obscurity deep into the nineteenth century. Composers like Maxim Berezovsky

(1745–1777) and Dmytro Bortniansky (1751–1825) were native Ukrainians who were sent to St. Petersburg and learned baroque music from Italian masters that influenced the composition of settings for the liturgy and, therefore, the audial experience for the faithful.[16] An interest in recovering indigenous musical traditions led to a creative compromise in nineteenth and early twentieth-century Russian music cultivated by the Moscow Synodal Choir. The Moscow Synodal Choir recovered native chants and arranged the melodies for choir. The spirit of the music, however, was not merely performative but was also designed to restore communal singing. New polyphonic compositions for choirs featured chant melodies with the choir essentially leading the people. The choir assumed a leadership role in this paradigm, performing the music so that everyone could sing it.

There is no single, universal rule for the performance of liturgical music in Orthodoxy. In general, the following principles apply in terms of the appointment of roles. Deacons chant all litanies and some of the responsorial psalmody, like the little litany and the prokeimenon. Chanters or a choir sing the responses to litanies, often (and ideally) accompanied by the people. Bishops and presbyters chant or intone the prayers. Usually, most of the prayers are recited quietly, with only the final exclamation chanted out loud for the people to hear.[17]

Responsorial psalmody is a central feature of Orthodox liturgy. Psalms with refrains are chanted at all services, even when there is no lesson appointed from the Bible. The three most common psalm refrains appointed to Orthodox liturgy are the Prokeimenon, the Alleluia, and God is the Lord (Ps. 117).

Some parishes have abbreviated and simplified this section of the liturgy. The prokeimenon might be intoned by a single cantor, with no refrain sung by a choir or people. Many parishes omit the psalm verses on the Alleluia. Some parishes have the presbyter read the Gospel from the solea, facing the people, even if a deacon concelebrates. These variations represent the diversity of practices in Orthodoxy.

To summarize, the fact that the Orthodox chant or sing almost everything in the liturgy reveals both the significance of music and the value the Orthodox have invested in their liturgy. Musical sounds are theological on their own, even without accompanying words. Music has an important role in shaping the meaning of the texts. While Orthodoxy embraced the development and influence of polyphonic music on their liturgy, they never annulled their chant traditions and sought to restore them in the nineteenth and twentieth centuries.

THE WEEKLY CYCLE

The Orthodox liturgy has a complicated relationship with time. A glance at the schedule of liturgies grants the appearance of an obsession with time. Some parishes have services on several days of the week. The Orthodox calendar is populated by numerous feasts, and seasons of fasting and feasting shape the people's practices and habits. Numbers also seem important. Many feasts have "afterfeast" periods during which the church sings the festal hymns and retains the liturgical colors. Fasting periods also follow time, with forty days of Lenten fasting for both Lent and the Christmas fast.

Alexander Schmemann described liturgy as an ascension into heaven.[18] He attempted to redefine the famous mystagogies of liturgy by medieval figures such as Germanus of Constantinople. Germanus, patriarch of Constantinople in the eighth century, had written a treatise on the liturgy that described each part of the liturgy in vivid visual detail relating to events in the life of Christ. Schmemann was not particularly fond of these descriptions because he thought they detracted from the inner meaning of the liturgy.[19] For Schmemann, the liturgy is a true participation in the life to come, where the church as a community ascends to heaven in the course of the liturgy and literally speaks to God, standing before his holy throne. Schmemann was essentially saying that the liturgy is an experience that takes its participants out of the present and into the future, keeping in mind that God, who has no limits and cannot be contained or confined, is both outside of and the creator of time. In this sense, then, Orthodox liturgy is a participation in the future life promised to all, or, as some liturgical theologians like to say, is a foretaste of eternal life. Orthodox liturgy, then, is something of a paradox, as it circulates around time and yet is timeless at the same time. Sunday is the heart of Orthodox liturgy, the organ that gives life and pumps blood to animate the body of the church. Sunday is the primary focus of the weekly rhythm, both its beginning and its end.

Orthodoxy has developed a weekly system that circulates around each Sunday. Each day of the week has specific themes expressed by the appointed hymns contained in a book called the *octoechos*.[20] This book provides the complete texts for the hymns of each week based on the number eight. In other words, there are eight sets of weekly services that rotate, going from one to eight and then starting at one again. Each number corresponds to a mode for the week. The modes, or tones, are melodies that govern the hymns for each week and vary in accordance with regional singing traditions. In one of the older Byzantine systems, tones 5 through 8 were variations of tones 1 through 4, in order. So, for example, tone 5 was the "plagal" or "grave" of tone 1, and tone 6 for tone 2.

In the Eastern Slavic tradition, Aleksei Lvov simplified the eight Kyivan tones to try to make them easier for smaller parish choirs to sing.[21] These simplified Kyivan tones are known as either "Bakhmetev" or, more often, "obikhod," which simply means customary. The bottom line is that each week will cycle through the eight tones and continue to rotate through them on almost all Sundays. A new tone begins on Sunday and is used throughout that week.

SUNDAY: THE HEART OF ORTHODOX LITURGY

Sunday is the heart of Orthodox liturgy because it is the original feast day of the Church. Sunday has always been important in Orthodoxy because it is the day of Christ's resurrection, sometimes known as the Lord's Day. Many pastors and theologians refer to Sunday as a "little" Easter, but it is actually the original Easter, in a certain sense.

The stories of Jesus' resurrection from the dead establish the centrality of Sunday. Jesus, risen from the dead, appears to his disciples at the end of each of the four gospels. He invites Thomas to touch his side and his hands, and most importantly, Jesus eats with them (Lk 24). The New Testament created a blueprint for the core meaning of Sunday morning. The disciples gather in a space with the risen Jesus, who is always with them.

This principle of Sunday as a day of resurrection, proclaiming God's word, and breaking bread with the Risen Lord is not exclusive to Orthodoxy. Mainstream Protestants and the Roman Catholic Church share the same core principle of Sunday as the heart of the church week.[22] For the most observant Orthodox Christians, Sunday is the most common occasion of gathering as a community.

Perhaps the most poignant description of Sunday comes from the nun Egeria, who made a pilgrimage to Jerusalem in the fourth century. Egeria describes the gathering of the community on the "Lord's Day," highlighting the large crowd, the splendor of the liturgical environment, the preaching and singing of psalms, and especially the emotional proclamation of the resurrection gospel, read by the bishop himself.[23]

RESURRECTION VIGIL (SATURDAY NIGHT/ SUNDAY MORNING)

The Sunday cycle begins on Saturday evening, following the Jewish notion of the liturgical day, with evening ending one day and beginning the next one. Orthodoxy observes the beginning of Sunday with a celebration of a Vigil service. This Vigil consists of a festive Vespers (known as Great Vespers) followed by Matins.

The order for services on Saturday evening varies somewhat in Orthodoxy. The ideal pattern of the Typikon, the liturgical book that governs the liturgical cycle, is to observe Great Vespers and Matins as one seamless celebration. Monasteries, many cathedrals, and some parishes follow this pattern. Communities that celebrate Vigil on Saturday evening observe Matins, a morning service, the night before Liturgy. Some pastors and theologians find this observance to be jarring, so they celebrate Vespers the night before and Matins on Sunday morning, before Liturgy. Other communities celebrate Vespers the previous evening and omit Matins. This pattern is common among parishes with Slavic lineage in North America. Many communities of Greek and Antiochian lineage start with Matins on Sunday morning and do not have Vespers the previous evening. In general, Orthodox people tend to ignore Vigil, regardless of their parish's schedule. Attendance is strongest for the Divine Liturgy.

The highlights of these services are the hymns that proclaim Christ's resurrection and the Gospel reading appointed to Matins. Psalm 140, "Lord, I have cried," is a feature of Vespers on ordinary weekdays and Saturday evening. The hymns sung on Psalm 140 on Saturday evenings, called *stichera*, tell the story of Christ's resurrection. The stichera are multifunctional, with historical, typological, and moral functions, often ending with an exhortation to act. The Theotokion-dogmatikon is one of the most important of these stichera.[24]

The clergy process from the sanctuary into the nave as the choir sings the Theotokion-Dogmatikon for the evening entrance. The deacon holds the censer high as the presider says the appointed prayer. This is one of the focal points of Vespers, as the offering of incense occurs first during Psalm 140 and again here. The choir sings a hymn, Gladsome Light, as the clergy and servers return to the sanctuary. This hymn originated in Jerusalem during a lamp-lighting ceremony. It is old, though scholars do not know the exact point of origin. St. Basil of Caesarea said that it was "ancient" in the fourth century.[25] Vespers continues with a Prokeimenon (responsorial psalmody), prayers and litanies, more hymns (Aposticha), and then the Canticle of Simeon (Lk. 2, "Lord, now let your servant depart in peace").

The focal point of Matins is the Gospel reading, but it occurs later in the service. Matins begins with much singing, including more hymns of the resurrection known as the evlogitaria, fixed verses that are the same from one week to the next. After the initial set of prayers and hymns, there is a prokeimenon for Matins followed by the Gospel. Orthodox consider the Matins Gospels to be very important because each reading is an account of Jesus' resurrection from the dead. There are eleven Matins Gospels that rotate from one week to the next, known as *eothina* Gospels.[26] The presider intones the Matins Gospel from the middle of the church, with the deacon holding the Gospel book.

After the Gospel, Psalm 51 is chanted, and the choir sings another set of hymns known as the Canon. The Canon has eight hymns numbered one through nine, because the second song is omitted. The canon originated with the singing of three biblical canticles and expanded to nine. The second song of the canon (called an "ode") remains in place on some weekdays of Lent, but participants will not hear it at a Saturday Vigil. Vigil still includes the ninth song, the Magnificat of Mary (Lk. 2), sung in its entirety. The deacon censes the entire church during this ninth canticle. He stops at the icon of the Virgin Mary on the iconostasis, holds up the censer, and intones, "the Theotokos and Mother of light, let us magnify in song!" He then censes the icon of Mary nine times and then censes throughout the rest of the church.

Matins begins to move toward the conclusion with the chanting of Psalms 148, 149, and 150, a handful of stichera sung "on the praises" (selected verses from these psalms), and then the Great Doxology, known as the Gloria to Christians of the Western tradition. The Great Doxology is another poignant moment, especially in the Greek Orthodox churches. The placement of the Doxology at the end of Matins means that some people are starting to arrive for the Divine Liturgy. Matins ends with litanies and prayers and a dismissal.

The ideal way to view the Vigil is that it begins the celebration of Sunday as the day of gathering in honor of Christy's resurrection. Egeria, the nun who made a pilgrimage to Jerusalem in the fourth century, reported that the Vigil of the resurrection was a central feature of Christian urban worship, filled with ritual, singing, and the reading of the Gospel account of the resurrection.[27] Today, the hymns, entrances, canticles, and especially the Gospel readings of Vigil proclaim the news that Jesus Christ is risen from the dead. These services begin a celebration that essentially continues with the Divine Liturgy.

THE DIVINE LITURGY: OVERVIEW

The Divine Liturgy on Sunday is the service most Orthodox faithful experience. It is not limited to Sunday. The Divine Liturgy can be celebrated on any day of the liturgical year except for the season of Great Lent, with one exception – for the feast of the Annunciation. Most people's experience of church will be at a Sunday Divine Liturgy.

The Orthodox Church uses three versions of the Divine Liturgy: St. John Chrysostom, St. Basil the Great, and St. James of Jerusalem.[28] The Chrysostom and Basil liturgies are identical in structure, with different prayers, whereas James' liturgy has its own unique structure. It is likely that John Chrysostom originally introduced the liturgy he knew as a presbyter in Antioch to Constantinople when he became archbishop of the imperial capital. The Byzantine church was using the liturgy ascribed to St. Basil until the tenth century.[29] The Church began to favor the Chrysostom liturgy at that point, but it never eliminated the liturgy of Basil. The Church continued to use the liturgy of Basil for special occasions, including liturgies on Christmas and Theophany, the Sundays of Great Lent, the Paschal

Vigil, and St. Basil's feast day (January 1). The use of St. Basil's liturgy on the Sundays of Lent has led some to believe that this liturgy is more suitable for the penitential season of Lent, but this is not the case. Popular liturgical traditions tend to be resilient during periods of change, and the liturgy of St. Basil remains the appointed one on the most special occasions of the Church year. Orthodox Christians rarely use the liturgy of St. James.

Certain elements of the liturgy one might take for granted have changed considerably in history. These include the preparatory rites, the original entrance (or introit), and the position of the Great Litany. The antiphons originated from the time of stational liturgy, when psalms with refrains were sung during a procession on the way to the appointed church for the Sunday liturgy. These antiphons became permanent fixtures of the liturgy when processions to the church began to fade from practice.[30] The Byzantine church did not sustain the practice of stational liturgy, where a procession would start in one appointed place, singing antiphons on the way, and end in the stational church – the one appointed for the liturgy of the day.[31] The diminishment of stational liturgy resulted in the new positioning of the antiphons. The Church retained them by affixing them to a position before the introit (entrance), the traditional beginning of the liturgy.

The Orthodox Liturgy contains elements from particular regions that are associated with historical events. Antioch, Jerusalem, Palestine, Constantinople, and Mount Athos are among the most important regions that influenced Orthodox liturgy.[32] The Divine Liturgy of St. John Chrysostom has Antiochene roots, especially since Chrysostom brought the liturgy he knew from Antioch to Constantinople. The liturgy of Jerusalem also influenced Orthodox liturgy, since pilgrims to Jerusalem witnessed the liturgy there, reported it, and brought traditions cultivated there to Constantinople. A tradition of composing new hymns began to blossom at the monastery of St. Sabas in Palestine in the seventh century, following the Persian invasions. The monastery revised its liturgy to make it sustainable, and an unofficial school of hymnographers (liturgical songwriters) began to blossom there. Theodore the Studite, abbot of the Studion monastery in Constantinople, was inspired by the hymnography in Jerusalem as he sought to revive liturgical life after the defeat of iconoclasm. Theodore adopted many of the hymns composed at St.

Sabas and developed his own school of hymnography in Constantinople. This is just one of the many ways in which Palestinian liturgy influenced Constantinople.

It is crucial to note that parishes did not worship according to the same rite and rule as monasteries. This does not mean that there was no intersection of liturgical traditions – there was – but monasteries wrote their own rules for their liturgical life without requiring the permission or blessing of a bishop or patriarch. The monastic style of liturgy became fused, in part, with the cathedral style as early as the ninth century, when monasteries provided the leadership for the victory of Orthodoxy over iconoclasm. Monastic influence on the liturgy increased in the thirteenth century with the fall of Constantinople to the crusaders. Liturgical life was not exactly the same as it had been when the capital became Orthodox again in 1261. Many monastic liturgical traditions became permanent, and the cathedral style of Constantinopolitan liturgy migrated to places like Thessalonika as the Byzantine Empire weakened under the shadow of the Ottomans.

The monks remained the most important stewards of liturgy, as they had in St. Sabas and the Studion monasteries. Mount Athos had a strong liturgical revival during the hesychastic movement in the fourteenth century, and the current form and order of the liturgy were mostly finalized in the Diataxis of Patriarch Philotheos.[33] Liturgy experienced change after the fourteenth century, but we will now turn to an explanation of the structure of the Divine Liturgy to maximize our comprehension of its meaning.

MINISTERS OF THE LITURGY

Orthodox liturgy has an order and something of a hierarchy. The entire community prays the Divine Liturgy, ordained ministers exercise assigned roles, and non-ordained laypeople also perform essential functions. The Divine Liturgy begins with God. God is the initiator of the liturgy, the one who calls and invites the people to come together in a place for worship. The notion of God taking action and reaching out to humanity underpins Orthodox liturgical theology. Robert Taft uses Michelangelo's painting of the creation of humanity in the Sistine Chapel, with God extending God's hand to give life to Adam, as a visual symbol of liturgy.[34] Taft says that liturgy occupies the tiny space separating God's outstretched hand from Adam's. The community gathers in that space to receive the touch of God.

The community of people is the next level of order. Orthodox Christians are baptized and anointed and considered members of the laity, or laics, as Nicholas Afanasiev was fond of saying.[35] Baptism and Chrismation essentially ordain people into the order of the laity, and the people act together at the Liturgy. Someone has to lead and preside at the liturgy, and this ministry belongs to the bishop. The bishop is the ordinary minister of all liturgies, but in practice, bishops usually serve in their urban cathedral churches, so Orthodoxy permits presbyters, also known as priests, to preside at liturgies. The bishop or presbyter will perform most of the core gestures and actions, such as the giving of peace, the recitation of prayers, and preaching. Deacons bear the responsibility of leading the community in prayer by intoning litanies and proclaiming the good news in the readings from the Scriptures. Bishops, presbyters, and deacons share the responsibility of distributing Holy Communion to the laity. Orthodoxy does not have an equivalent of an extraordinary minister of Holy Communion, so laypeople typically do not assist in giving people Communion. Laypeople can and usually do assist with performing appointed psalm and Scriptural readings and also lead and sing the music for the liturgy.

LITURGY OF THE WORD

One of the most convenient ways to explain the Divine Liturgy is through structure. The Divine Liturgy has two main sections: word and sacrament. This categorization does not mean that the Liturgy of the Word is not sacramental – it is. In fact, it is more accurate to describe the Divine Liturgy as one single movement – a sacrament consisting of actions that bring the community into the same place as God, to hear God speak, and to share food with God.

The Liturgy of the Word begins with the preparatory rites.[36] When the clergy arrive at church, they say special prayers before entering the sanctuary and while vesting. The presider or the lowest ranking of the presbyters will begin to perform the ritual of preparing the bread and the cup for the liturgy, known as the prothesis. People do not customarily see this ritual, as it is completed before the Divine Liturgy begins and occurs within the sanctuary, inaudibly and out of sight. The prothesis originated as a practical ritual. People would donate loaves of bread and bottles of wine to the church for the Liturgy. The deacons would supervise the collection of these items and would choose the best among them. Deacons once handled all of the details of this ritual. The Coptic church has its own distinct ritual of presenting several loaves of bread and having the presider select one of them for the Liturgy.[37] Holy Communion requires fresh bread, wine, and water, so the preparatory rite is a matter of preparing this food and drink for the service (Figure 6.3).

The Prothesis has a deeper meaning connected with the sacrifice of Christ. In its current form, the baker uses a special seal to imprint the letters IC XC NI KA around a cross on one of the loaves, with four more loaves also used without the seal. The presider carefully cuts most, but not all, of the bread in the square around the cross and letters and places it in the center of the discos, or large plate. He then takes several small triangles of bread from the same loaf and places them in order on the plate. The square portion is known as the lamb, representing Christ, the lamb of God offered for the life of the world. Most Orthodox use only the lamb for communion.

Figure 6.3 Liturgy of the preparation.

Much of the time devoted to completing this ritual involves a crucial component – adding small pieces from the other loaves for particular people. For example, the presider has his own list of people he prays for – family, friends, and colleagues, both living and dead. He will add a small piece from the loaves to the discos. Parishioners also provide names of the living and the dead to be remembered on the discos, so the presbyter will take small pieces from the loaves for all of these. Such lists can become long in larger communities! Essentially, the living and dead become part of the community's offering to God at the Liturgy, a most beautiful expression of love.

The presbyter prepares the cup by pouring sweet red wine and cool water into it. He places covers that usually match his vestments over the discos and the cup, and then a larger covering called an aer over both of them. He holds each cover over the censer and says a short prayer at each covering. The origins of this practice were practical, to keep insects from the bread and cup. The preparatory rite concludes with a final incensation of the covered bread and cup.

The preparatory rites were originally functional. Communities needed bread, wine, water, and vessels to celebrate the Eucharist. Preparing the diskos, chalice, bread, wine, and water is truly similar to hosting a meal with wine and an appetizer. The Orthodox Church gradually began to assign a theological meaning to this rite. Pouring wine and water into the chalice evoked the memory of the soldier piercing Jesus with his spear, with blood and water coming out (Jn. 19:34). Making incisions into the lamb evoked similar images, not only of Jesus' death but also of his birth.

The fundamental theological meaning of the preparatory rite is twofold. First, it anticipates the Church's offering made in memory of Jesus' death and resurrection. Offering bread and wine is a gift of thanksgiving from the Church to God – thanksgiving for Jesus Christ's salvation of humankind. The second meaning is associated with the remembrance of people who are named and set aside on the diskos, included in the offering. The Orthodox Church prays for the life and salvation of the world, beginning with its own – the bishops, presbyters, and deacons – then continuing with the civil authorities, and finally, the beloved of the community, both living and dead. The prothesis offers the Church of heaven and earth – one church encompassing both places – to God.

The presbyter gives the censer to the deacon after they complete the rite of preparation, and the deacon incenses the holy table, the sanctuary, the iconostasis, the people, and the entire interior of the church. He finishes the censing, returns to the sanctuary, opens the royal doors, and begins the opening dialogue of the Divine Liturgy with the priest.

This section of the Liturgy, its beginning, looks much different to Western Christians than their customary liturgical beginning. The presbyter and deacon bow three times while making the sign of the cross, then the presbyter raises both arms in the praying posture (orans) while the deacon holds his orarion high with his right hand. The presbyter prays the "Heavenly King" prayer most of the time – the Paschal Troparion, "Christ is risen from the dead," replaces this from Pascha to Pentecost. Then the presbyter says, "Glory to God in the highest and on earth peace, goodwill among men," twice, and "O Lord, open my lips and my mouth will declare your praise," once. The deacon asks the presbyter to remember him, receives his blessing, and exits the sanctuary, walking to the solea, saying "Lord, open my lips" three times. The liturgy begins when the deacon intones "Bless, master," and the presbyter raises the Gospel book high with "*Blessed* is the kingdom," making the sign of the cross once.

The deacon intones the Great Litany, followed by the first, second, and third antiphons. The deacon prays two "little" litanies, after the first and second antiphons, and returns to the sanctuary before the third antiphon. The presbyter, deacon, and servers bow three times, with the clergy kissing the holy table, the presbyter giving the gospel book to the deacon, and all processing out the "north" door (to the left, facing the iconostasis). The presbyter "blesses" the entrance, the deacon holds the gospel book high and intones, "Wisdom! Let us stand upright!" The choir sings "Come, let us worship," while the clergy and servers return to the sanctuary.

The choir sings a selection of appointed hymns, Troparia, and Kontakia. The presbyter blesses the deacon to go to the solea through the royal doors. The presbyter intones, "For you are holy, O our God, and to you we send up glory, to the Father, to the Son, and to the Holy Spirit, now and ever," and the deacon turns to the people, holding his orarion high, intoning "and unto ages of ages," reentering the sanctuary through the royal doors. The choir sings the Trisagion hymn, "Holy God, Holy Mighty, Holy Immortal, have mercy on us," while the presbyter and deacon go up to the "high place," usually a chair at the apse. The deacon intones, "let us be attentive," the presbyter gives the peace, and the first responsorial psalm, known as the Prokeimenon, begins, followed by the first reading from an epistle or Acts, a second responsorial psalm, and the appointed Gospel reading.

There is a great deal of variation in the details of what happens ritually during the Liturgy of the Word. For example, the deacon turns to the people and intones "dynamis!" before the final singing of the Trisagion, a command to sing it with greater power. The deacon reads the Gospel in most churches, but the presbyter reads in some, and the place for the Gospel reading differs significantly among Orthodox.

Observers will notice a difference in the selection of the antiphon, depending on the church they attend. All Orthodox churches sing the "Only begotten Son of God" Troparion after the second antiphon. The emperor Justinian composed this hymn in the sixth century.[38] The hymn expresses Orthodox Christology and Trinitarian theology and is analyzed in Chapter 3. It functions like a mini-Creed in the liturgy.

The third antiphon follows another little litany. A cantor intones a psalm verse followed by the primary Troparion (hymn) of the day in the Greek and Antiochian tradition. The Beatitudes (Mt. 5) are sung in the Slavic tradition, though an appointed psalm verse alternating with the Troparion is often used on major feast days. The Trisagion hymn was the primary entrance verse at one point in Orthodox liturgical history.[39] It is quite popular, as it is appointed to daily prayers, the rite of burial, at the end of the Great Doxology (Gloria), and for processions at various points of the liturgical year. The Trisagion is both Trinitarian and Christological, defining God, Father, Son, and Holy Spirit, as "Holy God, Holy Mighty, Holy Immortal," ending with the petition, "have mercy on us." The Oriental churches added a clause, "who was crucified for us," highlighting the Christological dimension of the hymn.[40]

The presbyter and deacon kiss the holy table and go to the high place for the two readings. The Orthodox Church uses an annual lectionary system, with the same readings appointed for each year, unlike the Catholic and Protestant three-year cycles. The readings draw from all four Gospels, along with many of the epistles of St. Paul and the Acts of the Apostles. The lectionary does not appoint any Old Testament readings to Sunday liturgy, although there is evidence suggesting that the church read from the Old Testament at one point in history, up until about the eighth century.[41]

The Orthodox Church's system of readings is mostly a selection so that the readings fit the theme of the day, in a system known as *lectio selecta*. There are certain seasons of the Church year that follow a continuous pattern of reading, known as *lectio continua*. The readings for the weekday services of Lent read continuously through Genesis, Proverbs, and Isaiah. The Church year begins with the Indiction feast on September 1, and the lectionary "jumps" to the Gospel of Luke shortly afterwards. The people will hear two readings on any given Sunday – one from an epistle or the Acts of the Apostles and another from one of the Gospels. Most presbyters will deliver a sermon following the Gospel reading, though some pastors prefer to preach at another point in the Divine Liturgy.

The ritual units and patterns of the Liturgy of the Word reveal its meaning. In its current form, the church assembles and begins with prayers and antiphons. The little entrance is the first main ritual action, followed by hymns that express the theme for the day, usually one of resurrection. The Trisagion hymn, responsorial psalmody, and appointed readings are the main courses.

Once assembled, the people present initial prayers to God, reflect on the themes of the day, and then hear the word of God. Hearing the proclamation of the word of God in the readings and the homily are the main features. When the presbyter offers peace ("Peace be unto all") before the prokeimenon, or first responsorial psalm, Christ is in the midst of the people and speaking to them through the readings. The most important aspect of assembly is that all are gathered together in the same space and place. There is no division of heaven and earth during the Liturgy of the Word. The people are with God – Father, Son, and Holy Spirit.

LITURGY OF COMMUNION

The Liturgy of Communion continues after the homily. Many more prayers are offered in litanies for the bishops, civil authorities, the dead, and the living. Another litany addresses catechumens, people who are not baptized but are present at the liturgy. The deacon instructs the catechumens to pray, and then he instructs the faithful to pray for them, that they would hear God's word and be received in the church in due course. The deacon dismisses the catechumens. Technically, any catechumens in church are supposed to leave at this point, though they typically remain for the rest of the liturgy. More prayers of the faithful occur before the next main feature, the Cherubikon (hymn) and the Great Entrance.

The Great Entrance has been a focal point in Orthodox imagination through the centuries. It has become such a prominent part of the Liturgy that Robert Taft wrote an encyclopedic study of its history. This portion of the liturgy concerns the next stage of the church's offering of a gift to God. The gifts offered are bread, wine, and water prepared during the prothesis before the Divine Liturgy begins.

The Great Entrance begins with the deacon performing a censing of the sanctuary, iconostasis, and the people, while he recites Psalm 50 quietly.[42] The presbyter recites the "nemo dignus" prayer, beginning with the words "no one who is worthy," a prayer asking for forgiveness of his own sins as he prepares the sequence of events that offer the church's gift to God. He recites the text of the Cherubikon with the deacon after the deacon completes the censing while the choir sings the hymn, often to sophisticated compositions. The presbyter and deacon go to the side table, where the presbyter wraps the large covering (aer) around the deacon's neck and hands him the discos with the bread, while the presbyter takes the chalice. The clergy and servers bring the bread and chalice in a solemn procession around the church, stopping at the solea to ask God to remember the bishops, civil authorities, and all Christians in his kingdom. They set the discos and chalice on the table, remove the coverings, cense them, and proceed to the next part of the Liturgy of Communion.

The Great Entrance has a rich and textured history with multiple meanings. It became famous in the liturgy of Hagia Sophia in Constantinople when the bread and chalice were brought into the main church from the smaller external structure called the skeuophylakion. The patriarch awaited the procession with these gifts, performed by the deacons, near the holy table. The grandiosity of the music accompanied by the pomp of the ritual revealed deep meaning. Something important was happening – the Church was offering its gift of bread and wine to God and was praying for its leaders, both church and state, at the same time.

The ritual portion of the offertory ends when the presbyter recites the texts of hymns recalling Jesus' burial. The Great Entrance came to signify Jesus' death and burial in the imagination of some theologians, who sought to inscribe meaning on the ritual during the long period of time when people were not receiving Holy Communion.[43] The grandiosity of the ritual was a way for the people to reflect on Jesus' gift to them – his death offered for the life of the world.

This section of the liturgy really has two core meanings that supersede a historic reflection on Jesus' death and burial. The first is the one of gift. The people of God gather to offer God the gift of food and drink, bread and wine made from God's good soil and their labor. Jesus himself is the one who offers this gift, keeping in mind that the Church is still gathered with him. The end of the presbyter's prayer is mindful of Jesus' presence: "For you are the offerer and the offered," the one who presents himself and the church as a community to God. The Great Entrance is the main act of the Church's gesture of gift-giving to God.

The second meaning is functional. The Liturgy of Communion requires eating and drinking. It is a meal shared with God. The clergy prepared the plates, cups, and spoons for the meal beforehand. They are now setting the table. A festive meal involves fancy dishes and some degree of pomp and circumstance in the presentation. The Great Entrance also marks an important transition. The presbyter asks the clergy to pray for him at this time because he is leading the community's main event – the thanksgiving they offer in prayer to God and in anticipation of receiving God's gift.

The deacon goes to the solea to offer a litany of supplication when the presbyter offers the peace to the people. Technically, the people are supposed to exchange the kiss of peace at this point, before they offer their central prayer to God. In practice, clergy exchange the kiss of peace. The deacon kisses the cross on his orarion to symbolize the exchange of the kiss of peace with all the other deacons in the order of the diaconate.

Everyone recites or sings the Nicene-Constantinopolitan Creed at this point, making the common confession of faith before completing the offering of the gift. The Orthodox liturgy proceeds into recitation of the Eucharistic Prayer, or anaphora, at this point. The Byzantine version of the anaphora of St. Basil is quite long, and the one of St. John Chrysostom is considerably shorter.

A brief word on the history of the anaphora is necessary here. First, there is no doubt that the anaphora has always been considered as the community's primary prayer offered to God in the liturgy. It is also clear that these versions of the anaphora address God the Father. They begin by praising God with some detail, in formal language, expressing the Church's understanding of God as loving, almighty, and beyond comprehension.

Both the Basil and Chrysostom prayers refer to the presence of angels and archangels to show that the Church is standing with the invisible powers in offering this service to God and singing the hymn sung at the liturgy of heaven – "holy, holy, holy, Lord God of Sabaoth" (Is. 6). In the next section of the anaphora, the prayers remember God's saving acts, sometimes in great detail (Basil) and briefly at other times (Chrysostom). Scholars refer to this section as anamnesis – the church giving thanks for everything God did for them, from liberation from Egypt over the Red Sea to sending Jesus to save the world. This anamnesis leads seamlessly into a more precise remembrance of Jesus' last supper with his disciples when he took the bread and cup, blessed them, gave thanks, and gave them to the disciples to eat his flesh and drink his blood for the forgiveness of their sins. The presbyter and deacon point to the bread on the discos and then the cup filled with water and wine at this point.

The presbyter then thanks God for Christ's death, burial, resurrection, ascension, and second coming. Then, the deacon takes the discos in his right hand and the cup in his left (in a criss-cross fashion) and lifts them high while the presbyter prays, on behalf of the people, "Offering you your own of your own, on behalf of all, and for all."[44] The choir finishes the hymn while the presbyter asks God to send his Holy Spirit upon the church and the gifts (bread and cup) to change them into Christ's body and blood so that those who partake of them in Holy Communion would be in fellowship with God and one another. The presbyter then censes the holy table and prays for the dead and living and commends all of humankind to God while the choir sings a song of praise to Mary, the Mother of God, and the deacon prays for the dead and living by name.

The text of this section in the Basil anaphora is particularly beautiful, even asking God to remember those whom the church has either forgotten or doesn't know.[45] The deacon goes out to the solea for another litany before the community prays "Our Father" and Holy Communion begins.

THE ANAPHORA (EUCHARISTIC PRAYER)

A short commentary on Orthodoxy's interpretation of the anaphora is in order. Orthodoxy believes that the bread and wine become truly and wholly Christ's body and blood. This is possible by the almighty power of God, the promise of Christ, and the descent of the all-holy Spirit upon the gifts. Much ink was spilled in the late Middle Ages concerning Orthodoxy's dispute with the Catholic Church on how this happens, with Catholics emphasizing the power of Jesus' words and Orthodox insisting upon the invocation (epiclesis) of God to send the Spirit. Catholics and Orthodox don't really dispute this matter any longer, with both churches insisting that the entire anaphora – all of its parts – functions as a single unified act of the Church thanking God for all of his divine acts, and God responding by giving the church the gift of Christ in the bread and cup. Orthodoxy does not use the Catholic doctrine of transubstantiation to explain how this happens. The main point is that God acts by sending the Holy Spirit, who then makes Jesus Christ truly present.

Sometimes, the clergy make a big deal out of this moment during the Divine Liturgy, and this seems to magnify the epiclesis – God sending down the Holy Spirit – as a special moment of consecration. Many clergy and people believe that it is the ultimate moment, but this misrepresents the inner meaning of the anaphora. The point of the Divine Liturgy is for the people to continue to grow into becoming like Christ by receiving him through his self-offering of food and drink. The miracle is one of people becoming holy through their intimate encounter with God, and not of God performing a magic trick by changing bread and wine into human flesh and blood.

After "Our Father," the presbyter lifts up the lamb (consecrated bread) and intones, "the holy gifts are for the holy," which is the original invitation for the people to come forth and receive Holy Communion.[46] He breaks the lamb set aside for communion into pieces (fracture) and puts the portion for the people into the chalice (commixture). Then the deacon pours hot – almost boiling – water into the chalice (Zeon). The hot water has come to represent Jesus' resurrection, but it originates from a Mediterranean tradition of adding hot water to cups of wine.[47] The presbyter calls the deacon to the altar and gives him a small portion of the lamb for Communion, and the two eat the bread. The presbyter drinks from the chalice and then gives the deacon communion of the blood of Christ before he places the rest of the lamb into the chalice.

At this point, the deacon receives the chalice from the presbyter, goes to the solea, and invites the people to Communion by intoning, "in the fear of God, with faith [and love], draw near." The presbyter (and deacon, if necessary) gives everyone Communion with a spoon, taking a very small piece of the bread from the chalice, usually with a little wine on the spoon. When the people have finished receiving Communion, the presbyter brings the chalice to the holy table, and the deacon places the rest of the small pieces on the discos into the chalice, wipes the discos clean, folds the coverings and places them on the discos, uses one of the covers for the chalice, and recites the hymns of resurrection. The presbyter censes the chalice, gives the discos to the deacon, blesses the people with the chalice, and brings it to the side table, where the deacon will consume everything remaining in the chalice after the Liturgy.

A few words of explanation are in order here. First, all of the people used to receive Communion in both kinds, separately, one after another, until the eleventh century in Orthodoxy.[48] The deacons would give them communion from the chalice in a similar fashion to the way the clergy receive it now. The spoon was initially introduced as early as the seventh century and became the customary practice by the eleventh century as a way to minimize spilling and also because there were fewer deacons on hand to manage large chalices.

Receiving communion from a spoon is called intinction.[49] The coronavirus pandemic challenged Orthodox theologians to explain how communicants would be protected from infection since people are sharing the same spoon. Most theologians argued that it was impossible to become ill from Communion because the body and blood of Christ could not make someone ill. Some parishes temporarily adopted the use of multiple bamboo spoons, which were burned after one use, so no one was sharing a spoon with someone else.[50] Other communities had the presbyter or deacon clean the spoon by swirling it in pure alcohol and wiping it after each person had received communion. Parishes in Ukraine and Africa offered communion as bread previously dipped in wine, the other form of intinction. Orthodoxy reverted to the use of the spoon for everyone after the pandemic ended. The church has yet to propose solutions for people suffering from celiac disease, other than to give them communion from a cup containing only the blood of Christ. The liturgy ends with prayers of thanksgiving for Communion and a dismissal.

A few more points on Communion will be helpful for readers. First, bishops, presbyters, and deacons are the only ministers of Holy Communion. Bishops and presbyters normally distribute Communion, and deacons distribute in some parishes, but not others. Deacons used to give Holy Communion from the chalice, as noted above. Deacons ceased assisting with Holy Communion for two reasons. People began to receive Communion infrequently – as early as the fourth century – and most parishes did not have deacons. Only one minister of Communion was needed – the presbyter. When Orthodoxy experienced a Eucharistic renewal in the twentieth century and people began to receive Communion regularly, some bishops authorized deacons to assist with distribution. Orthodoxy has not considered the creation of a lay ministry for distributing Communion, however, and it seems unlikely that the Church would create such a ministry. Clergy bring Communion to the sick from the reserved sacrament, consecrated on Holy Thursday each year. Occasionally, some bishops will permit deacons to lead a Typica service with Holy Communion in the absence of a presbyter.

The final service involving Communion is the Liturgy of Presanctified Gifts.[51] On the Sunday before, the presbyter includes one lamb for each Presanctified Liturgy the community will pray on the weekdays of Lent (usually one or two). He dips the lamb into the consecrated wine (the blood of Christ) or carefully places a few drops of wine into the center portion of the lamb and places it into a container. The church will use the lamb a few days later for a rather ornate evening service that culminates with receiving Holy Communion on the weekdays of Lent. Orthodoxy does not celebrate Divine Liturgy on Lenten weekdays to obey the principle of fasting (from offering the Liturgy). The most observant Orthodox tend to receive Communion more often during Lent. The practice also introduces the irregularity of receiving Communion in the evening, unless the Presanctified Liturgy is prayed in the morning. It can be difficult to fast for an entire day for some people, so the faithful tend to have a light breakfast and then fast for the rest of the day until having a meal after the liturgy.

WHAT SUNDAY LITURGY MEANS

Sunday is the heart of Orthodox worship because it is the day of resurrection, the day when the Orthodox people assemble, and the occasion with which almost all Orthodox people are familiar. It is, above all, an experience of the promise of eternal life because the Church comes together with God, Father, Son, and Holy Spirit, at liturgy. The people hear the story of God's acts, especially his sending of Jesus Christ and his death, resurrection, and burial, and receive Holy Communion. Receiving Communion has a higher purpose – to become more and more like God and to pursue the vocation of being God's chosen people, God's priests, prophets, and kings in daily life. The dismissal from liturgy is like an act of sending God's people into the world to bear witness to God and to represent God in their daily lives and interactions.

THE DAILY CYCLE (LITURGY OF THE HOURS)

The Orthodox Church has a longstanding tradition of daily communal prayer. All monasteries and some cathedrals and parishes have services other than the Divine Liturgy. Daily communal prayer follows the principle established by St. Paul to pray without ceasing (1 Thess. 5:17). Communal prayer follows a long tradition that originated in the apostolic age and developed with major contributions from the desert monastic traditions of Egypt and Palestine.[52]

The ideal of daily communal prayer in the Byzantine Orthodox tradition has the following services: Matins, first hour, third hour, ninth hour, Vespers, compline, and midnight office (mesonyktikon). The prayer book for each office is the psalter, with fixed psalms appointed to each hour. Once again, there is a tradition of continuous prayer that originated with Egyptian monasteries. Monks would take turns reading from the psalter continuously while they sat in the church working, often weaving baskets. The current form of Byzantine daily prayer comes from a fusion of monastic and cathedral traditions. It is important to note, however, that the ordinary forms of services like daily Matins differ from Sundays and major feast days. Special hymns are appointed to Sundays and feast days at Matins and Vespers that distinguish them from the simpler daily forms. The main features of Matins are the singing of the canon, the Marian Magnificat canticle, and the recitation of the doxology (Gloria). Psalm 140 with its hymns, the "Gladsome Light" hymn, and the Canticle of Simeon are the main fixtures of Vespers.

The vast majority of cathedrals and parishes do not observe a daily rotation of services because few people would attend. Some parishes schedule daily Matins or Vespers once or more each week to maintain some semblance of the principle of daily communal prayer. Some prayerbooks published by churches and distributed to people contain these services.

THE LITURGICAL YEAR

The Orthodox Church's observance of the liturgical year is one of its most fascinating features. The year is organized into a complex system of feasts. The fixed cycle consists of feasts appointed to specific dates on the calendar, meaning that the occasion is celebrated on the same day every year, like Christmas on December 25. The movable cycle involves feasts that depend on the Orthodox method for calculating the date of Pascha (Easter). The commemoration of saints belongs to the fixed cycle, and numerous saints are commemorated every day.

An important book governs the convergence of feasts – the Typikon.[53] This book originated as a manual containing a monastic community's rule, so it contains regulations other than liturgical ones. The Typikon expanded for monasteries so that it included descriptions of the order of services for the entire Church year. The Typikon includes stipulations for extraordinary occurrences, such as Annunciation during Holy Week or Pascha.

THE FIXED CYCLE

Orthodoxy's fixed cycle contains the feasts of the Lord, Mary, John the Baptist, and many saints. The liturgical year begins with the Indiction feast on September 1. Table 6.1 presents the order of the major feasts of the fixed cycle.

Table 6.1 Major Fixed Feasts

Date	List of Fixed Feasts
September 8	Birth of Mary, Mother of God
September 14	Exaltation of the Holy Cross
November 8	St. Michael and the Angels
November 21	Entrance of Mary into the Temple
December 6	St. Nicholas of Myra in Lycia
December 24–25	Birth of Jesus Christ
January 5–6	Theophany of Jesus Christ
February 2	Meeting of the Lord
March 25	Annunciation Feast
June 29	Apostles Peter and Paul
August 6	Transfiguration of Christ
August 15	Dormition of Mary

These are the primary feasts observed on a typical parish's cycle of services with a Divine Liturgy. There are numerous other feasts considered to be important, especially for local churches. These include the Birth (June 24) and Beheading (August 29) of St. John the Baptist, the Baptism of Rus' on July 15, the Protection of the Virgin Mary on October 1, and St. Demetrius' feast day on October 23. The commemoration of the Armenian genocide on April 24 is a significant new development in the liturgical year, with the canonization of the victims as martyrs by the Armenian church in 2015.[54]

The Marian feasts contribute to the shape and meaning of the liturgical year. Mary's birth on September 8 essentially begins the liturgical year as the first major feast. Mary's death, known by the Orthodox as Dormition, is the last major feast of the year. The Annunciation feast is on March 25, just after the spring equinox. This feast precedes Jesus' birth by exactly nine months, denoting the perfection of Christ's fulfillment of God's promise.

A MINOR FEAST OF MARY IS ALSO TELLING, THE CONCEPTION OF MARY BY ANNA ON DECEMBER 9

Orthodoxy does not define Mary's conception as immaculate, even though the Orthodox Church is clear in its teaching of Mary's incorruption and sinlessness in her life. The Roman Catholic solemnity of the Immaculate Conception of Mary is on December 8, exactly nine months before her birth on September 8. Orthodoxy's appointment of December 9 for this feast shows that only Jesus Christ himself is perfect.

Orthodoxy's celebration of the Dormition feast also reveals slight differences in Marian doctrine with the Catholic Church. The Orthodox Church appoints a two-week fast before the Dormition feast, and the feast itself includes lamentations and a procession with Mary's shroud, imitating the services of Holy Week devoted to Christ's death and burial.[55] Orthodoxy teaches that the Holy Spirit gathered all of the apostles to Mary in Gethsemane, where they witnessed her death. Christ himself received Mary, and she ascended into heaven, where she was received as Queen. Catholic teaching on the Dormition (known as Assumption in the Roman tradition) is quite similar, with one notable exception: the matter of Mary's actual death is ambiguous. One can interpret the Assumption feast as teaching that Christ received Mary without her experiencing death.[56]

THE MOVABLE CYCLE

Pascha is the feast that governs the movable cycle in the Orthodox Church. The seasons preceding and following Pascha are major contributors to Orthodox spiritual life, and the history and liturgical details can be overwhelming. This section presents a condensed description of the movable cycle[57] and emphasizes what it means for Orthodox people.

The Orthodox date for Pascha usually differs from the date appointed for the Western celebration of Easter. The council in Nicaea (325) directed that Pascha be celebrated on the first Sunday after the spring equinox and the first full moon. The Western and Eastern churches follow this method, with one major difference – the Eastern churches still use an Alexandrian method of calculation on the basis of different mathematical formulas for both the vernal full moon and the actual calendar date.[58] The outcomes vary each year. Pascha can be one, two, or even five weeks after Easter, and on rare occasions, on the same date.

The dates of Pascha govern the seasons preceding and following the feast of feasts. Orthodoxy begins to prepare for Lent one month in advance, with powerful Gospels assigned to the Sundays preceding Lent. Lent itself lasts for forty days and is the most solemn fasting season of the year. Lazarus Saturday and Palm Sunday provide a brief intermission separating Lent and Holy Week, and Pascha begins with a lengthy Vigil service that is usually celebrated on Holy Saturday. Paschaltide lasts for forty days until the feast of Christ's ascension into heaven, and then Pentecost comes on the fiftieth day.

PRE-LENT AND LENT

The pre-Lenten period gradually initiates the faithful into Lent with powerful Sunday gospel readings, the introduction of Lenten hymns, and a soft launch of fasting. The primary themes of the pre-Lenten Sundays are true humility, returning to God, true love for the least of Christ's brethren, and forgiveness. Orthodoxy does not have an Ash Wednesday. Lent begins on the Sunday evening of Cheesefare Sunday, when Lenten melodies are used, the vestments change to darker colors, and everyone asks forgiveness of one another. The first week of Lent is known as Clean Week and can include nightly prayer services with numerous prostrations. The tone is penitential, and the experience involves heavy use of the body. Many parishes have the Liturgy of Presanctified Gifts once or twice during the weekdays of Lent. The faithful are encouraged to fast from meat, dairy products, sex, and other indulgences during the fasting period. Many people relinquish social media apps during this time.

The Sundays of Lent feature diverse themes. The Triumph of Orthodoxy celebrates Orthodoxy's veneration of icons, and the third Sunday, of the cross, occurs at the midpoint of Lent to place the goal of the Christian life before all participants – to take up one's cross and follow Christ. The second, fourth, and fifth Sundays – St. Gregory Palamas, St. John Climacus, and St. Mary of Egypt – honor monastics who made extraordinary contributions to Orthodox identity. The spiritual practices of St. John and St. Mary are particularly relevant to Lent. Many parishes have a long evening service where they sing the penitential canon, a series of hymns of lament by St. Andrew of Crete, while reading the life of St. Mary of Egypt. Lent ends on the Friday before Lazarus Saturday.

Lazarus Saturday features the long Gospel from St. John on Jesus' raising of Lazarus from the dead. It became an occasion for Baptisms in the Orthodox Church, evidenced by the singing of "as many as have been baptized" instead of the Trisagion. Palm Sunday often involves the blessing and waving of palms before Holy Week begins.

HOLY WEEK

Orthodox Holy Week is like Lent in the profound solemnity assigned to the short season. The liturgical theology of Holy Week is anchored in an extensive series of Scriptural lessons, especially in the seemingly constant proclamation of the Gospel. The observant Christian who hears the proclamation of the Word attentively can receive incomparable blessings.

Orthodoxy has a common core with the Western Churches in its rich liturgical celebration of the Paschal Triduum, beginning with the offices of Holy Thursday through Paschal Vespers on Sunday afternoon. Parishes and monasteries that fulfill the ideal pattern of liturgical celebration pray the hours, Liturgy of Presanctified Gifts, and Bridegroom Matins on Monday, Tuesday, and Wednesday of Holy Week.

THE PASCHAL TRIDUUM

The Paschal Triduum begins with Holy Thursday. Holy Thursday consists of Vespers and the Liturgy of St. Basil in memory of Jesus' supper with his disciples. The presbyter consecrates and sets aside the reserved communion for the entire year during this service. The rest of the week follows a rather complicated schedule.

Orthodox Christians start observing Holy Friday on Thursday evening, with the first service of Friday, the Passion Gospels, and Matins of Holy Friday. This is an extraordinarily long service with twelve Gospel readings, a procession with a cross, and dozens of hymns reflecting on Jesus' passion, arrest, and crucifixion, along with Judas' betrayal and the scattering of the disciples. Two more services of Holy Friday take place on Friday: the Royal Hours and Vespers. The Vespers of Holy Friday has a long Gospel reading that draws from all four evangelists. People come to this service for the first appearance and procession with the shroud of Christ, known commonly as the epitaphios (Greek) or plashchanitsa (Slavonic). The only words to describe this event are that it is a "big deal." Some Orthodox people hold the veneration of the shroud to be equivalent to receiving Holy Communion, so they will attend one or more of the Holy Friday and Saturday services just to venerate the shroud (Figure 6.4).

The main service of Holy Saturday takes place on Friday evening – the Vigil at the tomb of Christ with Lamentations and a procession with the shroud. The lamentations are poems reflecting on Jesus' death, humanity's sin, Mary's sorrow at her son's passion, and Jesus' victorious descent into Hades. The service grants participants a view of salvation. They see and hear Christ resting in the tomb, a bodily sabbath rest, and also descending into Hades to complete his work by freeing humankind from the clutches of death. The ritual is quite intense, filled with drama, twists and turns, darkness and light, lament, and glimpses of joy. It includes a procession around the church with the shroud while singing the Trisagion funeral hymn. The people venerate the shroud and go home, having reflected upon Christianity's great paradox – the incarnate God, sinless and full of love and grace, is sentenced and put to death, only to rise from the tomb and lift up all of humanity to eternal life with God.

Figure 6.4 Plashchanitsa (Burial Shroud) at the Gorodets Local History Museum.

Pascha begins with the Vigil service. It starts with Vespers, with fifteen readings appointed, and often a smaller number taken since they were designed to cover for Baptisms led by the patriarch in the cathedral baptistry. The message of the resurrection and the breaking of the fast begin with the proclamation of Psalm 81, "Arise o God and judge the earth," instead of Alleluia, followed by the resurrection account from Matthew. All are vested in white at this point, and the Divine Liturgy is served. Receiving Holy Communion breaks the fast held in honor of Christ's sabbath rest. Pascha has begun.

The midnight services, beginning with Nocturne and proceeding through Matins and Liturgy, are quite popular, highlighted by a candlelight procession, almost nonstop singing, the traditional sermon of St. John Chrysostom, sharing boiled eggs, and numerous intonations and exchanges of "Christ is Risen!" "Truly, he is risen!" Many Orthodox parishes gather in the wee hours of the morning to share their favorite meats and sweets they had set aside for the fast. The joy that permeates many of these gatherings can be inexplicable. For many, it is the destination of a journey that began with Lent, and pastors delight in describing it this way to encourage people to attend services.

The day of Pascha itself is not the destination. Orthodox celebrate Pascha, with a similar fervor, for forty days until Ascension, refraining from fasting and singing the Paschal hymns. Pentecost is also a major feast, the authentic feast of "Church," where the Holy Spirit descends to reveal those who are gathered as God's chosen people, holy nation, priests, prophets, and kings. Orthodox parishes decorate the churches in late spring green, unlike the Western red, in honor of the Spirit. The Church resumed kneeling at Vespers on Pentecost, a feast that inaugurates Orthodox "ordinary" time – most of the Sundays and weeks of the entire liturgical year (Figures 6.5 and 6.6).

CONCLUSION

Liturgical participation is the primary experience of church for most Orthodox Christians. To be sure, people perform a number of rituals outside of liturgy expressing their Orthodox identity, from lighting candles to saying prayers from a prayerbook or app to continuing domestic traditions like a festive Pascha meal. People also live out their Christian identity in daily life. Liturgy is not the only way to be an Orthodox Christian, and no, no particular feast is the end-all,

Figure 6.5 Paschal candles at a service in Annunciation, Toronto, Canada.

Figure 6.6 Greek Orthodox Christian Easter ceremony procession in Athens, Greece.

be-all. For Orthodox, the point of Liturgy is to be with God and his community – Father, Son, Holy Spirit, and all of the saints, living and departed. Orthodox believe that heaven and earth become one at Liturgy, and that eternal life consists of life with God, anchored in love. Liturgy is the main portal to everlasting life and the primary way Orthodox begin and sustain their experience of being with God, humankind, and redeemed creation.

NOTES

1 Paul Bradshaw, *The Search for the Origins of Christian Worship*, 2d ed. (London: SPCK, 2002), 1–20, Robert Taft, "Comparative Liturgy Fifty Years After Anton Baumstark (d. 1948): A Reply to Recent Critics," *Worship* 73 (1999), 521–540.
2 Robert Taft, *A History of the Liturgy of St. John Chrysostom*, 4 vols. Orientalia Christiana Analecta 200, 238, 261, 281 (Rome: Pontifical Oriental Institute, 1975).
3 The list of Taft's disciples who are continuing to develop studies on Orthodox liturgy in the spirit of comparative liturgy includes Paul Meyendorff, Mark Morozowich, Nina Glibetic, Gabriel Radle, Alexander Rentel, Daniel Galadza, and Vassa Larin. Stefanos Alexopoulos, Alexander Lingas, Sharon Gerstel, Steylios Muksuris, Vasily Permiakov, and Teva Regule are other Orthodox scholars who excel in comparative liturgy.
4 For a thorough review of Schmemann's legacy of scholarship, see Robert F. Taft, "The Liturgical Enterprise Twenty-Five Years after Alexander Schmemann: The Man and His Legacy," *St. Vladimir's Orthodox Theological Quarterly* 53, nos. 2–3 (2009), 139–177.
5 For Schmemann's application of this phrase, see Alexander Schmemann, "Liturgical Theology, Theology of Liturgy and Liturgical Reform," in *Liturgy and Tradition: Theological Reflections of Alexander Schmemann*, ed. Thomas Fisch (Crestwood, NY: St. Vladimir's Seminary Press, 1990), 38–40.
6 See, for example, Alexander Schmemann, *The Eucharist: Sacrament of the Kingdom*, trans. Paul Kachur (Crestwood, NY: St. Vladimir's Seminary Press, 1984), 16–17.
7 Schmemann, *The Eucharist*, 231.
8 See Schmemann's detailed explanation of this matter in *The Eucharist*, 231–240.
9 For background, see Alexander Grishin, "Eastern Orthodox Iconography and Architecture," in *The Blackwell Companion to Eastern Christianity*, ed. Ken Parry (Malden, MA: Blackwell Publishing, 2007).
10 For an overview, see Jennifer Lord, "Vice Presidential Address: Their Proclamation has gone out into All the Earth: An Account of the Aural

Iconography of Orthodox Church Bells," *Proceedings of the North American Academy of Liturgy* (5–7 January 2017), 11–31.

11 See Bissera Pentcheva, *Hagia Sophia: Sound, Space, and Spirit in Byzantium* (University Park: The Pennsylvania State University Press, 2017), 141–149.
12 For a historical overview of Byzantine chant, see Alexander Lingas, "Byzantine chant," in *The Oxford Companion to Music* (Oxford: Oxford University Press, 2011), https://www.oxfordreference.com/view/10.1093/acref/9780199579037.001.0001/acref-9780199579037-e-1059 (accessed July 29, 2024).
13 Elizabeth M. Jeffreys, "Kontakion," in *The Oxford Dictionary of Byzantium* (Oxford:Oxford University Press,1991),https://www.oxfordreference.com/view/10.1093/acref/9780195046526.001.0001/acref-9780195046526-e-2916 (accessed July 29, 2024).
14 The Roman and Protestant churches tend to pause the singing of Alleluia during Lent. Orthodoxy continues to sing Alleluia at most of its offices through Lent.
15 See Vladimir Morosan, *Choral Performance in Pre-Revolutionary Russia*, Russian Music Studies no. 17 (Madison, CT: Musica Russica, 1986), 37–73.
16 For a detailed background on these two composers and their musical formation, see Lydia Korniy, *Історія української музики, vol. 2: Друга Половина XVIII ст.* (Kyiv: M.P. Kots, 1998), 170–175, 216–224.
17 Orthodox use the Greek word "ekphonesis" to refer to the exclamation.
18 Schmemann, *The Eucharist*, 50.
19 Schmemann criticizes "illustrative symbolism" in his essay "symbols and symbolism," in Schmemann, *Liturgy and Tradition*, 115–128.
20 Job Getcha, *The Typikon Decoded: An Explanation of Byzantine Liturgical Practice*, trans. Paul Meyendorff, Orthodox Liturgy series book 3 (Yonkers, NY: St. Vladimir's Seminary Press, 2012), 24–25.
21 Morosan, *Choral Performance in Pre-Revolutionary*, 78–81.
22 See Pope John Paul II, Dies Domini, Dies Domini (May 31, 1998) | John Paul II (https://www.vatican.va/content/john-paul-ii/en/apost_letters/1998/documents/hf_jp-ii_apl_05071998_dies-domini.html) (accessed July 30, 2024).
23 Anne McGowan and Paul Bradshaw, eds., *The Pilgrimage of Egeria: A New Translation of the Itinerarium Egeriae* (Collegeville, MN: Liturgical Press, 2018), 152–155.
24 For a precise definition of the types of hymns, see Johann von Gardner, *Russian Church Singing*, vol. 1: *Orthodox Worship and Hymnography*, trans. Vladimir Morosan (Crestwood, NY: St. Vladimir's Seminary Press, 1980), 34–53.
25 See Robert F. Taft, *Beyond East and West: Problems in Liturgical Understanding*, 2d ed. (Rome: Pontifical Oriental Institute, 2001), 179.
26 Getcha, *The Typikon Decoded*, 113–114.
27 See n. 23 above.

28 For a brief historical overview of the Liturgies used by the Eastern Orthodox Church, see Job Getcha, *The Euchologion Unveiled*, Orthodox Liturgy Series Book 4 (Yonkers, NY: St.Vladimir's Seminary Press, 2021), 43–54.
29 Stefanos Alexopoulos and Maxwell Johnson, *Introduction to Eastern Christian Liturgies* (Collegeville, MN: Liturgical Press, 2022), 63.
30 See the explanation of this shift in Alexopoulos and Johnson, *Introduction to Eastern Christian Liturgies*, 71–77.
31 Alexopoulos and Johnson, *Introduction to Eastern Christian Liturgies*, 74–76.
32 See Alexopoulos and Johnson, *Introduction to Eastern Christian Liturgies*, xxx–xxxiv for a concise synopsis.
33 Alexopoulos and Johnson, *Introduction to Eastern Christian Liturgies*, xxxiii–xxxiv.
34 Taft, *Beyond East and West*, 240.
35 Nicholas Afanasiev, *The Church of the Holy Spirit*, trans. Vitaly Permiakov, ed. Michael Plekon, foreword Rowan Williams (Notre Dame, IN: University of Notre Dame Press, 2007), 10.
36 Alexopoulos and Johnson, *Introduction to Eastern Christian Liturgies*, 74. See also Stelyios Muksuris, *Economia and Eschatology: Liturgical Mystagogy in the Byzantine Prothesis Rite* (Brookline, MA: Holy Cross Orthodox Press, 2013).
37 See the description of the offering of the lamb in the liturgy of St. Cyril, "A Coptic Reader."
38 Alexopoulos and Johnson, *Introduction to Eastern Christian Liturgies,* 73, 75.
39 Alexopoulos and Johnson, *Introduction to Eastern Christian Liturgies*, 73.
40 The clause was added in the fifth century. See Alexopoulos and Johnson, *Introduction to Eastern Christian Liturgies*, 76.
41 Juan Mateos, *La célébration de la parole dans la liturgie byzantine: étude historique*, Orientalia Christiana Analecta 181 (Rome: Pontifical Oriental Institute, 1971), 130–131.
42 Robert Taft, *A History of the Liturgy of St. John Chrysostom, vol. 2: The Great Entrance*, Orientalia Christiana Analecta 200, 4th ed. (Rome: Pontifical Oriental Institute, 2004), 9–10.
43 See Taft's discussion of this issue in *A History of the Liturgy*, 244–249.
44 Taft, *A History of the Liturgy*, vol. 2, 119.
45 Taft, *A History of the Liturgy*, vol. 2, 121.
46 Robert F. Taft, *A History of the Liturgy of St. John Chrysostom*, vol. 5: *The Precommunion Rites*, Orientalia Christiana Analecta 261 (Rome: Pontifical Oriental Institute, 2000), 230–232.
47 See Taft, *A History of the Liturgy*, vol. 5, 473–502.
48 For details on the development of the Communion spoon, see Daniel Galadza, "'Remember, o Lord…': Liturgy, History, and Communion Spoons in a Time of Pandemic," https://publicorthodoxy.org/2020/05/21/liturgy-history-and-communion-spoons/ (accessed August 6, 2024).
49 The other form of intinction is to dip a piece of bread into the cup and hand it to the recipient, so they are receiving the body and blood at the

same time. The Armenian church continues to follow this practice. See *The Divine Liturgy of the Armenian Apostolic Orthodox Church*, ed. Daniel Findikiyan (Los Angeles, CA: Western Diocese of the Armenian Church of North America, 2005), 119.

50 See Will Cohen, "Coronavirus and Communion," https://publicorthodoxy.org/2020/03/14/coronavirus-and-communion/ (accessed August 6, 2024).
51 Stefanos Alexopoulos, *The Presanctified Liturgy in the Byzantine Rite: A Comparative Analysis of Its Origins, Evolution, and Structural Components*, Liturgia Condenda 21 (Leuven: Peeters, 2009).
52 Robert Taft, *The Byzantine Rite: A Short History* (Collegeville, MN: Liturgical Press, 1992), 56–60.
53 Alexopoulos and Johnson, *Introduction to Eastern Christian Liturgies*, xxxiv.
54 Alexopoulos and Johnson, *Introduction to Eastern Christian Liturgies*, 142.
55 For an explanation of this feast, see Nicholas Denysenko, "Mary's Dormition: Liturgical Cliché, Summer Pascha," *Studia Liturgica* 43 (2013), 256–280.
56 For reference, see Pope Pius XII's Apostolic Constitution, Munificentissimus Deus, https://www.vatican.va/content/pius-xii/en/apost_constitutions/documents/hf_p-xii_apc_19501101_munificentissimus-deus.html (accessed August 8, 2024).
57 Most of the rest of this chapter synopsizes material taken from Nicholas Denysenko, *This Is the Day That the Lord Has Made: The Liturgical Year in Orthodoxy* (Eugene, OR: Cascade, 2023).
58 John Fotopoulos, "Some Common Misconceptions about the Date of Pascha/Easter," https://publicorthodoxy.org/2018/03/15/easter-date-2018/ (accessed October 16, 2024).

ORTHODOX ECCLESIOLOGY
Communities, Leaders, People

The Orthodox Church has an exclusive character – it defines itself as the one, holy, catholic, and apostolic church.[1] This exclusivity allows for some semblance of regional independence. Orthodoxy relies on a system of fifteen fully independent churches that share a limited degree of interdependence. Conciliarity sustains the inner unity of the church. This chapter introduces Orthodox principles of church by explaining the concepts of conciliarity, catholicity, and autocephaly. A brief historical snapshot of the emergence of autocephalous churches, especially in the modern era, is included. The Orthodox teachings on ordination and leadership are also explained here to familiarize readers with terms and figures such as patriarchs and metropolitans.

THE ORGANIZATION OF THE EASTERN ORTHODOX CHURCHES

The review of history outlined the original establishment of church centers in major metropolises. Apostles created communities by preaching the word of God in cities like Rome, Ephesus, and Antioch. The Christian church expanded outwards from these cities. Earlier, we emphasized the importance of apostolicity for Christian identity. A church community was considered legitimate when its origins were clearly connected to an apostle who preached or was martyred there. Early Christians revered Rome with special honor because Saints Peter and Paul were martyred and buried there. Antioch and Alexandria were also revered apostolic sees and intellectual centers. Constantinople became important when the emperor Constantine designated it as the new Rome and the new imperial capital.

DOI: 10.4324/9781003433217-8

The global Christian community originated as a constellation of communities held together by their common belief in Jesus Christ as the only-begotten son of God. Constantine's Edict of Milan in 313, which legalized Christianity in the Roman Empire, catalyzed mass conversions, and Christian communities began to spring up in and around cities quite rapidly. Faith in Christ and the Holy Trinity sustained Christian unity through numerous theological challenges. An administrative apparatus that drew from imperial blueprints began to take shape in the Christian church. Originally, the bishop was the pastor, presider, and overseer of one local community. The bishop was the normal presider of the regular celebration of the Eucharist. In Rome, presbyters were not permitted to preside at Eucharistic celebrations until sometime after the sixth century.[2]

TOWARD AN ORDER: FROM REGIONAL STRUCTURES TO AN ORDERED CHURCH

The rapid increase in Christian numbers necessitated the creation of new communities around the metropolis. It was impossible to appoint a bishop to oversee each and every community in a city and in its vicinity, so bishops authorized presbyters to preside at the Eucharist in these parishes. The bishop continued to preside at the primary city church and began to oversee the presbyters, who were leading communities in the vicinity of the bishop's church. The bishop's church became known as the cathedral, based on his designation as the leader of a regional community. Cathedra means chair, and the bishop's chair became a symbol of his status as the occupant of the seat in the line of successors to the original apostle who established the church in that city. The city of the bishop's cathedral became the center of a diocese, which many Orthodox call an eparchy.[3]

Church expansion led to this new development in administration. In the fourth century, as the church began to grow much more rapidly, the community adapted to its new needs by revising its offices of leadership. Bishops now oversee multiple communities within the vicinity of the city that functions as the main center. The bishop was the chief officer of both his cathedral church community and the smaller communities that fall within his region.[4] Presbyters became overseers of all the other parish communities. Deacons served in the parish communities, as well as deaconesses. Bishops, presbyters, deacons, and deaconesses constituted the clerical orders, while subdeacons and readers (chanters) made up the minor clergy.

THE MAJOR ORDERS OF THE CHURCH: BISHOP, PRESBYTER, DEACON

The New Testament identifies apostles as the chief leaders of communities on account of their preaching. Apostles established an order of deacons to assist with widows' needs (Acts 6:3). The apostles passed on their authority to preach to bishops, and presbyters likewise contributed to Christian community life. The New Testament also mentions the significance of ministers such as prophets, teachers, and widows. The church began the process of establishing administrative apparatuses led primarily by bishops, presbyters, and deacons as early as the second century.[5] Radu Bordeianu notes evidence from as early as the second century of bishops delegating presidency at the Eucharistic assembly to presbyters.[6]

These three major orders of bishop, presbyter, and deacon remained static for most of the history of the Eastern churches. The bishop oversaw the life of a regional church from his metropolis, the presbyter led a parish community, and the deacon served as needed in parishes. These three clerical offices remain the three major orders of ministry and leadership in the Orthodox Church to this day.

ORDER WITHIN ORDER: DIPTYCHS AND PENTARCHY

If the three major orders were essentially static, imperial culture influenced the church and created limited dynamism within the structures. The bishops of metropolises like Constantinople and Athens received the title of archbishop, which designates a bishop who ranks higher than other bishops and exercises leadership among them. Dynamism catalyzed ranks within each major order. A bishop leading a regional church was known as an archbishop or metropolitan (taken clearly from metropolis). As regional structures expanded, new bishops were appointed to lead the church in regions within a larger region, so the archbishop of the main metropolis would be the highest-ranking bishop among all of those belonging to a regional structure.

Presbyters also became known as priests because of their presidency at the Divine Liturgy. A ranking system emerged among presbyters. A protopresbyter was the highest ranking of the presbyters, usually on the basis of the number of years served. An archdeacon and protodeacon were the first among deacons of a regional church. Orthodoxy sustained this system of ranking because of the influence of imperial offices. The system remains in place to this day, with some variety.

ROME AND CONSTANTINOPLE

The ranking of regional churches is a much more important issue for the global Orthodox Church. The matter of seniority and authority emerged as early as the fourth century. The Christian communities regarded Rome as the senior of the churches, as mentioned before, on account of the apostle Peter's martyrdom and burial there. Rome began to assert its theological authority in the early medieval period by arguing that the bishop of Rome – also known as the Pope – was the inheritor of the authority Jesus granted to Peter as the leader of his disciples. Peter preached in Antioch, and the apostle Mark had established the church in Alexandria, so these two churches bore special authority as original apostolic sees.

The appointment of Constantinople as the New Rome garnered prestige in the Christian world, despite its late emergence as an important center. The imperial capital became a location for international gatherings, and its importance rivaled Rome's as early as 381, at the second ecumenical council. Multiple factors contributed toward a system of global church governance. First, the theological controversies that caused divisions among Christians in cities necessitated meetings to clarify teachings and ultimately resolve controversies. The meetings themselves included the bishops of the major regional centers – Rome, Antioch, Alexandria, and Constantinople. The Orthodox Church always considered these meetings of the representatives of the whole church, the ecumenical councils, to hold the highest authority in the church because they symbolized univocality – the church professing her belief and faith with one voice.[7]

Nevertheless, as we have already seen, Christians looked for the most authoritative voices within these conciliar gatherings. Christians always regarded Rome as possessing the honor of the highest authority.[8] The debate on authority generated a discussion on rank and order among the churches. Church leaders maintained lists called diptychs of the senior bishops presiding over each local church in order. It was customary for the senior bishop to pray for the leader of the other regional churches on that list at the Eucharistic liturgy as a way of expressing the unity of the global church.

The diptychs contained an order ranking the churches, beginning with the church bearing the highest dignity. The church of Constantinople was the most prestigious of the churches in the Eastern Christian world, and Constantinople had an affinity for systems of order, also known as *taxis*. All of the churches recognized five regional church structures as possessing a special dignity within the taxis by the middle of the fifth century. These were, in order, the churches of Rome, Constantinople, Antioch, Alexandria, and Jerusalem. The churches regarded one another as patriarchates, and the senior bishop who presided over each church was known as a patriarch. The bishop of Constantinople received new privileges at the Council of Constantinople in 381 and again at the Council of Chalcedon in 451.[9] Constantinople received the new privileges as the seat of the imperial capital with the title of New Rome and received more authority within the order of the church, second only to Rome itself. Jerusalem was granted the dignity of a patriarchate only at this council in 451 on account of its location as the site of Jesus Christ's death, burial, and resurrection. Christian scholars describe this list of five Christian centers as the *pentarchy*.

AUTOCEPHALY IN THE ORTHODOX CHURCH

It is essential to emphasize Orthodoxy's opinion that the highest-ranking senior bishops possess neither jurisdiction nor administrative oversight over the other churches. The Orthodox churches agree that the churches of Rome and Constantinople had special privileges possessed by none of the other church leaders but describe the exercise of these privileges as a primacy of honor only. Bordeianu offers a helpful clarification on the limits of the authority of the church of Rome when he writes that some of the best theologians appealed to Rome for confirmation of correct doctrinal teaching, but that Rome's jurisdiction over the global church – and claims to such jurisdiction – evolved over a long period of time.[10]

The separation of the Eastern Orthodox and Western Roman Christian worlds expanded largely on account of disagreements on both the nature of the senior bishops' authority and the structure of the global church.[11]

The Orthodox churches maintain that each regional structure is essentially independent and self-governing. This means that no regional church requires the permission of the bishops of Rome or Constantinople to govern its affairs. Eventually, scholars created a term that designated the legal status of such a regional structure – this term is *autocephaly*. An autocephalous church is a regional church that is completely self-governing. An autocephalous church elects and appoints its own bishops and leaders, manages its liturgical life, and makes all decisions in the broad areas of faith and order.

There are seventeen autocephalous Orthodox churches as of this writing: the churches of Constantinople, Alexandria, Antioch, Jerusalem, Russia, Georgia, Serbia, Bulgaria, Romania, Cyprus, Greece, Albania, Poland, the Czech Republic and Slovakia, America, Ukraine, and North Macedonia. The legitimacy of the churches in America, Ukraine, and North Macedonia are matters of dispute and unresolved.

One can speak of both one global Orthodox Church and seventeen autocephalous churches. There is one church because there is one Lord Jesus Christ, one God, and one Baptism. No Christian is baptized as a member of an autocephalous church – each person is baptized and anointed as a member of the one, holy, catholic, and apostolic church.

The unity of the Orthodox Church is real, invisible, and visible. The unity is visible when the leaders of the churches gather to celebrate Eucharist or pray for one another at the Divine Liturgy.[12] The Orthodox churches point to the celebration of the Eucharist as the sign of unity. Praying for the faithful of the church in other regions is a sign of universal unity. Orthodoxy continues to use the tradition of praying with diptychs as a symbol of the unity of the church in all places. Lists of people's names, the dead and the living, are on the diptychs, and praying for them is a way of expressing a gathering of all the dead, the living, and those in other places in one space – God's bosom. Orthodox also continue to observe the tradition of praying for church leaders who aren't present. The traditional place for this prayer is at the end of the Eucharistic prayer – a symbolic gesture that the whole church will partake of Holy Communion, wherever they are – in another city on earth or in the eternal city in heaven. The presbyter leads prayers for the local bishop at the end of the anaphora. When the local bishop presides, he prays for the head bishop of his synod at this time. When the primate of a church presides, he prays for all of the other Orthodox primates. All of these prayers, ranging from petitions for the dead and living to heads of churches praying for their fellow primates, express the unity of the church, with the Eucharist transcending visible separations of time and place.

The common adherence to the declarations of the first seven ecumenical councils and the Nicene-Constantinopolitan Creed are liturgical expressions of the unity of the seventeen churches. In this sense, the seventeen Orthodox churches are independent, and it is possible to simultaneously state that there is one Orthodox Church.

The seventeen churches are independent administratively and in governance. The Orthodox concept of autocephaly is similar to the notion of sovereignty and territorial integrity observed by nation-states. A few examples can illustrate this point. If the autocephalous church in Greece decides to introduce a new liturgical practice, its synod of bishops can make this change without asking for permission from another Orthodox Church. The church in America can decide to add a new saint to its calendar without receiving approval from another church. Autocephaly means that the regional church community is neither dependent upon nor subordinate to an external church body.

One of the consequences of the freedom of autocephaly, though, is that other churches might object to the introduction of a new practice. Orthodox leaders tend to be sensitive to the possibility of objections coming from another church, or even worse, from their own people, and are therefore hesitant to introduce practices or reforms that could face opposition. The adoption of the new calendar by many of the world's Orthodox churches in 1923 caused an outcry of opposition.[13] The result was that some churches observed holidays on the same dates as the churches of the West, with the exception of Easter.

In 2024, a bishop in Zimbabwe ordained a deaconess, which predictably elicited strong reactions.[14] Some commentators felt that the entire synod of the Alexandrian patriarchate should have made the decision, and not just one bishop. If the Alexandrian church continues to ordain deaconesses, an issue could arise at pan-Orthodox gatherings where other Orthodox churches could prohibit her from concelebrating. These hypotheticals are unlikely to become realities. They do, however, illustrate a vulnerability in Orthodoxy's preference for local independence if the local becomes too detached from the universal.

Perhaps the best example of autocephaly is with the election of a new senior bishop – an archbishop, metropolitan, or patriarch who presides over the regional structure. Let's use the church in Greece as an example. When the archbishop of Athens retires or dies, the synod (council) of bishops in Greece appoints an interim bishop to continue to lead the church until a new archbishop is elected and enthroned (installed). The Orthodox Church typically refers to interim leaders as *locum tenens*, Latin for "in the place of."

The Church of Greece will then nominate and elect a new archbishop of Athens who will preside over the synod of bishops and function as the chief bishop of the Church of Greece. The elected archbishop becomes archbishop when he is enthroned at a special Divine Liturgy on a date appointed by his fellow bishops on the synod. The new archbishop needs neither the approval nor the confirmation of any other Orthodox archbishop, metropolitan, patriarch, or synod. In this sense, it is similar to an election for political office. The leaders of other countries recognize the newly elected leader in most circumstances. The Orthodox Church has sustained a tradition from the early church of a newly elected head of the church sending a letter (called a synodikon) greeting the leaders of the other churches, in effect introducing himself and expressing his commitment to serving the Church.[15]

In summary, the Orthodox churches demand that the other Orthodox churches respect their sovereignty in administering their own affairs. Orthodoxy emphasizes independence, perhaps more than interdependence.

AUTOCEPHALY AND SOVEREIGN NATION-STATES

The historical trajectory of the creation of new autocephalous Orthodox Church structures has followed the general pattern of establishing and maintaining imperial and national borders. The churches of Antioch and Alexandria retained their status as ancient patriarchates despite becoming religious minorities in predominantly Islamic nation-states.

The fall of Constantinople in 1453 changed the Orthodox configuration of territory significantly. Constantinople retained its stature as first among equals in Orthodoxy, but its position was weakened without the support of the imperial state. The Ottomans granted Constantinople authority over other Christians in their Rum millet system. When nation-states began to emerge from the declining Ottoman, Habsburg, and Russian empires, Constantinople began to grant autocephaly to the churches within the borders of those nation-states. The re-establishment of patriarchates in Bulgaria, Serbia, and Romania, and the creation of churches in Greece, Albania, and Poland made it appear that autocephalous churches are always within the borders of sovereign nation-states. The nation-state is the prevailing model for Orthodox autocephalous churches, but there are also multinational structures. These include the patriarchates of Alexandria, Moscow, and Constantinople.

The historical trajectory of autocephaly shows that it develops in dynamic tension with political realities over time. The core principle is that a regional structure of churches with a center in an important city frequently constitutes an autocephalous church. Autocephaly is fluid and is not well-defined – it does not need to follow the blueprint of the modern nation-state.

Orthodoxy has adopted another model for a limited degree of self-governance in the modern era – autonomy. Autonomous churches began to emerge in the early twentieth century. An autonomous church has its own synod of bishops and is self-governing to a degree determined in agreement with the church it is dependent upon. Finland has a sizable Orthodox population and is an autonomous church within the patriarchate of Constantinople. The Moscow Patriarchate granted autonomy to the small church in Japan.

The most controversial example concerns the church in Ukraine. One of the two large Orthodox churches in Ukraine known as the Ukrainian Orthodox Church (UOC) received a *hramota* (certificate) from Patriarch Aleksy II of Moscow in 1990 granting it a broad degree of autonomy in governance and administration.[16] This *hramota* was not the same as granting the UOC autonomous status, and the ambiguity of the UOC's status symbolized autonomy's fluidity.

Technically, an autonomous Orthodox Church governs its internal life without supervision in most aspects.[17] An autonomous church is attached to the structure of a larger autocephalous church, however, and is somewhat subordinate to it. The autocephalous mother church must confirm the election of new chief bishops of an autonomous church, and the bishops of an autonomous church participate in the life of the autocephalous church. These stipulations apply to the relations between the autonomous church of Finland with Constantinople and the autonomous churches of Japan and Ukraine to the Moscow Patriarchate. In this sense, an autonomous church's relations with its mother church are similar to the relations of an Eastern Catholic Church with Rome. The Eastern Catholic churches have a certain degree of independence but belong to the larger structure of the Roman church and have some level of subordination.

CHALLENGES TO AUTOCEPHALY: IS IT NECESSARY?

Autocephaly is one of the constant topics of conversation among Orthodox insiders. People interested in Church politics want to know the ins and outs of autocephalous churches. Which church has autocephaly? Which church has requested autocephaly? Are there differences in the degrees of freedom among the autocephalous churches? Who has the right to grant autocephaly? And finally, is autocephaly even necessary?

The easy answer to the last question suggests that for Orthodox, yes, autocephaly is necessary because it is associated with freedom. Orthodox people tend to take autocephaly for granted, however. People in autocephalous churches recognized widely tend to describe autocephaly as a litmus test for legitimacy. When church bodies want autocephaly, it can become a contested issue. As mentioned earlier, the autocephaly of the churches in America and Ukraine is contested. Previously, the autocephaly of the churches of Poland and the Czech Republic and Slovakia was also disputed. The most important question requiring explanation is the one on the necessity of autocephaly. Reviewing some of the disputes about autocephaly can help us to answer this question.

The main topic of dispute concerns who has the right to grant autocephaly and the mechanism used to grant it. The situation of the

Church in Poland in the early 1920s is a helpful illustration.[18] Most of Poland had been annexed to the Russian Empire over a period of four partitions, beginning in the eighteenth century. A sizable population of Belorussian and Ukrainian Orthodox people lived in the Austro-Hungarian Empire. The climactic events of World War I and the collapse of the Austro-Hungarian and Russian empires resulted in reconfigured political and national entities in Eastern Europe. The sovereign republic of Poland was constituted after the Treaty of Versailles in 1919, and the eastern part of Poland included Galicia and Volyn' with its sizable Orthodox minority.

The small Orthodox Church was separated from the Moscow Patriarchate and was challenged on two fronts. First, intense Bolshevik persecution of the Moscow Patriarchate strangled its leadership and posed a potential security threat to Poland. Second, the Catholic Church dominated in Poland. Polish leaders believed that an autocephalous Orthodox Church would minimize the Bolshevik threat and add a significant Christian counterpoint to the Catholic majority. In 1923, the small synod of Orthodox bishops in Poland voted three to two in favor of autocephaly and then declared it. At this point, representatives of the Polish government worked with the Orthodox bishops to receive autocephaly from the Ecumenical Patriarchate of Constantinople, an event that took place in 1924.

The Church in Poland retained its autocephaly even when Hitler and Stalin partitioned Poland yet again in 1939. The Orthodox Church in Poland rescinded the autocephaly it had received from Constantinople in 1948, after Poland had a communist government and was firmly under the influence of the Soviet Union.[19] The Church in Poland received autocephaly yet again in the same year, but this time from the Moscow Patriarchate and not Constantinople.

This example from the church in Poland introduces many points of discussion that can help us understand the disputes surrounding autocephaly. The process began when church and government officials felt the need to strengthen the church's structure, both to insulate it from the potential external Bolshevik threat and also to mitigate the influence of the Catholic Church, which held an otherwise overwhelming religious majority in Poland. Orthodox clergy and people were not the only interested parties. The church structure itself carried political overtones with potential consequences for state security. This means that the matter of autocephaly is not limited to Church leaders – historically, government officials are also interested in religious structures and their relations with international leaders.

The method used for obtaining autocephaly was another matter of concern. Autocephaly did not begin externally but inside the church of Poland. The synod of bishops took up the matter initially, and a slim majority was enough to secure autocephaly, though not without controversy.[20] The final matter concerns the rescinding of autocephaly from Constantinople and receiving it anew from Moscow. The tomos of autocephaly Poland received from Moscow did not include the requirement that Poland receive its chrism from Moscow. Politics certainly motivated the exchange of one autocephaly for another in this instance, since Moscow claimed to be the original mother of the Orthodox in Poland and laid claim to historical jurisdiction over the church in Polish territory. All of these issues coalesce into the most contested topic by Orthodox pastors and scholars up until the explosion of the culture wars in the late twentieth and early twenty-first centuries.

The church in Poland was not the only one in history to simply declare itself as autocephalous. The Russian church declared its autocephaly in 1448, and the church in Greece also asserted its autocephaly in 1825 before engaging formal Orthodox mechanisms that normalized autocephalous status. The most controversial declarations of autocephaly, however, have involved the Ukrainian case, as we saw in our review of history in Chapter 3. Orthodox bodies in Ukraine have declared autocephaly on numerous occasions, beginning in 1921, and then again in 1922, 1942, 1989, and with the establishment of the Kyiv Patriarchate in 1992.[21]

There seems to be a difference between declaring autocephaly and requesting it from another church organization. Sometimes, churches declare autocephaly and then wait for other churches to recognize it. This method is similar to the formation of a new nation-state, which might declare independence and await recognition. The other option is to request that another church grant autocephaly to the church desiring it. In this case, the church requesting autocephaly is seeking independence from what is commonly known as its "mother" church. The dispute seems to circulate around the identity of the "mother" church. Russian Orthodox theologians have argued that any Orthodox Church can be a "mother" to a church seeking autocephaly, whereas Constantinople argues that it alone is the "mother" church because of its identity as the new Rome and first among equals in Orthodoxy.

The situation of Orthodoxy in North America was already complicated before the revolutionary war in Russia. After the revolution, the Moscow Patriarchate's Metropolia in the United States and Canada encountered the same political difficulties the church in Poland had feared because of Bolshevik persecution and exploitation of the Russian church. The bishops of the Metropolia worked with theologians, especially Alexander Schmemann and John Meyendorff, to propose autocephaly for the American Metropolia. Autocephaly would begin with the Metropolia, but the architects of the proposal envisioned that it would eventually embrace all of the other Orthodox churches in North America. The bishops of the Metropolia requested autocephaly from Moscow, and Moscow granted it in 1970. The Metropolia became the Orthodox Church in America (OCA).

The rest of the plan did not unfold as the American originators had hoped, however. First, the other Orthodox in America did not join the new autocephalous church, even though they created ethnic dioceses (Bulgarian, Albanian, and Romanian) as temporary entities to accommodate parishes and their native traditions until American Orthodoxy developed its own organic life. Second, only some of the world's Orthodox churches recognized the autocephaly of the OCA. Constantinople and the churches aligned with its position did not recognize it.

The obstacle to recognition was the dispute on who gets to grant autocephaly to a new church. Constantinople had argued that it alone had the authority to grant autocephaly to new churches, as it had in the late and post-Ottoman periods. Moscow argued that it had the authority to grant autocephaly to the OCA (and also to Poland and the Czechoslovakian churches) because it was their "mother" church. The dispute between Constantinople and Moscow had festered since the initial Soviet period, when Constantinople briefly recognized the renovationist church in Russia.[22] More importantly, Orthodox theologians and pastors knew that this was the most formidable obstacle to Orthodox unity, especially if church bodies would continue to seek autocephaly.

The commissions of scholars and theologians preparing for the pan-Orthodox council in Crete of 2016 created a process that had the potential to resolve the issue.[23] The nuts and bolts of the process called for the bishops of a church that desired autocephaly to initiate the process by requesting autocephaly from their "mother" church. The "mother" church would work with the "daughter" toward an agreement and an initial statute for the daughter church. Once the mother and daughter agreed, the ecumenical patriarch of Constantinople would enter the process by obtaining the approval of all of the other Orthodox churches. This part of the process was very important because it would honor one of Orthodoxy's most beloved core values – conciliarity. Once the ecumenical patriarch obtained everyone's agreement on the new church's autocephaly, he would create, sign, and bestow the tomos of autocephaly. Tomos simply means "part of a book," but it is significant because it is essentially the primary document that has the autocephaly of the new church inscribed upon it.

Unfortunately, this proposal of the preparatory commission for the pan-Orthodox council dissipated because of the objections of the Moscow Patriarchate. The agreement called for Constantinople to issue and bestow the tomos of autocephaly to the new church, and Moscow objected to this stipulation.[24] The proposed mechanism granted Moscow many of its desired elements, with one standing out above all – the involvement of all parties with a limitation on the part of Constantinople, which would essentially carry the baton to the end by confirming a prearranged agreement. This proposal was supposed to be declared as an agreed statement by the pan-Orthodox council, but Moscow's objection has rendered autocephaly one of Orthodoxy's most disputed topics.[25]

Another example illustrates why an acceptable, agreed-upon mechanism for autocephaly is needed. When Constantinople intervened in Ukraine in 2018, united two of the three churches into the Orthodox Church of Ukraine (OCU), and granted autocephaly to the OCU in 2019, new questions surfaced on the necessity of autocephaly. These questions came from the UOC in the context of Russia's invasion of Ukraine and the UOC's precarious position as a church that had traditionally belonged to the Moscow Patriarchate.

The UOC claimed that they revised their statute when they announced their separation from the Moscow Patriarchate in May

2022.[26] Upon examination, their statute had remained largely the same as the one they received in the hramota from Patriarch Aleksy II in 1990 that granted the UOC broad autonomy in administration and governance. The UOC claimed that this certificate of broad autonomy made them more independent than the OCU, which had a tomos of autocephaly from Constantinople.[27] The UOC argued that the OCU's tomos made them dependent on Constantinople because it contained language requiring the metropolitan of the OCU to consult with the ecumenical patriarch on important issues. The tomos of autocephaly also requires the OCU to receive the holy chrism for Baptisms and Chrismations from the ecumenical patriarch of Constantinople. The modern architect of Ukrainian autocephaly, Metropolitan Filaret (Denysenko), was also critical of the OCU's autocephaly because of its seeming subservience to Constantinople and his assertion that the OCU had every right and privilege to declare itself a patriarchate since it had attained canonical autocephaly.[28]

The UOC's argument that their autonomous statute grants them more independence than the OCU's autocephaly from Constantinople suggests that autocephaly does not deliver true independence. If this is true, then what is the purpose of autocephaly, and is it even necessary? It would seem to be the case for Orthodoxy since it has been the most controversial issue for over a century. Possessing a certificate of autonomy does not elevate a church's status in interchurch relations. The other Orthodox churches regard the UOC as a part of the Moscow Patriarchate because they are not autocephalous. That said, the UOC makes an important point about the inconsistency of autocephalous status in Orthodoxy. Some autocephalous churches seem to be completely independent in all aspects of their lives. Others have some kind of formal and subservient relationship with the Patriarchate of Constantinople.

We can conclude with a few assertions about autocephaly. Autocephaly preserves order in the Orthodox world by maintaining a list of legitimate church structures on the diptychs. One could argue that autocephaly is essential in this regard because autocephaly makes church relations possible without compromising independence. The problems that have surfaced with autocephaly are troubling, however, and the dissipation of the preparatory commission's proposal doesn't reduce the urgency needed to arrive at some kind of consensus on a mechanism for granting it. Orthodox theologian Cyril Hovorun has suggested that autocephalous structures are convenient but not essential.[29] No one should expect Orthodoxy to move away from autocephaly any time soon. But autocephaly will continue to be a matter of dispute in Orthodoxy if its pastors and theologians fail to renew potential revisions to its structures.

WHO'S IN CHARGE? THE DEBATE ON PRIMACY

The other major issue engulfing Orthodox ecclesiology is primacy – the matter of who is in charge. After centuries of heated polemical exchanges with the Roman church, Orthodox theologians engaged Catholic thinkers on the nature and role of primacy in the church. The simplest way to define primacy is by identifying the most authoritative theological sources and the officers who lead the Church. The debate with the Roman church has concerned the privileges and prerogatives exercised by the Pope. Pope John Paul II invited all global Christians to envision how the Pope might carry out his ministry, with the hope of reuniting all divided Christians into one church by the year 2000.[30] Orthodox dialogue with Catholics on primacy has revealed some common beliefs, but as is so often the case with Orthodoxy, diverse viewpoints on the inside prevent a consensus.[31]

JESUS CHRIST, SCRIPTURE, AND TRADITION

Orthodoxy views Jesus Christ himself as the highest authority of the Church, as revealed by the Holy Scriptures and tradition.[32] Tradition is an ambiguous term and has numerous interpretations within the Orthodox Church. From the perspective of theological and administrative authority, we can define tradition as the eyewitness accounts and teachings of the apostles and the teachings of the holy fathers and mothers of the church that have been received and sustained within the church. This previous assertion needs a little unpacking – what are the teachings of the "holy fathers and mothers" that have been received by the church?

Orthodox tend to describe tradition as holy tradition. The litmus test for holy tradition is sustenance and longevity. Athanasius' teaching on the incarnation and Basil's treatise on the Holy Spirit pass the litmus test because they have remained in the core of Orthodoxy's theological belief system. Teachings that are received, echoed, and find wide agreement within the church tend to be regarded by the Church as holy tradition. Anything that came to be declared or proclaimed by an ecumenical council also tends to be viewed as holy tradition.

Two examples illustrate the longevity of tradition. The ordination of a bishop requires three participating bishops, as stipulated by the Council of Nicaea in 325.[33] The three bishops bear witness to the eligibility and theological soundness of the candidate. Orthodoxy has not only retained this tradition since 325, but it has also resisted efforts to circumvent it. Another example is from the seventh ecumenical council of 787, also in Nicaea. This council legitimized the veneration of icons, but it also invited the faithful to adorn churches, homes, and public spaces with sacred images. This is another example where Orthodoxy has retained a tradition confirmed by an ecumenical council.

A good example of dynamism in tradition is the reverence with which clergy and faithful convey toward the holy shroud, known to the people as epitaphios or plashchanitsa, during the services of Holy Friday and Saturday. Veneration of the shroud is a central feature of Holy Week, to the point that some faithful regard kissing the shroud as an obligation as sacred as receiving Holy Communion or making an annual Confession.

The place of the shroud in the history of Holy Week is somewhat innovative. The shroud was not a part of the Holy Week services until the fourteenth century, which makes it one of the newest innovations of Orthodox practice.[34] Furthermore, the proclamation of the rich collection of Scripture lessons is the actual centerpiece of the Holy Week liturgies – not the veneration of the shroud. The introduction of the shroud to the services demonstrates the dynamic character of Orthodox tradition. Orthodoxy can accommodate new practices – it does, indeed, change. In fact, one could argue that this example shows that Orthodoxy refuses to reduce tradition to retaining the past. For Orthodox, encountering God and bearing witness to his truth is ritualized and taught in diverse ways that occasionally need to change.

It is also important to note that disagreements on tradition can become quite problematic for Orthodoxy. The Church has mechanisms in place for the people to hold leaders accountable, as mentioned with bishops who violated their vows of celibacy. Sometimes, groups of people in the church read tradition differently by enabling bishops to exploit others through power. This reading of tradition is one of entitlement, granting the bishop more protective immunity on account of his office.

The heart of tradition is not a text, book, ritual, or officeholder – it is the person of Jesus Christ himself. The actual head of the Orthodox Church is Jesus Christ. Orthodox primacy is anchored in Christ. For Orthodox, this means that no officeholder is infallible – any patriarch, metropolitan, or archbishop could stray from the faith, apostatize, lead the church into schism, or commit moral failings. The notion of the church's infallibility is complicated because Christ is the head of the church. If the church experiences a period of moral tribulation by inciting hatred, supporting an evil regime, or justifying an evil practice or cause, some portion of the church remains faithful to Christ, the Scriptures, and tradition. Orthodoxy rejects the assertions of Vatican I on the Petrine office on papal infallibility and the extraordinary magisterium because every officeholder is accountable to Christ.[35] The Orthodox Church does not dismiss the need for a visible head of the church, even at the universal level. There is no question that the Church needs a visible leader; the debate concerns the degree of authority the leader possesses and how he exercises his ministry of oversight.[36]

Authentic tradition originates with and is inspired by God and is therefore divine. The Church might exercise stewardship over a set of rituals or repository of dogma, but God is the ultimate author of everything and everyone that is holy. It is necessary for the Church to approach itself in a spirit of humility, lest the church succumb to glorifying itself – the trap of ecclesiolatry. David Bentley Hart suggests that the Church needs to exercise a certain kind of "hermeneutical piety" as it pertains to holy tradition, because tradition is essentially apocalyptic.[37] God is not only the beginning but also the end, and Orthodoxy worships a living God. God can and does disrupt the community's sense of tradition in continuity by eliciting an unanticipated awakening to a mystery that was previously unknown. Hart's warning reminds us of a staple feature of Orthodox liturgy – the community remembers the past in thanksgiving, ascends to the living God in the present, and asks God to continue to love the community in the future. Tradition is like liturgy in this way – dynamic, not static, and always venturing into eternity while remembering the past.

PRIMACY IN PRACTICE

There are several layers of primacy, and they are bound together with the Orthodox concept and practice of conciliarity. Here's how it works. Each and every bishop, from the leader of a diocese to the head of a large autocephalous church, is accountable first and foremost to Jesus Christ and the Gospel. The rite of ordination to bishop calls for the concelebrating bishops to hold the Gospel book over the head of the ordinand, showing that he is not the source of his own theology but draws from the Gospel, shapes his ministry upon the Gospel's proclamation, and is accountable to the witness of its teaching.[38] The requirement of three concelebrating bishops was mentioned earlier. The newly-ordained bishop does not stand alone but is accountable to his fellow bishops and also to the people of God, who bear witness to his ordination. An important part of the concept of synodality is bishops working together – they work together and attempt to speak with one voice.

Orthodox bishops appear to possess a great deal of authority and power, especially in churches where synods of bishops make all decisions unilaterally. The Orthodox concept and practice of conciliarity reveals a vision of the entire church gathered together and deliberating together. Numerous theologians have defined conciliarity, perhaps none more than Nicholas Afanasiev.[39] Afanasiev depicted a church filled with the Holy Spirit, like the descent of the Spirit on the apostles in Acts 2:1, when everyone was gathered together in one place. Afanasiev emphasized the importance of the laity in conciliarity. He argued that the laity also exercises Christ's priesthood, albeit in a way different from deacons, presbyters, and bishops.[40] Afanasiev also argued that the rites of Baptism and anointing with chrism are like an ordination to apostolic work. He did not seek to eliminate the distinct features of the church's orders but to envision a church that lives with all parts of her body working together.

The movement toward the restoration of conciliarity has a simple core. Essentially, Orthodoxy's preference for councils, which symbolize the whole church's univocality, needed to be manifest in its institutions. The practical implication would be to revise church governance to ensure that the entire church is participating in the process, and not just the bishops. Conciliarity can have different manifestations, but the basic idea is that the entire church should be represented at gatherings making important decisions. This means that women and men, along with deacons and priests, should play a part in deliberating and even making decisions. It also means that bishops are neither outside of nor above the church in any way. Councils are not composed only of bishops, so bishops and their elected leaders are accountable to the entire church gathered in council.

One of the issues causing problems in contemporary Orthodoxy is the uneven and inconsistent application of conciliarity. The Moscow Patriarchate restored the patriarchal office and created conciliar structures that granted lower clergy and laity much more access to participation and governance in church life. Small churches like the Orthodox Church in America (OCA) and the Western European exarchate of the Patriarchate of Constantinople adopted similar structures. In recent decades, Orthodoxy has reduced access to laity for governance and restored more power to synods of bishops and especially the primates of the churches. Conciliarity tends to be an idea that garners broad appeal and applause in theory but is difficult to identify in practice. The strains of geopolitical crises have taken a toll on the church. Some clergy of the Moscow Patriarchate who protested the war or simply prayed for peace instead of victory were deposed from holy orders.[41] This kind of punitive action for expressing an opinion reveals the gap separating theory from practice in the Orthodox application of conciliarity.

The final issue concerns the primacy given to one of the church leaders of an apostolic see, Rome and Constantinople.[42] Orthodoxy acknowledges that the entire church recognized Rome as the first among equals until the Latin Catholic and Eastern Orthodox primates excommunicated one another in 1054. There is also general agreement among Orthodox that the patriarch of Constantinople exercises a kind of primacy. The disagreement concerns the details on what the primate of the church can and cannot do. Orthodox unilaterally reject the notions of the Pope exercising universal jurisdiction over the church, possessing infallibility, and teaching with the extraordinary magisterium. Occasionally, some Orthodox depict the ecumenical patriarch as overreaching his authority in his exercise of the primatial ministry, another illustration of divisions over primacy within Orthodoxy.

The late Orthodox theologian Kallistos Ware summarized the position on the Pope's exercise of his ministry concisely and clearly.[43] Ware wrote that the Orthodox Church agrees with two of the three levels the Roman Catholic Church uses to define the ministry of the Pope. The Catholic Church understands the Pope as the bishop of Rome, the first level. Orthodoxy has never challenged the Pope's ministry to his own diocese. The Catholic Church understands the second level of the pope as the first among the patriarchs. Again, Orthodoxy confirms this claim. Ware describes this second level as akin to the "elder brother" within the worldwide Christian family, a "first among equals" (primus inter pares) who enjoys certain "rights of seniority."[44]

The third level – universal jurisdiction – is rejected by Orthodoxy. Ware astutely noted that the Orthodox aren't completely in agreement on this matter, since some admit that there are "strong grounds historically" for allowing the Pope some measure of "appellate jurisdiction" over the Christian East.[45] Ware added, however, that even this concession to a small measure of jurisdiction falls far short of the supreme and universal jurisdiction ascribed to the Pope by the First Vatican Council.[46] Orthodoxy adheres to a balance of regionally independent structures within an ordered system of seniority, with Rome functioning as "the elder brother," on the basis of history.

ORIENTAL ORTHODOX ECCLESIOLOGY

The Oriental Orthodox churches are generally aligned with the Eastern Orthodox in their views on primacy and conciliarity. The structures of the Oriental churches are similar to the Eastern Orthodox.[47] Each Oriental church has a primate, who governs the church with a synod of bishops, and has some level of lay participation. The Armenian Apostolic church grants more authority to its primate, the catholicos, on the basis of Armenian tradition. The catholicos has privileges belonging only to his office, including the right to ordain bishops (with two or three other bishops, but the catholicos must participate) and to consecrate chrism. Furthermore, the Armenian catholicos is the only bishop consecrated.[48] Otherwise, differences between Oriental and Eastern Orthodox structures are not particularly significant, as the individual primates of the autocephalous

Eastern Orthodox churches have varying degrees of authority on the basis of their statutes.

Here it is important to note the differences between the Eastern Orthodox, Oriental Orthodox, and Eastern Catholic churches on the historical legacy of conciliarity.[49] On the one hand, all the churches state their reverence for conciliarity. On the other hand, the Oriental churches are unwilling to honor the ecumenical nature of the councils after Ephesus in 431, and the Eastern Orthodox count seven, with Nicaea II in 787 the final one. Furthermore, there is no agreement on the mechanism for convening a new ecumenical council were the churches to act on taking further steps toward unification.

DISPUTES ON CONSTANTINOPLE'S AUTHORITY

The primacy claimed by Constantinople has caused problems in recent decades, especially as it pertains to matters of international church order. Constantinople's assertion of its right as the mother of all Orthodox churches and sole giver of autocephaly is rejected by several churches. Many Orthodox describe Constantinople as the first among equals, while Archbishop Elpidophoros rather famously argued that it is the first without equals.[50] The most urgent crises arise when there is a severe dispute either within an autocephalous church or between two churches, and there is no mediator possessing the authority to intervene and act. The churches of Antioch and Jerusalem have a longstanding dispute over parishes in Qatar that caused schism. The crisis in Ukrainian Orthodoxy needed more firm intervention long before Constantinople entered the picture in 2018. The Orthodox churches will have to weigh all of their options as they continue to consider how primacy should be exercised. One thing is clear: Orthodox will always consider Jesus Christ to be the head of the church and the Holy Scriptures and tradition to be its primary sources for faith and order.

ECCLESIOLOGY FOR ORDINARY PEOPLE: PARISH, DIOCESE, PRIEST, BISHOP

The overview of Orthodox ecclesiology reveals a view of the Church as presented by specialists. Most people experience church at the most local and intimate level – their home parish. Parishioners who belong to the same parish over an extended period of time are likely to know their own pastor, perhaps a deacon and other assistants, and the choir director. On some occasions, Orthodox parishes come together for special occasions, like a temple feast, and parishioners get to know clergy and parishioners from other churches. The diocesan bishop will schedule visits to the parishes in his diocese, so a parish might see their bishop on occasion, though not usually more than once a year. The life of the parish is usually limited to their local experience of their pastor and assisting clergy, with these exceptions noted. How, then, does the parish itself represent the other marks of Orthodox ecclesiology, such as the oversight of the bishop? Who exercises authority within the parish, and how?

Orthodoxy does not have a universal model for parish administration. In principle, the pastor is the parish's leader, but it is customary for the pastor to work together with the people in administering the community. The pastor typically has complete authority over the parish's liturgical practices. The people can request and suggest modifications, and the pastor can adopt them, with the bishop's permission. Most parishes have a council, and the pastor works with this group in administering the parish.

Orthodox parish councils vary in their level of authority. In many instances, the pastor cannot make unilateral decisions, and occasionally, parishes handle clergy compensation and review. In some instances, the diocesan or national church structure will create guidelines for clergy compensation, and the parish must adhere to these. Parish councils also cannot supervise clergy, at least in principle. The bishop oversees clergy conduct and may appoint a dean (senior priest) to regulate local issues.

Parish participation in diocesan and national church life is important, and this matter can become complicated, especially with the turbulence that has afflicted Orthodoxy in the post-Soviet period. When a diocese needs a new bishop, each church has different procedures for nominating and selecting a new leader. In some instances, the laity can nominate candidates and participate in electing them at a diocesan assembly. In other instances, the bishops nominate and elect candidates. The issue can become quite contentious at the highest level, the primate of an autocephalous or autonomous church. The Moscow Council here is instructive. In the council's initial ballot, Metropolitan Antony (Khrapovitsky) won the most votes, with Metropolitan Tikhon (Bellavin) second. The council of 1917–1918 elected the patriarch by renewing the practice of drawing lots, which would indicate God's choice. Tikhon was elected and enthroned patriarch, despite Antony's majority in the initial round of voting.

The Moscow Council employed a conciliar method of nominating and electing a candidate. The inclusion of laypeople in the process was unprecedented, considered to be a restoration of older church practices in which all of the people participated. Some of the Orthodox churches reserve the election of a new leader to the bishops alone. This was the process used by the church of Bulgaria in their recent process of enthroning Patriarch Daniel in 2024. Only the bishops participated in the process of nominating and electing the new patriarch.

The Coptic church has a distinct tradition of electing a new pope.[51] The Coptic church establishes a nominating committee that works with the entire church, including the laity, to receive nominations. The process even permits a fifteen-day period of time for people to challenge the nominations, which the committee reviews. Elections are held on the 150th day after the death of the previous pope, yielding three finalists. The names of the finalists are placed in a sealed "altar ballot," and a boy between the ages of five and eight is selected at random to draw the name of the new pope from the box – the boy is blindfolded during the drawing.

Many Orthodox churches have lay representation in the deliberation processes of the institutional church structures. For example, a parish would typically send their priest and one or more laypeople to a diocesan or all-church assembly. The inclusion of laypeople honors the fullness of the priesthood of the laity while preserving the hierarchical structure of the church. The reservation of ordination to all major orders to men in the Eastern Orthodox churches reveals a major gender gap in church decision-making processes.

CONCLUSION

This chapter began with a bold assertion: the Orthodox Church defines itself as *the* one, holy, catholic, and apostolic church. Orthodoxy's exclusivist character shapes its structures, relations among the Orthodox churches, interactions with other churches and religious organizations, and view of the world. The survey of ecclesiological issues also reveals diverse opinions among Orthodox on the dynamics of their relationships with others.

This diversity occasions a closing reflection on the role the Orthodox Church could exercise in moving toward Christian unity. The human catastrophes caused by the wars of the twentieth century compelled some Orthodox figures to advocate for urgent progress toward reunion with the Catholic and Anglican churches. The Catholic Church's period of openness renewed dialogue with the Orthodox Church at a number of levels. Catholics and Orthodox created joint theological commissions to study the issues that had separated the churches historically and rediscovered common ground, especially in the church's conciliar tradition and its sacramental heritage. Catholics have taken several steps toward union with Orthodoxy, including recognizing the Eastern churches as fully legitimate sister churches and attempting to repair the relationship with Russia. The annulment of anathemas and exchange of the kiss of peace between Pope Paul VI and Patriarch Athenagoras of Constantinople in 1964 moved the two churches closer to an agreement.

The Eastern and Oriental Orthodox churches also renewed dialogue and made significant progress toward resolving the issues that had divided them since the Council of Chalcedon (451). In 1989 and 1990, a joint theological commission issued statements that the Oriental and Eastern Orthodox churches arrived at an agreement on their christological viewpoints, recommended the lifting of the anathemas, and the restoration of intercommunion between the churches.[52]

The fall of the Soviet Union and freedoms given to the Orthodox churches of the emerging nations placed additional stress on inter-Orthodox relations, which were already fragile. Divisions among the Orthodox deepened over these jurisdictional disputes. Orthodoxy's general turn toward increased moral rigor generated some tension with Roman Catholics, who were in a constant crisis with the cultural wars. Ultimately, Orthodoxy's failure to heal its own internal divisions pushed it further away from the pursuit of Christian unity that had characterized much of the twentieth century. The achievement of that unity seems as distant as ever, but the Orthodox Church has not remained static in its history, so new impulses toward unity remain within the realm of possibility.

NOTES

1. See "Relations of the Orthodox Church with the Rest of the Christian World," Relations of the Orthodox Church with the Rest of the Christian World – The Holy and Great Council of the Orthodox Church (holycouncil.org) (accessed August 12, 2024).
2. See John Baldovin, "The Fermentum at Rome in the Fifth Century: A Reconsideration," *Worship* 71, no. 1 (2005), 50–53.
3. An eparchy is based on the Roman province, a regional unit defined for administrative purposes. See Cyril Hovorun, *Scaffolds of the Church: Towards Poststructural Ecclesiology* (Eugene, OR: Cascade Books, 2017), 60.
4. Hovorun, *Scaffolds of the Church*, 50–72.
5. John Zizioulas, *Eucharist, Bishop, Church: The Unity of the Church in the Divine Eucharist and the Bishop during the First Three Centuries*, trans. Elizabeth Theotikroff (Brookline, MA: Holy Cross Orthodox Press, 2001), 111–125.
6. Radu Bordeianu, *Icon of the Kingdom of God: An Orthodox Ecclesiology* (Washington, DC: The Catholic University of America Press, 2023), 236–243.
7. Bordeianu, *Icon of the Kingdom of God*, 255–256.
8. Bordeianu, *Icon of the Kingdom of God*, 279–281.
9. Brian Daley, "The Meaning and Exercise of 'Primacies of Honor' in the Early Church," in *Primacy in the Church*, vol. 1, ed. John Chryssavgis (Crestwood, NY: St. Vladimir's Seminary Press, 2016), 35–37.
10. Bordeianu, *Icon of the Kingdom of God*, 281.
11. For a summary of central events, see Bryn Geffert and Theofanis Stavrou, eds., *Eastern Orthodoxy: The Essential Texts* (New Haven, CT: Yale University Press, 2016), 218–265.
12. For more on this matter, see Nicholas Denysenko, "The Eucharist and Orthodox Ecclesial Unity," in *Autocephaly. Coming of Age in Communion. Historical, Canonical, Liturgical, and Theological Studies*, eds. by Edward G., Farrugia, S.J., and Željko Paša, S.J. *Orientalia Christiana Analecta* 314–315 (Rome: Pontifical Oriental Institute, 2023), 843–863.
13. Dagmar Heller, "The (Holy and Great) Council of the Orthodox Churches: An Ecumenical Perspective," *The Ecumenical Review* 69, no. 2 (2017), 290 (288–300).
14. Carrie Frederick Frost, "Reflections on the Ordination of Deaconess Angelic," Reflections on the Ordination of Deaconess Angelic – Public Orthodoxy (accessed September 6, 2024).
15. Alexander Kazhdan, "Synodikon," in *The Oxford Dictionary of Byzantium*. https://www.oxfordreference.com/view/10.1093/acref/9780195046526.001.0001/acref-9780195046526-e-5255 (accessed September 13, 2024).
16. Frank Sysyn, "The Third Rebirth of the Ukrainian Autocephalous Orthodox Church and the Religious Situation in Ukraine, 1989–1991," in

Religion and Nation in Modern Ukraine, eds. Serhii Plokhy and Frank Sysyan (Edmonton: Canadian Institute of Ukrainian Studies, 2003), 92–93.
17 See Pan-Orthodox Council, "Autonomy and the Means by Which It Is Proclaimed," Autonomy and the Means by Which It Is Proclaimed – The Holy and Great Council of the Orthodox Church (holycouncil.org) (accessed September 9, 2024).
18 For an overview of the Orthodox church in Poland, see Edward Wynot, *The Polish Orthodox Church in the Twentieth Century and Beyond: Prisoner of History* (Lanham, MD: Lexington Books, 2015), 31–34.
19 Wynot, *The Polish Orthodox Church*, 62–64.
20 Wynot, *The Polish Orthodox Church*, 32.
21 See Nicholas Denysenko, *The Orthodox Church in Ukraine: A Century of Separation* (DeKalb, IL: Northern Illinois University Press, 2018).
22 John Erickson, "The Orthodox Church in America: Its Place in American and Global Orthodoxy," in *Autocephaly. Coming of Age in Communion. Historical, Canonical, Liturgical, and Theological Studies*, eds. by Edward G., Farrugia, S.J., and Željko Paša, S.J. *Orientalia Christiana Analecta* 314–315 (Rome: Pontifical Oriental Institute, 2023), 598.
23 See the translation of the 1993 text by John Erickson in Alexander Bogolepov, *Toward an American Orthodox Church*, foreword John H. Erickson (Crestwood, NY: St. Vladimir's Seminary Press, 2001), xvi–xix. The draft text is titled "Autocephaly and the Way it is to be Proclaimed."
24 Alexander Bogolepov, *Toward an American Orthodox Church*.
25 Secretariat for the Preparation for the Holy and Great Council of the Orthodox Church, *Synodika XII: IV Conférence Orthodoxe Préconciliaire, Chambésy 6–13 Juin 2009* (Chambésy: centre Orthodoxe du Patriarcat Oecuménique, 2015), preambule.
26 See "Resolutions of the Council of the Ukrainian Orthodox Church on May 27, 2022," Resolutions of the Council of the Ukrainian Orthodox Church of May 27, 2022 – Ukrainian Orthodox Church (uoc-news.church) (accessed September 6, 2024).
27 "Фактичний статус УПЦ більш автокефальний, ніж має «ПЦУ»," Фактичний статус УПЦ більш автокефальний, ніж має «ПЦУ» – Українська Православна Церква (church.ua) (accessed September 6, 2024).
28 "Філарет каже, що ПЦУ має стати самостійною і оновити статут," Філарет каже, що ПЦУ має стати самостійною і оновити статут | Українська правда (pravda.com.ua) (accessed September 6, 2024).
29 Hovorun, *Scaffolds of the Church*, 197–198.
30 See John Paul II, *Ut Unum Sint*, Ut Unum Sint (25 May 1995) | John Paul II (https://www.vatican.va/content/john-paul-ii/en/encyclicals/documents/hf_jp-ii_enc_25051995_ut-unum-sint.html) (accessed August 26, 2024).

31 See "Ecclesiological and Canonical Consequences for the Sacramental Nature of the Church: Ecclesial Communion, Conciliarity and Authority," Ravenna Document | Ecclesiological and Canonical Consequences of the Sacramental Nature of the Church. Ecclesial Communion, Conciliarity and Authority (https://www.christianunity.va/content/unitacristiani/en/dialoghi/sezione-orientale/chiese-ortodosse-di-tradizione-bizantina/commissione-mista-internazionale-per-il-dialogo-teologico-tra-la/documenti-di-dialogo/testo-in-inglese.html) (accessed August 26, 2024). This common statement of Catholic and Orthodox theologians is known as "The Ravenna Document."

32 See "Ecclesiological and Canonical Consequences," nos. 11–15.

33 Norman Tanner, ed., Decrees of the Ecumenical Councils (Washington, DC: Georgetown University Press, 1990), 7.

34 Robert Taft, "Holy Week in the Byzantine Tradition," in *Between Memory and Hope: Readings on the Liturgical Year,* ed. Maxwell Johnson (Collegeville, MN: Liturgical Press, 2000), 176–178 (155–181).

35 For an explanation of the original objectives of Vatican I concerning Papal infallibility, see Paul McPartlan, *A Service of Love: Papal Primacy, The Eucharist, and Church Unity* (Washington, DC: The Catholic University of America Press, 2023), 45–52.

36 See Alexander Schmemann, "The Idea of Primacy in Orthodox Ecclesiology," in *Primacy in the Church*, vol. 1, ed. John Chryssavgis (Crestwood, NY: St. Vladimir's Seminary Press, 2016), 345–347.

37 See David Bentley Hart, *Tradition and Apocalypse: An Essay on the Future of Christian Belief* (Grand Rapids, MI: Baker, 2022), 139–143.

38 For a detailed explanation, see Nicholas Denysenko, "Primacy, Synodality, and Collegiality in Orthodoxy: A Liturgical Model," *Journal of Ecumenical Studies* 48, no. 1 (2013), 20–44.

39 Nicholas Afanasiev, *Трапеза Господня* (Kyiv: Temple of St. Agapit, 2003), 11–14.

40 See Nicholas Afanasiev, *The Church of the Holy Spirit*, trans. Vitaly Permiakov, ed. Michael Plekon (Notre Dame: University of Notre Dame Press, 2007), 23–32.

41 Ksenia Luchenko, "The Anti-War Faction in the Russian Orthodox Church has Yet to Find Its Voice," https://carnegieendowment.org/russia-eurasia/politika/2024/02/the-anti-war-faction-in-the-russian-orthodox-church-has-yet-to-find-its-voice?lang=en (accessed October 18, 2024).

42 See Will Cohen's discussion of Constantinople's "Secondness" in *The Concept of 'Sister Churches' in Catholic-Orthodox Relations Since Vatican II,* Studia Oecumenica Friburgensia 67 (Eugene, OR: Wipf and Stock, 2017), 263–265, and McPartlan, *A Service of Love*, 55–58.

43 Kallistos Ware, "The Orthodox Church and the Primacy of Peter: Are We Any Closer to a Solution?" in *The Primacy of the Church*, vol. 2: *The Office of Primate and the Authority of Councils*, ed. John Chryssavgis (Crestwood, NY: St. Vladimir's Seminary Press, 2016), 868–869.
44 Ware, "The Orthodox Church."
45 Ware, "The Orthodox Church," 869.
46 Ware, "The Orthodox Church."
47 See the helpful descriptions of Oriental Orthodox church structures in Pro Oriente, *The Vienna Dialogue: Five Pro Oriente Consultations with Oriental Orthodoxy*, on Primacy, bk. 4 (Horn: Ferdinand Berger and Sohne, 1993), 56–67.
48 Oriente, *The Vienna Dialogue*, 61.
49 Oriente, *The Vienna Dialogue: Five Pro Oriente Consultations with Oriental Orthodoxy*, bk. 1 (Horn, Austria: Ferdinand Berger and Sohne, n.d.), 71.
50 Archbishop Elpidophoros (Lambridianis), "First Without Equals: A Response to the Text on Primacy by the Moscow Patriarchate," FIRST WITHOUT EQUALS – A Response to the Text on Primacy of the Moscow Patriarchate – Orthodox Christian Laity (ocl.org) (accessed August 26, 2024).
51 See "The Papal Selection Process for the Coptic Orthodox Church," The Coptic Orthodox Church UK: Search Results for Altar Ballot (copticcentre.blogspot.com) (accessed September 4, 2024). See "Bishop gives details for final details of Coptic Church's papal selection," Bishop Gives Details about Final Stage of Coptic Church's Papal Elections – Politics – Egypt – Ahram Online (accessed September 4, 2024).
52 See "First Agreed Statement (1989)," for a sample of the work accomplished by the Joint Commission at First Agreed Statement (1989) « Orthodox Unity (Orthodox Joint Commission) (wordpress.com) (accessed September 6, 2024).

ORTHODOXY IN THE TWENTY-FIRST CENTURY

The Orthodox Church has a reciprocal relationship with culture. Orthodoxy has contributed to the formation of local cultures, and the people have inscribed their culture on Church traditions and rituals. Orthodoxy has struggled most intensely in its encounter with modern culture. I'm using "modern" as an adjective quite loosely here, because many readers might ask about post-cultural modifiers. How has Orthodoxy confronted post-modernism? The arrival of the post-Christian era? Many Orthodox view secularism suspiciously and urge the church to resist the temptations of secularism.

Orthodoxy's difficulty in responding to public trends and cultural movements follows the patterns of many other Christian churches and faith communities. The Orthodox Church defines itself as the one, holy, catholic, and apostolic church, and therefore seizes exclusive Christian authority for itself. This exclusivity is naturally polarizing because Orthodox people tend to view themselves as in the world but not of it. Orthodoxy's encounter with culture, then, has yielded diverse outcomes. Sometimes, Orthodoxy clothes itself in culture, an implicit stamp of approval. At other times, the Orthodox Church takes an oppositional stance on cultural issues. There are also occasions on which Orthodoxy's positions on cultural issues are divided or inconsistent.

ECUMENICAL AND INTERRELIGIOUS DIALOGUE

The story of Orthodoxy's separation from the Roman church sounds dramatic, given the mutual excommunications between Rome and Constantinople in 1054. Scholars have suggested that the schism never penetrated the entire Orthodox world.[1] The Fourth Crusade

DOI: 10.4324/9781003433217-9

of 1204 and the ensuing destruction of Constantinople were probably the main cause of Orthodox grievances against the Catholic Church at least in the Greek-speaking part of the Orthodox world.

Orthodoxy's traditional aversion to pursuing reunion with the Roman church shifted during the catastrophes of the twentieth century. Bloody wars, shocking persecution of Christians by revolutionaries, the Holocaust and other genocides, and the human rights movement all contributed to a sense of urgency to set aside differences and find pathways for reunion. Russian Orthodox theologians participated in serious discussions with the Anglican church for the restoration of communion.[2] The Roman church made serious gestures of recognizing the fullness of Orthodoxy, especially in *Unitatis Redintegratio* of Vatican II and the doctrinal document *Dominus Iesus* of the Congregation for the Doctrine of Faith.[3] Pope Paul VI and Patriarch Athenagoras of Constantinople exchanged the kiss of peace and annulled the excommunications in 1964.

These gestures of openness for reconciliation are countered by Orthodox who argue for withdrawal from participation in interfaith dialogue groups and common prayer services.[4] Ardent opponents of ecumenism call for the rebaptism of Christians baptized in non-Orthodox churches and consider prayer with non-Orthodox to be forbidden. The strongest opponents of ecumenism discourage Orthodox Christians from praying for other Christians and other people.[5] At the official level, some Orthodox have demonstrated their displeasure with ecumenism by withdrawing delegations from ecumenical organizations. The Antiochian Archdiocese of North America withdrew their delegation from the National Council of Churches in 2005 to protest left-wing and right-wing extremist positions they deemed incompatible with Orthodoxy.[6]

In summary, there are two polarizing positions on ecumenism in Orthodoxy, along with an existing middle. At the official level, opponents of ecumenism claim that all non-Orthodox are not legitimately Christian because Orthodoxy is the church – the exclusivist position. Supporters of ecumenism promote dialogue, common prayer, education, and social ministry. Some Orthodox ecumenists push for the restoration of Eucharistic communion on the basis of the *una sancta*, the existence of one church despite disputes and divisions leaders cite to justify exclusivity.[7]

The middle ground is one that exists in practice, among the people. Many Orthodox people married to non-Orthodox spouses participate in both faiths. The Orthodox Church prohibits an Orthodox person from partaking of sacraments of a non-Orthodox Church, but many clergy are unaware of such instances or simply unwilling to enforce the rules. There is a living Orthodox ecumenism on the ground, among the people, even if officials do not acknowledge it.

MODERN ISSUES

We now turn to the topic du jour – gender, family life, and sexuality, the issues that divide all Christians, including Orthodox. The following sections briefly analyze how these issues are affecting the Orthodox Church.

HUMAN SEXUALITY

Orthodoxy teaches that God created human beings as sexual beings designed to procreate. Procreation is the primary purpose of sexuality, but not the only one. People can enjoy sexual activity together, but within the strict confines of a marriage between one husband and one wife. Orthodoxy teaches that all sexual activity outside of the marital bond is sinful.[8] These activities include fornication, masturbation, and same-sex activity. Fornication applies to any sexual activity between a man and a woman outside of marriage, and not only to people engaged in sexual activity before marriage.

The feast of the Conception of Mary Theotokos by Anna on December 9 symbolizes Orthodoxy's affirmation of sexuality as an expression of love. The icon for this feast depicts Mary's parents, Joachim and Anna, embracing one another. The Orthodox Church does not point to this feast as proof that Mary was also born without sin, like the Roman Catholic doctrine of the Immaculate Conception. Orthodoxy also does not emphasize conjugal love in the marital bond on this feast, but it is a secondary notion. For Orthodox marital sex between a husband and a wife is good, and the church urges couples to refrain from sex only during fasting periods.

It is essential to note here that the Orthodox Church permits laypeople to be married up to three times.[9] For Orthodox, second and third marriages are exceptions and concessions. Orthodoxy adheres to one marriage as the ideal for all people. The rules for clergy reveal Orthodoxy's preference for one marriage.[10] A married man who meets theological and other moral qualifications can be eligible for ordination to the diaconate and the priesthood. He must be married before the ordination – he cannot receive ordination and then marry.

By rule, any deacon or priest who divorces must be deposed unless he and his wife mutually agree to take on monastic vows. Widowed deacons and priests are forbidden from remarrying. There have been many attempts to allow a second marriage to widowed clergy in Orthodox Church history. Some bishops permit it in accordance with the principle of *oikonomia*, interpreting the canon within a case-by-case context. The Ecumenical Patriarchate of Constantinople is the first Orthodox Church that has publicized its new policy of allowing a second marriage to deacons and priests on the basis of examining a request.[11] The principles of an ideal Orthodox marriage apply to the spouse in these cases – she must be Orthodox and not previously married.

The main reason for prohibiting a second marriage to widowed and divorced clergy is sexual purity. Engaging in sexual relations with a second wife violates the norm of sex confined to one marital bed with one spouse. This norm supersedes mercy for the member of the clergy who bears no responsibility for his wife's death. Proponents of adherence to this rule note that the church does permit widowed clergy to remarry without the penalty of excommunication. They simply cannot remain active in ministry if they are married a second time.

CONTRACEPTION

Orthodoxy's positive appraisal of sex does not exclude questions about contraception and alternative methods of conception. The rite of marriage and Orthodox culture promote procreation. The Church does not have a consensus on contraception within marriage, though the Ecumenical Patriarchate of Constantinople permits contraception for married couples.[12] The Patriarchate of Constantinople acknowledges that some families have physical, psychological, spiritual, and financial impediments that make it wise to forego or delay having children, which warrant contraception.[13] The Russian Orthodox Church vehemently opposes most alternative means of conception, including in-vitro fertilization.[14]

AUTHORITY IN MARRIAGE

The Orthodox Church does not have an official teaching on the relationships between husband and wife in marriage. The church stayed out of marriage for most of the first millennium, until the desire of an emperor to marry multiple times intervened. The pastoral and theological thrust of marriage is that of blessing, joy, abundance, bearing witness to one another, and having children. There is nothing in the rite of marriage that states the authority of the husband over the wife. The appointed reading from Ephesians (5:20–33) includes the passage of the wife respecting her husband. Some clergy have taken this passage and interpreted it to mean that the wife must be subordinate to the husband. Others emphasize the theological theme of the rite – the two becoming one and submitting themselves to one another, which is also in the Ephesians passage. Some couples have requested a different reading to replace the Ephesians pericope. Paul Evdokimov described the denigration of women as the desecration of love, filled with lies and hypocrisy, and appealed for a vision of marriage that was true to the Gospel.[15] Alkiviadis Calivas expresses the mainstream Orthodox view of marriage by describing the spouses as equal, yet relating to one another according to an order established by God, with the husband taking the lead and the two complementing one another.[16]

Carrie Frederick Frost has recently addressed issues of women in the church and gender-based authority. Frost has compared the edenic view of gender with the eschatological.[17] The edenic paradigm makes the relationship between Adam and Eve in Genesis 3 paradigmatic for male-female relationships in the world. The priestly editor of this foundational biblical story presented the story within a patriarchal context. Christian exegesis of the story does not require the wife to be subordinate to her husband, despite the fact that the edenic perspective assumes that humanity's state after the fall from paradise (sometimes called postlapsarian) remains intact even after the incarnation of Jesus Christ. Frost maintains that the patriarchal model of female subordination to men is antithetical to Orthodox theological anthropology.[18] Some might say that the eschatological perspective makes more sense because humanity is in a constant state of becoming, and human nature will no longer be gendered in the next age, in God's kingdom. Frost suggests that the eschatological perspective need not diminish features that come with gender but instead calls upon Orthodox theologians to consider how the different gifts of the sexes might lead to deification.[19]

Another approach to understanding the relationship between spouses comes from Baptism in Christ. Baptism and anointing make each person into a priest, prophet, and king, and also a servant of God.[20] Baptism does not eliminate gender or other worldly identities. One can be both a servant of God and a husband, wife, parent, grandparent, and single person. Baptism does not erase these roles and identities, but it makes each person equal before God. No husband ranks ahead of his wife in the church because both are baptized and anointed.

Ultimately, Orthodox families work these issues out on their own without asking for the Church's opinion. The husband is the head of some households, the wife presides over others, and elsewhere, the two work things out as they go through their marriage. One might laughingly dismiss the famous line from My Big Fat Greek Wedding, when Maria tells Tula that the husband is the head, but the wife is the neck who governs the head's direction. The statement runs true in some families. Overemphasizing authority in the household can cause problems, however. The sacramentality of marriage draws from a constant exchange of love and mutual bearing witness to the cross. Orthodox couples that focus on loving one another won't need to worry about authority because it will fall into its proper place within the dynamic stream of mutual love in Christ.

SAME-SEX ATTRACTION AND RELATIONSHIPS

Orthodoxy is one of many conservative churches that firmly opposes same-sex relationships.[21] Many of the autocephalous churches have criticized the legalization of same-sex marriage in civil society. None of the Orthodox churches blesses the rite of marriage for same-sex couples. Orthodoxy's teaching is based on biblical passages that condemn same-sex activity and a theological anthropology asserting that same-sex attraction is contrary to human nature.

Orthodox positions on same-sex relationships in the church vary outside of the opposition to marriage.[22] Brandon Gallaher and Gregory Tucker note that Orthodox are divided on baptizing children of same-sex families, giving communion to people in same-sex partnerships and marriages, differentiating between same-sex attraction and activity, and conversion therapy.[23] Some Orthodox scholars believe that same-sex attraction and relationships are not only natural but also represent a healthy exchange of love. People in this group suggest that the church needs to respect the basic human dignity and rights of homosexuals and that sexual attraction is not a matter of doctrine.

The most ardent opponents of tolerating same-sex couples in the Church assert that sexual orientation is a theological issue because God created humans as male and female and instructed them to procreate. Adherents of this school of thought believe that tolerating same-sex relationships is heretical because it violates the basic tenets of theological anthropology.

A recent episode in Greece caused a controversy. Archbishop Elpidophoros of the Greek Orthodox Archdiocese of America baptized two children of a same-sex couple in Athens, despite the objections of the Church of Greece.[24] This act raised questions on how a rigorous church position applies to the children of people living in a manner the church disapproves.

COHABITATION, POLYAMORISM, AND PAN-SEXUALITY

Studies of contemporary relationships reveal new emerging patterns. Marriage itself is in decline, and many couples cohabitate instead of marrying. Orthodoxy views marriage as a sacrament, and the church would urge couples to marry instead of cohabitating. The church regards cohabitation as sinful, even in instances where one of the partners risks the loss of financial benefits if they choose to marry.[25] Two new trends have emerged that the church has yet to address. These are polyamorism and pan-sexuality. Polyamorism embraces having multiple partners simultaneously, and pan-sexuality is embracing all types of sexual partnerships. The church's endorsement of the marriage of a husband and wife excludes the possibility of approving polyamorism and pan-sexuality, though the church has yet to comment officially on these new trends.

The final issue concerns the vocation of the single person who does not have a monastic vocation. The number of people who identify as single with no intention of marriage or even dating is increasing in society. Some people create chosen families and opt to live together under one household without blood relations or committed monogamous or polygamous relationships. Orthodoxy is in the beginning stages of developing a public vision for the Christian vocation of the single person.

In conclusion, the Orthodox Church assumes that people will opt either for married family life consisting of one husband and one wife or live as celibates. The church rejects a number of defined relationships that openly embrace sexual activity outside of a heterosexual conjugal union. The church's affirmation of the sacramentality of marriage with the assumption of procreation is the primary motivator for rejecting alternative committed relationships. The church defines marriage as a union of love, with Christ standing at the center of the love of a husband, wife, and their children. Orthodoxy would encourage people who claim to be in committed heterosexual relationships to seek marriage because love and commitment are intertwined. The varying positions on same-sex relationships and the absence of commentary on other relationship patterns reveal both the church's loyalty to heterosexual marriage as its preferred norm (along with celibacy) and its articulation of theological anthropology as a work in progress. Society and culture are changing rapidly, and Orthodoxy refuses to conform under duress. Orthodoxy is in the process of coming to terms with its core values as it considers the cultural changes happening around it. It is not surprising that the church would issue public comments on teachings at its own pace.

THE ORDINATION OF WOMEN

The chapter on liturgy noted that the Orthodox Church once ordained deaconesses and never abolished the practice. The first ordination of a woman to a presiding order of ministry took place in a Protestant denomination in the nineteenth century. Numerous mainline Protestant churches began to ordain women as pastors in the late twentieth century.[26] The Orthodox Church participated in the public theological discourse on the possibility of ordaining women, with varying opinions.[27] Conservative theologians like Alexander Schmemann opposed the practice, whereas Kallistos Ware thought it was theologically possible. Orthodox participation in the public discussion was limited mostly to ecumenical engagement with other Christians.

The twentieth and twenty-first centuries have witnessed a resurgence in debate on the possibility of ordaining women to ministry in Orthodoxy.[28] Most of the discussion has concerned the possibility of reinstituting the order of deaconess. Numerous historians and theologians, such as Evangelos Theodorou, Kyriaki FitzGerald, Valerie Karras, and Carrie Frederick Frost, have supported the reinstitution of the order of deaconess. The Patriarchate of Alexandria appointed four deaconesses to perform missionary work in 2017. They did not use the medieval Byzantine form for the ordination of a deaconess, but used a modified ritual designed for minor clergy. Alexandria's commitment to ordaining deaconesses remained intact. In 2024, on Holy Thursday, the diocese of Zimbabwe ordained a deaconess in traditional diaconal vestments, who then exercised the usual ministry of deacons at the Divine Liturgy.[29] None of the other Orthodox churches commented publicly on the ordination, though it generated numerous objections on social media. There is no evidence suggesting that other Orthodox churches are going to adopt the recent practice of the Alexandrian Patriarchate, as of this writing.

The question of women's service in the Orthodox Church emerged in the late nineteenth century. Historians and theologians of the Russian Orthodox Church adopted a positive outlook on the restoration of the female diaconate, noting the need for woman-to-woman ministry in the church.[30] Women's ministries had existed in the period following the disappearance of deaconesses and the modern era. Female monastics performed numerous ministries in monasteries throughout the Orthodox world. Abbesses and advanced monastics can hear confessions (without granting absolution), and women perform the chanting and singing and lend the assistance needed in and near the altar.

Blueprints for a restored female diaconate differed. Some imagined a ministry limited to celibate, older women who would be responsible for catechizing women, providing spiritual direction, and exercising healing ministries. Advanced blueprints called for a female diaconate that was exactly the same as the male – women performing all ministries belonging to the diaconate, from assisting at Eucharistic liturgies to bringing Holy Communion to the sick.[31]

A protest to the call for a female diaconate surfaced, especially in North America. Two figures are the primary ideologues opposing the restoration of the female diaconate: Lawrence Farley, a priest of the Orthodox Church in America, and Brian Patrick Mitchell, a deacon of the Russian Orthodox Church Outside of Russia.[32] Farley contends that there is no discernible pastoral need for deaconesses. Presbyters and deacons can handle the necessary ministries, and the answer to expanding ministry to all is to restore tasks that once belonged to the laity, which would allow all lay men and women access to certain ministries. Mitchell argued that the female diaconate was small, geographically confined, and fell into disuse because it was no longer needed. Both Farley and Mitchell believe that the restoration movement is motivated by leftist politics. Some opponents of a restored order of deaconess refer to the introduction of women to ordained ministry in Protestant churches as a false blueprint to follow, noting that this decision was politically motivated. They tend to argue that restoring deaconesses would function like a trojan horse and pollute Orthodoxy with leftist politics.

Women's ministries have evolved in the Orthodox Church. The veneration of Mary became widespread in the fifth century, especially with the dedication of numerous churches to her, along with a vibrant following of women devoting themselves to virginity. The Church honored the sanctity of other women, including St. Helen (Constantine's mother), St. Nino (evangelizer of Georgia), and St. Macrina, the sister of saints Basil and Gregory, the great Cappadocians. Stories written in honor of the sanctity of these women established blueprints for female saints who stood on equal footing with men in the Church.

In the modern era, women were introduced into choirs in the eighteenth century, and women began to lead choirs, performing a crucial ministerial function. Women also began to preside over parishes in lay capacities, often as members or presidents of parish councils.[33] The Philoptochos Society of the Greek Orthodox Church is a formidable women's group that serves the church. Women can chant, but they are not typically tonsured as chanters. At some point in Orthodox Church history, the office of reader (or chanter) became connected to the priesthood. Orthodoxy began to define the minor orders as steps one must take before they are ordained priest. Bishops tonsured readers only so they could take the next steps toward ordination to priest. The restoration of the office of reader could open the doors to women exercising the office – especially since they perform the task frequently.

Readers should note that the Orthodox Church's Eucharistic revival did not entail a broad expansion of which ministers were blessed to distribute Holy Communion. Many, but not all, Orthodox churches restored the practice of permitting deacons to assist with Communion distribution. Some Orthodox churches refuse to even permit deacons to assist. Orthodoxy does not have a ministry of extraordinary ministers of Holy Communion like the Roman church, where some lay people are blessed to distribute Communion.

While Orthodoxy never abolished the order of deaconess, the church has never ordained women as presbyters (priests) or bishops. For most of its history, the Orthodox Church did not explain its rationale for ordaining only men as bishops and priests, as men presided in Christian congregations of all backgrounds until the nineteenth and especially twentieth centuries. When the Episcopalian Church's ordination of the Philadelphia Eleven in 1974 blazed a path for women to ministry, the Catholic and Orthodox churches did not follow suit. Pope John Paul II attempted to permanently prevent Catholics from discussing the matter with his encyclical letter *Ordinatio Sacerdotalis*.[34] John Paul II essentially argued that Jesus's appointment of only men as apostles did not permit the Church to ordain women.

Orthodox theologians joined the ecumenical discussion on the possibility of ordaining women as priests. Prominent theologians found themselves on opposite sides. Kallistos Ware stated that there was no theological prohibition against women's ordination.[35] Many Orthodox adopt the same rationale as John Paul II, claiming that ordaining women would violate Jesus's institution of the priesthood. Other Orthodox theologians argue that only men can be priests because they are icons of Jesus himself, who was incarnate as a male human. Thomas Hopko argued that ordained ministry is masculine.[36] Hopko stated that men and women are indeed equal before God but also different, so ordained ministry was gendered. Currently, some Orthodox scholars are challenging the prevalence of gender essentialism, the status quo of declaring Orthodox men and women to be equal but different, as a justification for prohibiting women from exercising leadership in the church.[37]

The relationship between political leanings and the revival of the ministry of deaconess tends to be overstated within the broader

Orthodox community.[38] The Armenian apostolic church had historically ordained deaconesses, whose ministries were not identical to those of the male deacons. The Armenian female diaconate originated as early as the ninth century in female monasteries.[39] The Armenian rejuvenation of the order of deaconess in the twentieth century occurred concurrently with an attempt to bolster female monastic life and also to strengthen catechetics in parish communities.[40] The Armenian Christian people rank near the top in their conservative views on social issues among the Orthodox in the world.[41] Their social conservatism has not impeded a revival of the female diaconate for the purpose of strengthening parish ministry. The Armenian ordination of deaconesses serves as a reminder that the Churches draw from their own historical traditions to appoint men and women to perform the ministries established by Jesus Christ and the apostolic tradition.

Orthodox theologians and people find themselves all over the map on the question of the ordination of women to ministry. The discussion on ordaining women to the priesthood (or episcopate) has not evolved into a movement within the church and is unlike the restoration of the female diaconate in this way. Some of the leaders of the restoration of the deaconess, like Carrie Frost, have stated that they are seeking to restore an existing order and not use the movement to push women into the priesthood or episcopate.

The changes that occurred in Protestant churches with women's ministry and the movement to restore deaconesses in Orthodoxy had two certain outcomes. First, both movements catalyzed a debate on the history and theology of ordained ministry and raised important new questions on theological anthropology. Second, the changes introduced fear that reviving the deaconess order would be a Trojan horse for liberalizing the church among some Orthodox clergy and people. This fear stimulated defensive postures and an appeal for maintaining the status quo of men only in ministry. The ordination of deaconesses in the Alexandrian patriarchate shows that the movement has yielded a local restoration of deaconesses. Only time will tell if any of the other Orthodox churches adopt the blueprints of the Alexandrian and Armenian churches.

Perhaps the most important issue concerning women in the church is the depiction of their characteristics and behaviors. Alice-Mary Talbot observed that the ideal ascetic life for female monastics was described with male metaphors.[42] Talbot says that women monastics were expected to have masculine qualities and to rise up above the frailty of their gender to obtain the strength necessary to overcome powerful adversaries.[43] Honoring the sanctity of women who follow God with symbols and language anchored in non-masculine metaphors remains an ongoing task for Orthodox theology.

PEACE AND NONVIOLENCE

Orthodoxy's preference for regional church structures and its acceptance of national identity have created problems in the twenty-first century. There have been numerous instances of oppression of national and religious minorities in the Church's history. The Bulgarian push for autonomy in the declining years of the Ottoman Empire represented the frustration of national minorities with the preferential treatment for Greeks practiced by the Ecumenical Patriarchate of Constantinople within the Ottoman Rum millet. The entire history of the movement for Ukrainian autocephaly has featured their frustration with the Russian Orthodox Church prohibiting the use of Ukrainian for liturgical celebration. The emergence of nation-states in the nineteenth through the twenty-first centuries revealed multiple instances of the Church endorsing political slogans and even justifying the use of violence. This issue is frequently debated – one might object to a criticism of Russian bishops encouraging soldiers to defeat Nazi invaders in World War II as a justifiable use of violence.

The culture war erupted, however, with the Russian invasion of Ukraine that began in 2014 and escalated with a full-scale invasion in 2022. The violence began when President Victor Yanukovych authorized the Berkut riot police to use deadly force to dispel protesters in Kyiv in 2013. The crowd was protesting Yanukovych's reversal of Ukraine's accession to the European Union. When Ukraine forced Yanukovych out of office and elected a new president who resumed the course to association with the European Union, Russia began to use military force in Crimea and Donbas, in part to punish Ukraine.

More importantly, the Russian Orthodox Church justified the use of violent force on several occasions, beginning with the sermon of Patriarch Kirill on March 6, 2022, that depicted the war on the ground as an image of a metaphysical war between good and evil.[44] Kirill complained that Ukraine's government forced gay parades on the people of Donbas against their will as an example of alleged persecution. Kirill's rhetoric developed over time to eventually include a labeling of the Ukrainian government as a persecutor of the Orthodox Church and a successor to the Bolshevik regime in July 2023.[45] The boldest action was the Russian church's adoption of the Russian World Foundation's identification of Russia as the Restrainer anointed by God to defend the world against assaults on Christianity and Christian values.[46]

Russia's invasion of Ukraine reveals a serious fault line in Orthodoxy's encounter with the culture wars. Ukraine's desire for accession to the European Union was designed to preserve sovereignty and territorial integrity, provide more economic and educational opportunities for their citizens and businesses, and stabilize their currency. Russia had contested Ukraine's statehood and attempted to keep Ukraine within its economic and cultural orbit since the fall of the Soviet Union. Russian politicians perceived the Euromaidan protest as Ukraine's betrayal of Russia on multiple fronts. One of these was moral and cultural, as belonging to the European Union could amount to a rejection of Orthodox moral values.[47] Church leaders like Patriarch Kirill justified the use of violence to protect Russia from alien moral values approaching its border via Ukraine. The problem, though, is that Ukrainians remain somewhat conservative socially and would argue that they weren't abandoning moral values that posed a threat to Orthodoxy. Many Ukrainians argued that Russia's use of violence was morally reprehensible.

Russia's invasion of Ukraine has caused a human catastrophe on the largest scale since World War II. The war reveals a problem afflicting Orthodoxy before the events of 2014 – the absence of a firm position on war, peace, and nonviolence. Orthodox ethicist Perry Hamalis has recently proposed Orthodoxy's adoption of just peacemaking and Christian realism as the anchors for its war ethics.[48]

The bottom line, however, is that Orthodox people disagree on the tactics the Orthodox Church might adopt to preserve its values. Some Orthodox Church leaders and people support the Russian church's endorsement of Russia's invasion of Ukraine. Others support the use of violence to defend nation-states that adhere to more conservative religious morals and values.

TWO SOCIAL CONCEPT TEACHINGS

Two important documents have been published by the Orthodox Church in the last twenty-five years. These are the *Basis of the Social Concept of the Russian Orthodox Church*, released in 2000 by the Moscow Patriarchate (BSC). The second is *For the Life of the World: Toward a Social Ethos of the Orthodox Church* (FLOW), published by the Ecumenical Patriarchate of Constantinople in 2021. Regina Elsner, a Catholic theologian specializing in Orthodox theology, summarizes the context of the creation of the two documents aptly.[49] Elsner describes the context of the writing of BSC as taking place during a time of significant political and social turmoil during the 1990s, written to fill a glaring pastoral need, to state the church's position, teachings, and guidance in the first years of the Russian Federation following the fall of the Soviet Union.[50] FLOW was written by a team of theologians representing diverse backgrounds, many of whom teach and research in multidisciplinary contexts of non-Orthodox universities.[51] BSC is not as extensive as flow because the need to compose and publish a serviceable text addressing areas did not give the authors the luxury of time for repetitive engagement. The diverse backgrounds explain the differences in the two texts, but they remain significant because they address issues that are central to Orthodox thought and identity in the present.

THE SOCIAL CONCEPT OF THE RUSSIAN ORTHODOX CHURCH (2000)

The Russian Orthodox Church published BSC in 2000, just nine years following the fall of the Soviet Union and the ushering in of new freedoms for Orthodoxy. This document became an important reference for Orthodox teachings. Orthodoxy relies on the ecumenical councils and the corpus of canon law for its doctrine, but it is unlike the Roman Catholic, Lutheran, and Anglican churches in that it does not have a particular compendium of documents that represents the core of its teachings. The Roman Catholic Church has both the lengthy declarations of the Second Vatican Council and numerous letters and apostolic constitutions of popes that belong to the highest level of Catholic teaching. The Lutheran churches have the Augsburg confession, and the Anglican communion has the Articles of Religion.

BSC has sixteen sections discussing a number of core issues for the church, beginning with relations between the church and nation and church and state and continuing with topics like war and peace and bioethics before concluding with a chapter on international relations. The section on church and nation endorses a healthy Christian patriotism and claims that a country with a monoconfessional Orthodox community can be considered an Orthodox nation.[52] The section on church and state generally calls upon the people to obey civil authorities but also endorses resistance and refusal to cooperate in certain instances.[53] The sections discussing specific instances of church-state relations balance separation of the two entities with potential areas of intersection that fall far short of the possibility of the church promoting or carrying out a political agenda.[54] It does, however, permit the formation of Orthodox political organizations and units within larger political parties, as long as participation is limited to the laity.[55]

The section on personal, family, and public morality holds up a traditional Orthodox model. This section denounces sexual activity outside of marriage and even states the Church's disapproval of second marriage quite clearly while allowing for it as a concession.[56] This section holds up the family as the most important social institution of society and, perhaps most significantly, asserts the fundamental equality of men and women and their clear distinction in gender and gender roles.[57] BSC states that any attempt to minimize the natural differences between men and women in social fields is "alien to the church mind."[58] BSC explicitly condemns pornography and forms of mass media that might be harmful to young people but clarifies that this caution should not be received as discouraging healthy sexual relations between a married couple.[59] BSC describes these relations as "blessed by God."[60]

BSC's declarations on conception and contraception are notable. BSC condemns abortion and also medical methods of conception that are outside of God's design, calling upon a couple struggling to conceive to accept "childlessness" as a special calling in life.[61] BSC also condemns surrogate motherhood, cloning, stem cell research, and certain forms of organ donation and transplant. The condemnation stated with perhaps the most fervor is that of homosexuality, which BSC "unequivocally deplores" and calls a "vicious distortion" of God's creation.[62]

BSC's condemnation of homosexuality extends to disapproving of homosexuals being allowed to educate young people and prohibits transsexuals from ordination to holy orders.[63]

BSC's final section addresses international relations, globalization, and secularism. The document sends mixed messages on these matters, dancing carefully around international relations, prioritizing advocacy for national interests over those of other nations, and calling for severe restraint in the use of armed forces – only as a last resort.[64] The section on established conventions for respecting sovereignty and territorial integrity is problematic, however. BSC states that there is a contradiction between respect for sovereignty and territorial integrity and movements for state independence. BSC becomes more clear in its intention by arguing that the Church "grieves" when the historical community of a people is destroyed through the division of a multiethnic state.[65] The document adds that the division of a multiethnic state is justified only when one of the people is oppressed or a majority of the people do not wish to remain within the multiethnic state. The opacity of this statement cannot conceal the reality of Russian political ideology of the 1990s and in the years following, where Russians overwhelmingly believed that Russians, Ukrainians, and Belorussians were one and the same nation.[66] The final notable statement of BSC concerns the Russian church's reservation of the right to reject a world order anchored in a "human personality darkened by sin."[67] This statement previews the church's reservation of its right to push for the inscription of Christian values on global structures.

FOR THE LIFE OF THE WORLD (ECUMENICAL PATRIARCHATE OF CONSTANTINOPLE)

FLOW was released in the midst of the coronavirus pandemic, when the social issues constantly confronting church and society converged and exploded. FLOW addresses issues with a degree of authority often sparse in Orthodoxy. FLOW cautions Orthodox from subscribing to the nostalgia of a select golden age, such as the Byzantine empire or the age of the apostles.[68] FLOW also warns Orthodox Christians on the perils of using political coercion to advance their opinions or agendas, and calls upon the people to refrain from demonizing others, even if their positions do not align with Orthodoxy.[69] FLOW welcomes pluralism and advises the people to refrain from fearing diversity.[70]

FLOW makes an original contribution in calling upon Orthodox Christians to "protect and advance human rights everywhere" as a fundamental right that honors the fullness of the human dignity of each person.[71] The document condemns racism and calls upon Orthodoxy to fight against slavery in all of its forms.[72] The document emphasizes the church's responsibility to protect the vulnerable in this world and prioritizes the protection of children and even the necessity of divorce in certain instances for the sake of protecting a family's most vulnerable members.[73] FLOW also mentions the Church's responsibility to provide mental, emotional, and material support to single parents and to offer Baptism to all children, regardless of the "manner in which they were conceived or adopted."[74]

FLOW provides perhaps the most nuanced and careful language on the thorny matter of sexuality. The document explains the cultural moment, noting that the process of a young person leaving their parents and starting their own household has evolved drastically, along with the evolution of sexuality into both a consumer strategy and consumer product.[75] FLOW uses this statement to foreground the commentary on sexual identity. The document affirms the "basic right" of each person to have a sexual identity that is free from persecution and legal disadvantage in society.[76] It goes on to state, however, that human identity is not exclusively sexual. Being made in the image and likeness of God is the core of human identity for everyone. FLOW holds two teachings together that have potentially major pastoral consequences. First, everyone is called to observe sexual continence, both inside and outside of marriage. Second, Orthodox Christians must not discriminate or hate anyone on the basis of their sexual identity.

FLOW addresses gender issues and shares a similarity with BSC by acknowledging the differences and distinctions among men and women, held together by equality.[77] FLOW laments the development of certain ritual practices that exclude, diminish, and even punish women because of menstruation or other forms of bleeding. FLOW also acknowledges the possibility of renewing the female diaconate.[78]

FLOW provides a much-needed update and an essential resource document for Orthodox Christians to navigate the world they inhabit.

The document is not immune to criticism. Will Cohen notes the absence of examination of primacy, especially with regard to relations with the Roman Catholic Church – he calls it the "elephant" in the room.[79] Evgeny Pilipenko argues that FLOW indulges in an oversacralization of creation, stating that it takes the language too far.[80] Teachings like BSC and FLOW simply won't satisfy everyone, especially when they are created by communities of theologians. The documents are different, and they represent Orthodox Christianity's diversity.

CONCLUSION

The revolutions of the twentieth and twenty-first centuries have permeated the Orthodox Church. Orthodoxy has had to respond to pastoral issues on its relationship with the state, the legitimate use of force and violence, its public positions on abortion and contraception, its opinions on the roles of women in the church, and its policies on the participation of LGBTQ people in church life. The public perception of Orthodoxy is that it adopts a more conservative approach on cultural issues, and while survey data supports this assertion in general, Orthodox people hold diverse opinions on all of these issues. The publication of BSC and FLOW shows a concerted pastoral effort on the part of the Orthodox Church to engage an ever-changing world. The divergences of the two documents reveal a consistency in Orthodoxy – there is no absolute consensus within the church on responding pastorally and theologically to the issues of the twenty-first century.

NOTES

1 See David Bentley Hart, "The Myth of Schism," in *Ecumenism Today: The Universal Church in the 21st Century,* eds. Francesca Murphy and Christopher Asprey (Lanham, MD: Ashgate, 2008). Online version: Clarion: Journal of Spirituality and Justice – The Myth of Schism – David Bentley Hart (clarion-journal.com) (accessed August 30, 2024).

2 See the history of the Fellowship of St. Alban and St. Sergius at History | Fellowship of St Alban & St Sergius (fsass.org) (accessed August 30, 2024). For a rigorous exploration of these issues, see Brandon Gallaher, "Bulgakov and Intercommunion," *Sobornost* 24, no. 2 (2002), 9–28.

3 Second Vatican Council, "Unitatis Redintegratio," Unitatis redintegratio (https://www.vatican.va/archive/hist_councils/ii_vatican_council/documents/vat-ii_decree_19641121_unitatis-redintegratio_en.html) (accessed August 30, 2024). Congregation for the Doctrine of Faith, "Declaration 'Dominus Iesus' on the Unicity and Salvific Universality of Jesus Christ and the Church," Dominus Iesus (https://www.vatican.va/roman_curia/congregations/cfaith/documents/rc_con_cfaith_doc_20000806_dominus-iesus_en.html) (accessed August 30, 2024).
4 For a thorough overview of renowned anti-ecumenists and their arguments, see Paul Ladouceur, "Neo-Traditionalist Ecclesiology in Orthodoxy," *Scottish Journal of Theology* 72, no. 4 (2019), 398–413.
5 Some churches that use prayer lists adopt a middle ground by including "non-Orthodox" as a category.
6 "Antioch Exits National Council of Churches," https://www.tmatt.net/columns/2005/08/antioch-exits-national-council-of-churches (accessed August 30, 2024).
7 For a classical argument of the existence of the *una sancta*, see Nicholas Afanasiev, "Una Sancta," in *Tradition Alive: On the Church and the Christian Life in our Time*, ed. Michael Plekon, foreword John H. Erickson (New York: Rowman and Littlefield, 2003), 3–30.
8 See Pan-Orthodox Council, "The Sacrament of Marriage and Its Impediments," The Sacrament of Marriage and its Impediments – The Holy and Great Council of the Orthodox Church (holycouncil.org) (accessed August 30, 2024).
9 Pan-Orthodox Council, "The Sacrament of Marriage and Its Impediments."
10 See John Erickson, "The Council in Trullo: The Issues Relating to Clergy," *Greek Orthodox Theological Review* 40, nos. 1–2 (1995), 186.
11 See Ecumenical Patriarchate of Constantinople, "For the Life of the World: Toward a Social Ethics of the Orthodox Church," Social Ethos Document – Greek Orthodox Archdiocese of America – Greek Orthodox Archdiocese of America (goarch.org), no. 22 (accessed August 30, 2024). FLOW hereafter.
12 FLOW no. 24.
13 FLOW no. 24.
14 See Basis of the Social Concept of the Russian Orthodox Church (BSC hereafter), XII. Problems of bioethics | The Russian Orthodox Church (mospat.ru), no. 12 (accessed August 30, 2024).
15 Paul Evdokimov, *The Sacrament of Love: The Nuptial Mystery in the Light of the Orthodox Tradition*, trans. Anthony Gythiel and Victoria Steadman, foreword Olivier Clement (Crestwood, NY: St. Vladimir's Seminary Press, 1986), 30.

16 Alkiviadis Calivas, *The Liturgy in Dialogue: Exploring and Renewing the Tradition*, Essays in Theology and Liturgy, vol. 5 (Brookline, MA: Holy Cross Orthodox Press, 2018), 129.
17 Carrie Frederick Frost, *Church of Our Granddaughters*, foreword Vigen Guroian (Eugene, OR: Cascade Books, 2023), 21–27.
18 Frost, *Church of Our Granddaughters*, 31.
19 Frost, *Church of Our Granddaughters*, 30.
20 Nicholas Denysenko, *Chrismation: A Primer for Catholics* (Collegeville, MN: Liturgical Press, 2012), 118–139.
21 See, for example, the statement of the synod of bishops of the Orthodox Church in America, "Statement on same-sex relationships and sexual identity," Holy Synod – Encyclicals – Statement on same-sex relationships and sexual identity – Orthodox Church in America (oca.org) (accessed August 30, 2024).
22 Thomas Arentzen, *The Orthodox Church and Same-Sex Love: Resources for a Challenging Conversation* (Oslo: The Oslo Coalition on Freedom of Religion or Belief, Norwegian Center for Human Rights, 2022) is a helpful introductory resource laying out a variety of perspectives and opinions.
23 See *Eastern Orthodoxy and Sexual Diversity: A Report on Challenges from the Modern West*, eds. Brandon Gallaher and Gregory Tucker (n.p.: British Council, 2019), 51–57.
24 See Nikolaous Asproulas, "Baptism a la carte: Or Why the Orthodox Need to Discuss Human Identity Seriously," https://publicorthodoxy.org/2022/10/14/baptism-a-la-carte-or-why-the-orthodox-need-to-discuss-human-identity-seriously/ (accessed August 30, 2024). FLOW 23 states unequivocally that the Church should baptize all children.
25 Stated clearly in "The Sacrament of Marriage and its Impediments," https://holycouncil.org/marriage (accessed August 30, 2024).
26 The most sensational ordinations took place in the Episcopalian Church of the USA when eleven women were ordained in Philadelphia during an event known as the Philadelphia 11. See https://www.episcopalchurch.org/glossary/philadelphia-eleven-the/ (accessed August 30, 2024).
27 See *Women and the Priesthood*, ed. Thomas Hopko (Crestwood, NY: St. Vladimir's Seminary Press, 1999), for diverse opinions on the topic.
28 The most vocal proponent was Elisabeth Behr-Sigel. See Behr-Sigel and Kallistos Ware, *The Ordination of Women in the Orthodox Church* (n.p.: Counsel Oecumenique, 2000).
29 For a complete description of the ordination, see Carrie Frost, "Reflections on the Ordination of Deaconess Angelic," https://publicorthodoxy.org/good-reads/ordination-of-deaconess-angelic/ (accessed August 30, 2024).
30 See Hyacinthe Destivelle, *The Moscow Council (1917–1921): The Creation of the Conciliar Institutions of the Russian Orthodox Church*, eds. Michael Plekon and Vitaly Permiakov, trans. Jerry Ryan (Notre Dame: University of Notre Dame Press, 2016), 132–134.

31 See the recently published proposed guidelines by the St. Phoebe Center for the Deaconess, https://orthodoxdeaconess.org/proposed-guidelines/ (accessed September 4, 2024).
32 See, for example, Lawrence Farley, "The Call for Deaconesses: A Look at Scholarly Claims," https://nootherfoundation.ca/the-call-for-deaconesses-a-look-at-the-scholarly-claims (accessed September 4, 2024); Lawrence Farley, "The Need for Deaconesses in the Orthodox Church Today," https://nootherfoundation.ca/the-need-for-deaconesses-in-the-orthodox-church-today (accessed September 4, 2024); Brian Patrick Mitchell, *The Disappearing Deaconess: Why the Church Once Had Deaconesses and then Stopped Having Them* (Alexandria, VA: Eeremia Publications, 2021).
33 On this matter, see the thorough overview by Nadieszda Kizenko, "Feminized Patriarchy? Orthodoxy and Gender in Post-Soviet Russia," *Signs* 38, no. 3 (2013), 601.
34 John Paul II, *Ordinatio sacerdotalis*, https://www.vatican.va/content/john-paul-ii/en/apost_letters/1994/documents/hf_jp-ii_apl_19940522_ordinatio-sacerdotalis.html (accessed September 4, 2024).
35 See Kallistos Ware, "Man, Woman, and the Priesthood of Christ," in *Women and the Priesthood*, ed. Thomas Hopko (Crestwood, NY: St. Vladimir's Seminary Press, 2000), 33, 52–53.
36 Thomas Hopko, "Presbyter/Bishop: A Masculine Ministry," in *Women and the Priesthood*, ed. Hopko, 139–64.
37 See, for example, Ashley Purpura, "Innovating 'Traditional' Women's Roles: Byzantine Insights for Orthodox Christian Gender Discourse," *Modern Theology* 36, no. 3 (2020), 642 (641–661).
38 See Gevorg S. Kazaryan, "Институт диаконисс в традиции Армянской Апостольской Церкви," *Российский журнал истории Церкви* 3, no. 2 (2022), 5–22, and Marcin Bider, "Rights and Duties of the Deaconesses of the Armenian Apostolic Churches: A Historic and Legal Perspective of the 17th to the 21st Century," *KOŚCIÓŁ I PRAWO* 12, no. 25 (2023), 145–159.
39 Kazaryan, "Институт диаконисс," 9.
40 Bider, "Rights and Duties," 156.
41 See the samples of Orthodox views on social issues in the 2021 Pew Research Center survey, https://www.pewresearch.org/religion/2017/11/08/orthodox-take-socially-conservative-views-on-gender-issues-homosexuality/ (accessed September 4, 2021).
42 Alice-Mary Talbot, "A Comparison of the Monastic Experiences of Byzantine Men and Women," *Greek Orthodox Theological Review* 30, no. 1 (1985), 9.
43 Talbot, "A Comparison of the Monastic Experiences."
44 Patriarch Kirill of Moscow, "Патриаршая проповедь в Неделю сыропустную после Литургии в Храме Христа Спасителя," http://www.patriarchia.ru/db/text/5906442.html (accessed September 4, 2024).

45 See the Assembly of Russian Bishops meeting in July 2023,"Постановление Архиерейского Совещания (Свято-Троицкая Сергиева лавра, 19 июля 2023 года, день Собора Радонежских святых)," http://www.patriarchia.ru/db/text/6043699.html (accessed September 4, 2024).
46 "Наказ XXV Всемирного русского народного собора «Настоящее и будущее Русского мира»," http://www.patriarchia.ru/db/text/6116189.html (accessed September 4, 2024).
47 See the informed analysis by Mikhail Suslov, "The Russian Orthodox Church and the Crisis in Ukraine," in *Churches in the Ukrainian Crisis*, eds. Andrii Krawchuk and Thomas Bremer (New York: Palgrave Macmillan, 2016), 133–162.
48 Perry Hamalis, "Just Peacemaking and Christian Realism: Possibilities for Moving beyond the Impasse in Orthodox Christian War Ethics," in *Orthodox Christian Perspectives on War*, eds. Perry Hamalis and Valerie Karras (Notre Dame, IN: University of Notre Dame Press, 2018), 335–361.
49 Carrie Frederick Frost, Nadieszda Kizenko, et al, "For the Life of the World: Toward a Social Ethos of the Orthodox Church," *Journal of Orthodox Christian Studies* 5, no. 1 (2022), 119–139.
50 Frost et al., "For the Life of the World," 127.
51 Frost et al., "For the Life of the World," 128.
52 BSC II.3.
53 BSC III.2.
54 BSC III.8.
55 BSC V.4
56 BSC X.3.
57 BSC X.5.
58 BSC X.5.
59 BSC X.6
60 BSC X.6.
61 BSC XII.4.
62 BSC XII.9.
63 BSC XII.9.
64 BSC XVI.1.
65 BSC XVI.1.
66 See Maria Popova and Oxana Shevel, *Russia and Ukraine: Entangled Histories, Diverging States* (Hoboken, NJ: Polity Press, 2024), 41–47.
67 BSC XVI.4.
68 FLOW 2.10.
69 FLOW 2.12.
70 FLOW 2.12.
71 FLOW VII.61.
72 FLOW VII.65.

73 FLOW III.22.
74 FLOW III.23.
75 FLOW III.18.
76 FLOW III.19
77 FLOW III.29.
78 FLOW III.29.
79 Frost et al., "For the Life of the World," 124, 126.
80 Frost et al., "For the Life of the World," 135.

CONCLUSION

This book has taken us on a swift journey through Orthodoxy, with extended reflections on the Church's main features and core values. To conclude, we will offer a brief review of these main themes and offer a reflection on Orthodoxy's short- and long-term future possibilities.

ORTHODOXY'S MOST PRECIOUS CORE VALUE IS THE CHRISTOLOGY OF THE ECUMENICAL COUNCILS

Contemporary historians and theologians have noted that Orthodoxy tends not to have a repository of teaching texts for general reference like the Catholic Church's Vatican II or the Augsburg Confession for Lutherans. The absence of a ready-to-use theological reference system does not do justice to the sophistication of Orthodox theology. The Eastern Orthodox and Catholic churches refer consistently and unapologetically to the christological repository of the ecumenical councils, including Chalcedon. The Oriental Orthodox churches also cherish the theological heritage of the councils but continue to reject Chalcedon, professing the faith of the definitions of the Council of Ephesus instead.

The liturgical traditions of Alexandria and Antioch express and contribute to the Christological traditions central to Orthodox identity. These prayers continue to function like wells providing fresh water to the prayer and spiritual lives of the churches. The christological foundation is central to church identity. The letter to the Hebrews (attributed to Paul) states, "Jesus Christ is the same yesterday, today, and forever" (Heb. 13:8). All of the Orthodox churches take this matter to heart and regard the confession of faith in Christ as God and human to be a mark of the church's authenticity.

DOI: 10.4324/9781003433217-10

ORTHODOXY RETAINS THE TRINITARIAN THEOLOGY OF THE COUNCILS, ESPECIALLY IN ITS LITURGICAL LIFE

Jesus Christ is the beginning and end, the alpha and omega, of Christian faith. The Orthodox churches confess their faith in Father, Son, and Holy Spirit and decline to adopt alternative names for the Holy Trinity. God the Father is the same God who created the universe, humankind, and all living creatures; created and confirmed covenants with Noah, Abraham, Moses, and, through them, the Hebrew people; promised deliverance to Israel through the prophets; redeemed Israel by sending his only-begotten Son to the world; and adopted all of humankind through the death and resurrection of Jesus Christ. The Holy Spirit is the comforter who proceeds from God the Father, who revealed Jesus as the Son of God at his baptism in the Jordan, and who makes Christ present among the people by descending on them when they gather in his memory.

All of the Orthodox churches confess the Trinitarian theology expressed by the Council of Constantinople in 381 that completed the creed by adding the clauses on the Holy Spirit. The Orthodox churches have not revised the Nicene-Constantinopolitan Creed by adding the filioque clause that originally appeared in the sixth century and was adopted by the Roman church in the ninth century.

Orthodoxy refers to numerous manifestations of the Holy Spirit in the life of the faithful and places particular emphasis on the epicleses that take place in the church's liturgy. The epiclesis of the Divine Liturgy takes place when the people call upon the Father to send the Holy Spirit upon the people and the gifts and to make Christ present. This divine activity of God sending the Spirit to make Christ present among the people is a fundamental expression of Orthodox theology of the Holy Spirit.

ORTHODOXY BELIEVES IN THE COMMUNION OF SAINTS

Orthodoxy continues to profess faithfully that God has called all people to holiness and that many people have attained holiness through divine grace. Holy men and women are central to Orthodox spirituality and devotion, as people pray to their patron saints, venerate icons of beloved adopted saints, and install and revere relics of saints. The icons and relics bridge the gap separating heaven and earth by maintaining the tangible, physical presence of the saints in communities. Orthodoxy believes that the saints intercede on behalf of the world and the church before God's throne and inscribe the stories of holy people on the historical memories of the people.

ORTHODOXY BELIEVES THAT GOD GRANTS ETERNAL LIFE TO HUMANKIND AND THAT THEY CAN BECOME LIKE GOD

Orthodoxy accepts the classical story of humankind's fall, expulsion from paradise, and subjection to corruption and death. God restores the divine image in each Christian through baptism and anointing, and Christians become capable of living without sin, pursuing righteousness, and inheriting the promise of the kingdom – through continued reception of the divine grace, especially in the Eucharistic assembly. Orthodoxy tends to emphasize a positive view of humankind in its sacramental theology, expressing confidence that each person can become like God through a life of prayer, ascetical struggle, and – above all – love for God and their neighbors. Orthodoxy continues to profess its firm belief that the righteous will be admitted into God's realm and that God will grant them eternal rest in the resurrection at Christ's second coming.

THE ORTHODOX CHURCH MAKES AN EXCLUSIVE CLAIM AS THE ONE TRUE CHURCH

Orthodoxy is exclusivist – the church identifies itself as "the" one, holy, catholic, and apostolic church, without qualification or apology. Orthodoxy expresses its exclusivist claim through the practice of closed communion. Only baptized and anointed Orthodox Christians can receive Holy Communion. Catholics, Protestants, and all other Christians can attend Orthodox worship but cannot receive communion. The exclusivism applies to other mysteries as well. The Orthodox Church permits marriage only for two Orthodox Christians, although in practice, many bishops permit the rites of marriage between an Orthodox and non-Orthodox Christian.

Orthodoxy is divided in its positions on dialogue toward restoring communion with other Christians. Many Orthodox theologians have participated in official theological dialogues with representatives of other churches and have made progress on difficult theological and ecclesiological issues, especially with Catholics and Oriental Orthodox. The Roman Catholic adherence to papal primacy remains a stumbling block for intercommunion for Orthodox. The theological dialogue between Eastern and Oriental Orthodox concluded that miaphysite and diaphysite christologies are essentially the same, so constructing a path toward the restoration of communion is a natural next step for the leaders of the churches – one they have yet to realize. While some Orthodox are more open to and encouraging of dialogue to restore communion, the vast majority of Orthodox Christians maintain that the Orthodox Church has an exclusive claim to the Christian church's apostolic heritage and theological foundations.

ORTHODOXY'S HISTORICAL LEGACY IS HEAVILY WEIGHTED TOWARD RELIGIOUS HEGEMONY IN ORTHODOX-DOMINANT EMPIRES

Historians tend to loathe the identification of any particular epoch as a golden age, but Orthodoxy tends to view the life of the church in Orthodox-dominant empires as favorable. Eastern Orthodoxy continues to gravitate toward a type of symphonia, a collaboration and mutual agreement with governments in Orthodox-majority countries – a vestige from the imperial past. The relationship between the Orthodox Church and the state is dynamic and not static. Sometimes, the church collaborates with the state, and occasionally the ruling authorities exploit the church and attempt to fold its teachings into their political ideologies. Orthodoxy is still adapting to its status as a minority faith community in liberal democracies. The churches have frequently suffered from severe persecution at the hands of rulers hostile to Christians, especially during the Soviet era. Survival, resilience, and martyrdom have become three of the most prominent identity markers for both Eastern and Oriental Orthodox Christian communities.

THE EMERGENCE OF THE SOVEREIGN NATION-STATE HAS RESHAPED ORTHODOX IDENTITY

Orthodox ecclesiology honors the living out of faith through regional cultural idioms: music, art, and language in particular. Orthodoxy's preference for regional independence and autonomy in governance is mostly compatible with the current model of one church in a nation-state. The tendency for nation-states to construct historical narratives that unite their citizens lends itself to an organic adoption of nationalism by the church. Sometimes, church leaders and ideologues contribute to these historical narratives. The emergence of the nation-state and Orthodox preference for local structures have contributed to the church's adoption of national identity and, occasionally, the outright promotion of nationalism. Multiple instances of Orthodox churches promoting nationalistic platforms have been problematic since the late nineteenth century, leading the Ecumenical Patriarchate of Constantinople to condemn *ethnophyletism* as a heresy. The temptation to adopt nationalism continues to plague the Orthodox churches.

ORTHODOX SPIRITUALITY REMAINS VIBRANT AND DYNAMIC

Orthodoxy celebrates its rich heritage of public liturgy while continuing to support a vibrant tradition of spiritual practices. The people remain steadfastly devoted to reciting daily prayers (both official and extemporaneous), venerating their favorite icons, making pilgrimages to shrines, and upholding beloved communal and domestic traditions. Orthodoxy survived modern persecution because of the people's fervent observance of spiritual practices. The cultivation and sustenance of a veritable spiritual life remained a constant for Orthodoxy through wars, the global coronavirus pandemic, and the ups and downs of national political turbulence.

The final section offers a reflection on the primary challenges confronting Orthodoxy in the twenty-first century. These challenges include the occasionally explosive relationship between the academy and the clergy, the tension of conciliarity and hierarchical structures, divisions over sharp disputes on gender and human sexuality, and ministry to Gen Z and successive generations.

ATHENS VS. JERUSALEM? THE ORTHODOX ACADEMY AND THE CHURCH

Christianity has a contentious relationship with the academy. On the one hand, the Christian heritage itself was one of study and contemplation. Seven hundred of the best Greek scholars translated the Hebrew Bible into Greek in Alexandria. The same city was host to an early catechetical school that produced influential thinkers like Clement and Origen of Alexandria. The Cappadocian fathers, Basil of Caesarea, Gregory Nazianzen, and Gregory of Nyssa, were among the most brilliant thinkers whose theological treatises clarified, corrected, advanced, and – most important of all – edified the Christian world. On the other hand, the original apostles were not deep philosophical thinkers or accomplished writers. They grounded their ministry in labor, love, perseverance, affection for the afflicted, and love for the church. They were simple fishermen and accountants who heard Jesus and heeded his call to follow him. Some of the most brilliant theologians were also edgy, and the church considered their teachings too dangerous. These include the aforementioned Origen, along with Arius and Theodore of Mopsuestia.

The education of the masses and equal access to higher education were among the accomplishments of the cultural revolutions of modernity. Women outnumber men in many colleges and universities. Most parents still send their adult children for advanced education, despite the high cost of higher education. The ordinary faithful can now read the text of the liturgy on their own time and then discuss and debate its meaning, along with the other topics du jour, in small groups and on online forums.

The advent of higher education in Western and Central Europe and the commitment of churches and Christian organizations to founding confessional colleges and universities created theology faculty positions. Clergy and monastics originally dominated these posts, but they are now shared with lay men and women, some of whom are unchurched. Pedagogical strategies and the evolution of religious, historical, and textual scientific methods led to multidisciplinary approaches to theological education. The period immediately following the Second Vatican Council witnessed a surge in the establishment of liturgy faculty positions, and these are now in decline. There are still Orthodox scholars who work in the fields of biblical studies, patristics, liturgy, and church history, but many now specialize in new fields such as gender studies, political theology, and queer theology.

The rapid development of trends and methodologies in higher education has converged with an enormous financial bubble, creating a burden for students and their families. Furthermore, the investigation of theological questions through new disciplines and methodologies has challenged longstanding foundations of Orthodox Church practice and dogma. This study introduces a few of the contentious topics, namely the female diaconate and same-sex relationships, but the larger issue is the decline of trust separating church pastors from the academy.

Scholars seeking careers in academia will learn new methodologies as necessities of advancing their own careers. The study of theology through innovative methods has the potential to clarify, correct, and edify – and also to lead astray, confuse, and divide. One of the most urgent tasks for the church, especially its leaders, is to create and sustain a healthy dialogue with the academy. The object is to maintain an ongoing dialogue, not for the academy to correct church leaders. A healthy dialogue between the theologians and the church increases the chances of the church exercising stewardship over its theological heritage by keeping the dialogue within the church.

THE FUTURE OF CONCILIARITY

This study has demonstrated Orthodoxy's veneration for ecumenical councils and conciliarity in general. The Moscow Patriarchate created a conciliar structure that involved the participation of lower clergy and laity in church administration, governance, and ministry at the Moscow Council in 1917–1918. The Western European Exarchate and the Orthodox Church in America retained these conciliar structures, and other Orthodox Church communities throughout the world adopted variations of conciliarity as well in the twentieth and twenty-first centuries. A battle for authority has ensued within Orthodoxy, despite these developments. Some churches have redefined authority by granting more to the primate, or the synod, and some do not include the laity in major events and decisions, such as the nomination and election of new leaders.

A discussion has emerged on the nature of hierarchy itself, whether or not it is essential for the church, and the consequences of adhering loyally to hierarchical structures. Orthodoxy has considered mild revision of its structures. There has been no serious proposal for eliminating or minimizing the episcopal ministry, but there have been discussions on widening eligibility or even assigning a required retirement age. The larger issue concerns the potential role of the laity. Many regarded Tsar Peter I's Spiritual Regulations as protestantizing the Orthodox Church, especially with the appointment of a lay oberprocurator. Some theologians have argued that the laity is a liturgical order exercising a priestly ministry. We reviewed some of these developments in this book. Once again, what's at stake is not a review of the review, but the future of church governance. Will Orthodoxy consider revisions that retain hierarchical structures while allowing for shared governance? Is the creation and revision of conciliar structures the most optimal way of accomplishing this proposed task?

MEN, WOMEN, AND SAME-SEX MARRIAGE

The official Orthodox position on gender is one of equality – God has endowed men and women with the divine image. Orthodoxy reserves the vast majority of its ministerial offices for a few men – only some men are eligible for ordination to deacon, presbyter, and bishop. Eastern Orthodoxy once had female deacons, and the Armenian church has restored a female diaconate, while the Patriarchate of Alexandria ordained a deaconess in 2024, but the possibility of a renewal of the female diaconate in the entire Eastern Orthodox Church is hotly debated. There is also a debate on the gendering of ministries and spaces in the church, along with the church's ethical teachings. Some contend that a cultural resurgence of masculinity has occurred in the Orthodox Church as well, with others looking for a return of traditional roles from a previous era.

Cultural patterns are always evolving, ever dynamic, so it's no surprise that some Orthodox people fuse trends toward masculinity or feminism with church order and ethics. Orthodoxy has resisted change to the triumvirate of episcopate-presbyterate-diaconate, and the recent ordination of a deaconess in Zimbabwe ignited heated debate on social media. No religious organization is required to change with culture, and Christianity certainly has had dozens of countercultural movements. The question for the Orthodox Church concerns its pastoral approach to these issues. Will the church extend a hand of outreach to the LGBTQ community? Can Orthodoxy maintain its position of gender complementarity for the long run? One thing is certain – the discussion will continue among pastors and theologians.

MINISTRY TO GEN Z AND ITS SUCCESSORS

The Orthodox Church's approach to ministry has developed concurrently with its systems of theological education. Many priests were trained to know the liturgical services and lead them competently and to provide a basic ministry of presidential leadership during occasionally turbulent times. Some bishops became famous because of the rich theology and rhetorical brilliance of their homilies, but many pastors had limited training, and theological education was sparing, especially in periods of persecution or restrictions on religious freedoms.

Pastors no longer have the luxury of simply knowing the services to lead their people. Economic growth, access to education, and religious pluralism gave people the freedom to choose – to remain Orthodox, make another religious commitment, or have no affiliation at all. The degree of religious observance declines with each generation, from boomers to Gen Z, but interest in religious communities continues to persist. Pastors will be looking for new ways to engage Gen Z, understanding the challenges posed by social and digital media. Pastors also have to account for the surge in mental health awareness, society's discovery of widespread trauma, and the removal of the stigma of addiction. Younger people are committed to self-care and self-love and also engage in the therapies of counseling and medical assistance for mental and emotional health needs. The Orthodox Church has the capacity to support and encourage self-care and needs to consider the relationship between its strong impulses to self-denial and ascetical practices with self-love. The Orthodox Church will have to develop pastoral ministries in pace with Gen Z to maintain a viable outreach to the youngest people in the churches, especially since community is increasingly elusive for many who depend on connecting via digital media.

In conclusion, Orthodoxy has thrived, survived, suffered, and persevered through its two-thousand-plus years of existence. The Orthodox Church has certainly lived up to its reputation as a steady anchor in a stormy sea, and yet it has changed more than it would like to admit. One truth remains constant for the Eastern and Oriental Orthodox churches – they remain faithful to Jesus Christ as the only begotten son of God who came into the world to save humankind and reconcile it, with all of creation, to eternal life with the Father and the Holy Spirit.

BIBLIOGRAPHY

Afanasiev, Nicholas. *The Church of the Holy Spirit*. Trans. Vitaly Permiakov, ed. Michael Plekon, foreword Rowan Williams. Notre Dame, IN: University of Notre Dame Press, 2007.

Afanasiev, Nicholas. *Трапеза Господня*. Kyiv: Temple of St. Agapit, 2003.

Afanasiev, Nicholas. "Una Sancta." In *Tradition Alive: On the Church and the Christian Life in our Time*, ed. Michael Plekon, foreword John H. Erickson, 3–30. New York: Rowman and Littlefield, 2003.

Alexopoulos, Stefanos. *The Presanctified Liturgy in the Byzantine Rite: A Analysis of its Origins, Evolution, and Structural Components*. Liturgia Condenda 21. Leuven: Peeters, 2009.

Alexopoulos, Stefanos and Maxwell Johnson. *Introduction to Eastern Christian Liturgies*. Collegeville, MN: Liturgical Press, 2022.

Allen, Pauline and C.T.R. Hayward. *Severus of Antioch*. The Early Church Fathers series. New York: Routledge, 2004.

Arentzen, Thomas. *The Orthodox Church and Same-Sex Love: Resources for a Challenging Conversation*. Oslo: The Oslo Coalition on Freedom of Religion or Belief, Norwegian Center for Human Rights, 2022.

Arkjakovsky, Antoine. *The Way: Religious Thinkers of the Russian Emigration in Paris and Their Journal, 1925–1940*. Trans. Jerry Ryan, eds. John Jillions and Michael Plekon, foreword Rowan Williams. Notre Dame, IN: University of Notre Dame Press, 2013.

Asproulas, Nikolaous. "Baptism a la carte: Or Why the Orthodox Need to Discuss Human Identity Seriously." Accessed August 30, 2024. https://publicorthodoxy.org/2022/10/14/baptism-a-la-carte-or-why-the-orthodox-need-to-discuss-human-identity-seriously/. Accessed August 30, 2024.

Athanasius of Alexandria. *On the Incarnation*. Intro C.S. Lewis, trans. John Behr. Popular Patristics Series 44b. Yonkers, NY: St. Vladimir's Seminary Press, 2011.

Baldovin, John. "The Fermentum at Rome in the Fifth Century: A Reconsideration." *Worship* 71, no. 1 (2005): 38–53.

Barkey, Karen and George Gavrilis. "The Ottoman Millet System: Non-Territorial Autonomy and Its Contemporary Legacy." *Ethnopolitics* 15, no. 1 (2015): 24–42.

Basil of Caesarea. *On the Holy Spirit*. Trans. and intro. Stephen Hildebrand. Popular Patristics Series 42. Yonkers, NY: St. Vladimir's Seminary Press, 2011.

Basil of Caesarea. *On the Human Condition*. Trans. Nonna Verna Harrison. Crestwood, NY: St. Vladimir's Seminary Press, 2005.

Behr, John. *Formation of Christian Theology*, vol. 1: *The Way to Nicaea*. Crestwood, NY: St. Vladimir's Seminary Press, 2001.

Behr, John, ed. *Gregory of Nyssa: On the Human Image of God*, Oxford Early Christian Texts. Oxford: Oxford University Press, 2023.

Behr-Sigel, Elizabeth and Kallistos Ware. *The Ordination of Women in the Orthodox Church*. n.p.: Counsel Oecumenique, 2000.

Bider, Marcin. "Rights and Duties of the Deaconesses of the Armenian Apostolic Churches: A Historic and Legal Perspective of the 17th to the 21st Century." *Kościół I Prawo* 12, no. 25 (2023): 145–159.

"Bishop Gives Details for Final Details of Coptic Church's Papal Selection." Bishop Gives Details about Final Stage of Coptic Church's Papal Elections – Politics – Egypt – Ahram Online. Accessed September 4, 2024. https://english.ahram.org.eg/NewsContent/1/64/56962/Egypt/Politics-/Bishop-gives-details-about-final-stage-of-Coptic-C.aspx

Bociurkiw, Bohdan. *The Ukrainian Greek Catholic Church and the Soviet State (1939–1950)*. Edmonton: Canadian Institute of Ukrainian Studies, 1996.

Bogolepov, Alexander. *Toward an American Orthodox Church*. Foreword John H. Erickson. Crestwood, NY: St. Vladimir's Seminary Press, 2001.

Bordeianu, Radu. *Icon of the Kingdom of God: An Orthodox Ecclesiology*. Washington, DC: The Catholic University of America Press, 2023.

Bradshaw, Paul. *The Search for the Origins of Christian Worship*, 2d ed. London: SPCK, 2002.

Bradshaw, Paul and Maxwell Johnson. *The Eucharistic Liturgies: Their Evolution and Interpretation*. Collegeville, MN: Liturgical Press, 2012.

Brock, Sebastian. "Syrian Christianity." In *The Blackwell Dictionary of Eastern Christianity*, eds. Ken Parry et al., 467–476. Malden, MA: Blackwell, 2001.

Brubaker, Leslie. *Inventing Byzantine Iconoclasm*. Studies in Early Medieval History. London: Bloomsbury, 2012.

Bulgakov, Sergius. *The Bride of the Lamb*. Trans. Boris Jakim. Grand Rapids, MI: Eerdman's, 2002.

Bushkovitch, Paul. *A Concise History of Russia*. Cambridge: Cambridge University Press, 2012.

Calivas, Alkiviadis. *The Liturgy in Dialogue: Exploring and Renewing the Tradition*: vol. 5, *Essays in Theology and Liturgy*. Brookline, MA: Holy Cross Orthodox Press, 2018.

Chirovsky, Andriy. "Can I Pray with This Icon If It's Only a Print? Toward a Pastoral Interpretation of Orthodox Iconography." In *Icons and the Liturgy, East and West: History, Theology, and Culture*, ed. Nicholas Denysenko, 164–190. Notre Dame, IN: University of Notre Dame Press, 2017.

Chrysostom, John. "The Paschal Sermon." The Paschal Sermon – Orthodox Church in America (oca.org). Accessed September 11, 2024.

Chryssavgis, John. *Confession and Repentance in the Orthodox Church*. Brookline, MA: Holy Cross Orthodox Press, 1990.

Coakley, J.F. "Jacobite." In *The Blackwell Dictionary of Eastern Christianity*, eds. Ken Parry et al., 262. Malden, MA: Blackwell, 2001.

Cohen, Will. *The Concept of 'Sister Churches' in Catholic-Orthodox Relations Since Vatican II*. Studia Oecumenica Friburgensia 67. Eugene, OR: Wipf and Stock, 2017.

Cohen, Will. "Coronavirus and Communion." https://publicorthodoxy.org/2020/03/14/coronavirus-and-communion/. Accessed August 6, 2024.

Congar, Yves. *I Believe in the Holy Spirit*, vol. 3: *The River of the Water of Life (Rev. 22:1) Flows in the East and the West*. New York: Crossroad Publishing, 2004.

Congregation for the Doctrine of Faith. "Declaration 'Dominus Iesus' on the Unicity and Salvific Universality of Jesus Christ and the Church." Dominus Iesus (https://www.vatican.va/roman_curia/congregations/cfaith/documents/rc_con_cfaith_doc_20000806_dominus-iesus_en.html). Accessed August 30, 2024.

Coogan, Michael. "Septuagint." In *The Oxford Companion to the Bible*. Accessed September 30, 2024.

Coptic Orthodox Diocese of Southern USA. "Coptic Reader." Apple App Store, Vers. 2.84 (2020). https://suscopts.org/coptic-reader/. Accessed November 11, 2024.

Cox, Daniel. "The Societal Cost of Marriage Decline." The Societal Cost of the Marriage Decline | Institute for Family Studies (ifstudies.org). Accessed July 30, 2024.

Cyril of Jerusalem. *Lectures on the Christian Sacraments: The Procatechesis and the Five Mystagogical Catecheses ascribed to St. Cyril of Jerusalem*. Trans. and intro Maxwell Johnson. Yonkers, NY: St. Vladimir's Seminary Press. 2017.

Daley, Brian. "The Meaning and Exercise of 'Primacies of Honor' in the Early Church." In *Primacy in the Church*, vol. 1, ed. John Chryssavgis, 35–50. Crestwood, NY: St. Vladimir's Seminary Press, 2016.

Dallen, James. *The Reconciling Community: The Rite of Penance*. Studies in the Reformed Rites of the Catholic Church, vol. 3. Collegeville, MN: Liturgical Press, 1991.

Davis, Leo. *The First Seven Ecumenical Councils (325–787): Their History and Theology*. Collegeville, MN: Liturgical Press, 1983.

"Declaration on the Russian World." https://publicorthodoxy.org/2022/03/13/a-declaration-on-the-russian-world-russkii-mir-teaching/. Accessed July 26, 2024.

Denysenko, Nicholas. *Chrismation: A Primer for Catholics.* Collegeville, MN: Liturgical Press, 2012.

Denysenko, Nicholas. "The Eucharist and Orthodox Ecclesial Unity." In *Autocephaly. Coming of Age in Communion. Historical, Canonical, Liturgical, and Theological Studies,* eds. Edward G. Farrugia and S. J. Željko Paša, 843–863. *Orientalia Christiana Analecta* 314–315. Rome: Pontifical Oriental Institute, 2023.

Denysenko, Nicholas. "Exploring Ukrainian Autocephaly: Politics, History, Ecclesiology, and the Future." *Canadian Slavonic Papers* 62, nos 3–4 (2020): 426–442.

Denysenko, Nicholas. "Mary's Dormition: Liturgical Cliché, Summer Pascha." *Studia Liturgica* 43 (2013), 256–280.

Denysenko, Nicholas. *The Orthodox Church in Ukraine: A Century of Separation.* DeKalb: Northern Illinois University Press, 2018.

Denysenko, Nicholas. "Primacy, Synodality, and Collegiality in Orthodoxy: A Liturgical Model." *Journal of Ecumenical Studies* 48, no. 1 (2013): 20–44.

Denysenko, Nicholas. "Ressourcement or Aggiornamento? An Assessment of Modern Liturgical Reforms." *International Journal for the Study of Systematic Theology* 20, no. 2 (2018): 186–208.

Denysenko, Nicholas. *This Is the Day That the Lord Has Made: The Liturgical Year in Orthodoxy.* Eugene, OR: Cascade, 2023.

Destivelle, Hyacinthe. *The Moscow Council (1917–1918): The Creation of the Conciliar Institution of the Russian Orthodox Church.* Trans. Jerry Ryan, eds. Michael Plekon and Vitaly Permiakov. Notre Dame, IN: University of Notre Dame Press, 2016.

Dostoyevsky, Fyodor, Susan McReynolds Oddo, Constance Garnett, and Ralph E. Matlaw. *The Brothers Karamazov: A Revised Translation, Contexts, Criticism*, 2nd ed. New York: W. W. Norton & Co., 2011.

Ecumenical Patriarchate. *The Documents Speak: Ecumenical Throne and the Church of Ukraine.* https://www.ecupatria.org/2018/10/04/the-ecumenical-patriarchate-and-the-church-of-ukraine-the-documents-speak/. Accessed August 17, 2024.

Ecumenical Patriarchate. *For the Life of the World: Toward a Social Ethos of the Orthodox Church.* https://www.goarch.org/social-ethos?fbclid=IwAR2RSPrgYRhPfAgT9p2iIQkd9wqtOYJ74Gtjnpmyq9xYdxshwqr6U1FJFiY. Accessed July 26, 2024.

Elpidophoros, Archbishop. "First without Equals: A Response to the Text on Primacy by the Moscow Patriarchate." FIRST WITHOUT EQUALS – A Response to the Text on Primacy of the Moscow Patriarchate – Orthodox Christian Laity (ocl.org). Accessed August 26, 2024.

Ephrem the Syrian. *Selected Prose Works.* Trans. Edward G. Mathews, Jr. and Joseph P. Amar, ed. Kathleen McVey. Fathers of the Church 91. Washington, DC: The Catholic University of America Press, 1994.

Erickson, John. "The Council in Trullo: The Issues Relating to Clergy." *Greek Orthodox Theological Review* 40, nos 1–2 (1995): 183–199.

Erickson, John. "The Orthodox Church in America: Its Place in American and Global Orthodoxy." In *Autocephaly. Coming of Age in Communion. Historical, Canonical, Liturgical, and Theological Studies*, eds. Edward G., Farrugia, S. J., Željko Paša, 571–610. *Orientalia Christiana Analecta* 314–315. Rome: Pontifical Oriental Institute, 2023.

Evdokimov, Paul. *The Sacrament of Love: The Nuptial Mystery in the Light of the Orthodox Tradition* Crestwood, NY: St. Vladimir's Seminary Press, 1985.

Farag, Lois. "The Early Christian Period (42–642): The Spread and Defense of the Christian Faith Under Roman Rule." In *The Coptic Christian Heritage: History, Faith, and Culture*, ed. Lois Farag, 23–38. London: Routledge, 2014.

Farley, Lawrence. "The Call for Deaconesses: A Look at Scholarly Claims." https://nootherfoundation.ca/the-call-for-deaconesses-a-look-at-the-scholarly-claims. Accessed September 4, 2024.

Farley, Lawrence. "The Need for Deaconesses in the Orthodox Church Today." https://nootherfoundation.ca/the-need-for-deaconesses-in-the-orthodox-church-today. Accessed September 4, 2024.

"Fasting-Like Diet Reduces Risk Factors for Disease, Reduces Biological Age for Humans." https://gero.usc.edu/2024/02/20/fasting-mimicking-diet-biological-age/#:~:text=The%20FMD%20is%20a%205,people%20to%20complete%20the%20fast. Accessed September 30, 2024.

Florovsky, Georges. *Ways of Russian Theology*. Belmont, MA: Notable and Academic Books, 1987.

Fotopoulos, John. "Some Common Misconceptions about the Date of Pascha/Easter." https://publicorthodoxy.org/2018/03/15/easter-date-2018/. Accessed October 16, 2024.

Freeze, Gregory. "Handmaiden of the State? The Church in Imperial Russia Reconsidered." *Journal of Ecclesiastical History* 36, no. 1 (1985): 82–102.

Frost, Carrie, Nadieszda Kizenko et al. "For the Life of the World: Toward a Social Ethos of the Orthodox Church." *Journal of Orthodox Christian Studies* 5, no. 1 (2022): 119–139.

Frost, Carrie Frederick. *Church of Our Granddaughters*. Foreword by Vigen Guroian. Eugene, OR: Cascade Books, 2023.

Frost, Carrie Frederick. *Maternal Body: A Theology of Incarnation from the Christian East*. New York: Paulist Press, 2019.

Frost, Carrie Frederick, ed. *The Reception of the Holy and Great Council: Reflections of Orthodox Christian Women*. Faith Matters Series. New York: Greek Orthodox Archdiocese of America, 2018.

Frost, Carrie Frederick. "Reflections on the Ordination of Deaconess Angelic." Reflections on the Ordination of Deaconess Angelic – Public Orthodoxy. Accessed September 6, 2024. https://publicorthodoxy.org/good-reads/ordination-of-deaconess-angelic/

Galadza, Daniel. *Liturgy and Byzantinization in Jerusalem*. Oxford Early Christian Series. Oxford: Oxford University Press, 2018.

Galadza, Daniel. "'Remember, o Lord…': Liturgy, History, and Communion Spoons in a Time of Pandemic." https://publicorthodoxy.org/2020/05/21/liturgy-history-and-communion-spoons/. Accessed August 6, 2024.

Gallaher, Brandon. "Bulgakov and Intercommunion." *Sobornost* 24, no. 2 (2002): 9–28.

Gallaher, Brandon and Gregory Tuckers, eds. *Eastern Orthodoxy and Sexual Diversity: A Report on Challenges from the Modern West*. n.p.: British Council, 2019. https://www.britishcouncil.us/sites/default/files/exeterfordham_report_final_reduced.pdf

Gaufman, Elizaveta. "Come all ye Faithful to the Russian World: Governmental and Grass-Roots Spiritual Discourse in the Battle over Ukraine." In *Religion during the Russian-Ukrainian Conflict*, eds. Elizabeth A. Clark and Dmytro Vovk, 54–68. New York: Routledge, 2020.

Gavrilyuk, Paul. *Georges Florovsky and the Russian Religious Renaissance*. Oxford: Oxford University Press, 2014.

Gavrilyuk, Paul. "Universal Salvation in the Eschatology of Sergius Bulgakov." *Journal of Theological Studies* 57 (2006): 110–32.

Geffert, Bryn and Theofanis Stavrou, eds. *Eastern Orthodox Christianity: The Essential Texts*. New Haven, CT: Yale University Press, 2016.

Getcha, Job. *The Euchologion Unveiled*. Orthodox Liturgy Series Book 4. Yonkers, NY: St. Vladimir's Seminary Press, 2021.

Getcha, Job. *The Typikon Decoded: An Explanation of Byzantine Liturgical Practice*. Trans. Paul Meyendorff. Orthodox Liturgy Series Book 3. Yonkers, NY: St. Vladimir's Seminary Press, 2012.

Gillet, Lev. *In Thy Presence*. Crestwood, NY: St. Vladimir's Seminary Press, 1998.

Goraïnoff, Irina and Serafim Sarovski. *SéRaphim de Sarov: Sa Vie*. Paris, Bégrolles-en-Mauges: Les Editions du Cerf; Abbaye de Bellefontaine, 2019.

Graef, Hilda. *Mary: A History of Doctrine and Devotion*, vol. 1: *From the Beginnings to the Eve of the Reformation*. New York: Sheed and Ward, 1963.

Greek Orthodox Archdiocese of North America. Funeral Service for Infants – Greek Orthodox Archdiocese of America – Greek Orthodox Archdiocese of America (goarch.org). Accessed July 30, 2024.

Griffin, Sean. *The Liturgical Past in Byzantium and Early Rus*. Cambridge Studies in Medieval life and Thought 112. Cambridge: Cambridge University Press, 2019.

Grishin, Alexander. "Eastern Orthodox Iconography and Architecture." In *The Blackwell Companion to Eastern Christianity*, ed. Ken Parry, 371–387. Malden, MA: Blackwell Publishing, 2007.

Hamalis, Perry. "Just Peacemaking and Christian Realism: Possibilities for Moving beyond the Impasse in Orthodox Christian War Ethics." In *Orthodox Christian Perspectives on War*, ed. Perry Hamalis and Valerie Karras, 335–361. Notre Dame, IN: University of Notre Dame Press, 2018.

Harrison, Verna. "Perichoresis in the Greek Fathers." *St. Vladimir's Theological Quarterly* 35, no. 1 (1991): 53–65.

Hart, David Bentley. "The Myth of Schism." Clarion: Journal of Spirituality and Justice – The Myth of Schism – David Bentley Hart (clarion-journal.com). Accessed August 30, 2024.

Hart, David Bentley. *Tradition and Apocalypse: An Essay on the Future of Christian Belief.* Grand Rapids, MI: Baker, 2022.

Hedda, Jennifer. *His Kingdom Come: Orthodox Pastorship and Social Activism in Revolutionary Russia.* DeKalb: Northern Illinois University Press, 2008.

Heller, Dagmar. "The (Holy and Great) Council of the Orthodox Churches: An Ecumenical Perspective." *The Ecumenical Review* 69, no. 2 (2017): 288–300.

Heo, Angie. "Imagining Holy Personhood: Anthropological Thresholds of the Icon." In *Praying with the Senses: Contemporary Orthodox Christian Spirituality in Practice*, ed. Sonja Luehrmann, 83–102. Bloomington: Indiana University Press, 2018.

Heppell, Muriel. "Bulgaria." In *The Blackwell Dictionary of Eastern Christianity*, eds. Ken Parry et al., 93–97. Malden, MA: Blackwell, 2001.

Herbel, Dellas Oliver. *Turning to Tradition: Converts and the Making of an American Orthodox Church.* Oxford: Oxford University Press, 2014.

Hopko, Thomas, ed. *Women and the Priesthood.* Crestwood, NY: St. Vladimir's Seminary Press, 1999.

Hovorun, Cyril. "Kollyvadic Fathers." In *The Encyclopedia of Orthodox Christianity*, vol. 1, ed. John McGuckin, 365. Chichester: Wiley-Blackwell Publications, 2011.

Hovorun, Cyril. *Political Orthodoxies: The Unorthodoxies of the Church Coerced.* Minneapolis, MN: Fortress Press, 2018.

Hovorun, Cyril. *Scaffolds of the Church: Towards Poststructural Ecclesiology.* Eugene, OR: Cascade Books, 2017.

Ignatius of Antioch. *The Apostolic Fathers*, vol. 1. Trans. Francis X. Climm et al. Washington, DC: The Catholic University of America Press, 1962.

Jasper, Ronald C.D. and Geoffrey J. Cuming. *Prayers of the Eucharist: Early and Reformed*, 3d ed. Collegeville, MN: Liturgical Press, 1990.

Jeffreys, Elizabeth M. "Kontakion." https://www.oxfordreference.com/view/10.1093/acref/9780195046526.001.0001/acref-9780195046526-e-2916. Accessed July 29, 2024.

John Paul II, Pope. "Address of John Paul II to His Beatitude Christodoulos, Archbishop of Athens and Primate of Greece." https://www.vatican.va/content/john-paul-ii/en/speeches/2001/may/documents/hf_jp-ii_spe_20010504_archbishop-athens.html. Accessed November 8, 2024.

John Paul II, Pope. "Apostolic Letter Dies Domini." Dies Domini (May 31, 1998) | John Paul II (vatican.va). Accessed July 30, 2024.

John Paul II, Pope. "Apostolic Letter Ordinatio Sacerdotalis." https://www.vatican.va/content/john-paul-ii/en/apost_letters/1994/documents/hf_jp-ii_apl_19940522_ordinatio-sacerdotalis.html. Accessed September 4, 2024.

John Paul II, Pope. *Ut Unum Sint*. Ut Unum Sint (25 May 1995) | John Paul II (vatican.va). Accessed August 26, 2024.

Kalkandijeva, Daniela. *The Russian Orthodox Church, 1917–1948: From Decline to Resurrection*. London: Routledge, 2015.

Kazaryan, Gevorg S. "Институт диаконисс в традиции Армянской Апостольской Церкви." Российский журнал истории Церкви 3, no 2 (2022): 5–22.

Kazhdan, Alexander. "Synodikon." In *The Oxford Dictionary of Byzantium*. https://www.oxfordreference.com/view/10.1093/acref/9780195046526.001.0001/acref-9780195046526-e-5255. Accessed September 13, 2024.

Kizenko, Nadieszda. "Feminized Patriarchy? Orthodoxy and Gender in Post-Soviet Russia." *Signs* 38, no. 3 (2013): 595–621.

Kizenko, Nadieszda. *Good for the Souls: A History of Confession in the Russian Empire*. Oxford: Oxford University Press, 2021.

Kizenko, Nadieszda. "Written Confessions to Father John of Kronstadt, 1898–1908." In *Orthodox Christianity in Imperial Russia*, ed. Heather Coleman, 152–171. Bloomington: Indiana University Press, 2014.

Korniy, Lydia. *Історія української музики,* vol. 2: *Друга Половина XVIII ст.* Kyiv: M.P. Kots, 1998.

Ladouceur, Paul. *Modern Orthodox Theology: 'Behold, I Make All Things New'*. New York: Bloomsbury, 2019.

Ladouceur, Paul. "Neo-Traditionalist Ecclesiology in Orthodoxy," *Scottish Journal of Theology* 72 (2019): 398–413.

Larchet, Jean-Claude. *Life after Death According to the Orthodox Tradition*. Trans. G. John Champoux. Jordanville, NY: The Printshop of St. Job of Pochaev, 2021.

Lazor, Paul, ed. *Baptism*. New York: Department of Religious Education, the Orthodox Church in America, 1972.

Lerner, Konstantin. "Georgia, Christian history of." In *The Blackwell Dictionary of Eastern Christianity*, eds. Ken Parry et al., 210–217. Malden, MA: Blackwell, 2001.

Lingas, Alexander. "Byzantine Chant." https://www.oxfordreference.com/view/10.1093/acref/9780199579037.001.0001/acref-9780199579037-e-1059. Accessed July 29, 2024.

Löhr, Helmut. "The Epistles of Ignatius of Antioch." In *The Apostolic Fathers: An Introduction*, ed. Wilhelm Pratcher, 91–116. Waco, TX: Baylor University Press, 2010

Lossky, Olga and Michael Plekon. *Toward the Endless Day: The Life of Elisabeth Behr-Sigel*. Notre Dame, IN: University of Notre Dame Press, 2010.

Luchenko, Ksenia. "The Anti-War Faction in the Russian Orthodox Church Has Yet to Find Its Voice." https://carnegieendowment.org/russia-eurasia/politika/2024/02/the-anti-war-faction-in-the-russian-orthodox-church-has-yet-to-find-its-voice?lang=en. Accessed October 18, 2024.

MacCulloch, Diarmaid. *Christianity: The First Three Thousand Years*. London: Penguin, 2011.

Mack, John. "Peter the Great and the Ecclesiastical Regulation: Secularization or Reformation?" *St. Vladimir's Theological Quarterly* 49, no. 3 (2005): 243–269.

Mateos, Juan. *La célébration de la parole dans la liturgie byzantine: étude historique*. Orientalia Christiana Analecta 181. Rome: Pontifical Oriental Institute, 1971.

Mateos, Juan, ed. *Le typicon de la grande église*, vol. 2: *Le cycle des fêtes mobiles*. Orientalia Christiana Analecta 166. Rome: Pontifical Oriental Institute, 1963.

Mathewes-Green, Frederica. *Praying the Jesus Prayer*. Belmont, MA: Paraclete Press, 2011.

Maximus the Confessor. *On the Cosmic Mystery of Christ*. Trans. Paul Blowers and Robert Louis Wilken, Popular Patristics Series. Crestwood, NY: St. Vladimir's Seminary Press, 2003.

McGowan, Anne and Paul Bradshaw, eds. *The Pilgrimage of Egeria: A New Translation of the Itinerarium Egeriae*. Collegeville, MN: Liturgical Press, 2018.

McGuckin, John. *The Eastern Orthodox Church: A New History*. New Haven, CT: Yale University Press, 2020.

McKenna, John. *Eucharist and Holy Spirit: The Eucharistic Epiclesis in 20th Century Theology*. Alcuin Club Collections no. 57. Great Wakering: Mayhew-McRimmon, 1975.

McPartlan, Paul. *A Service of Love: Papal Primacy, the Eucharist, and Church Unity*. Washington, DC: The Catholic University of America Press, 2023.

Meyendorff, Paul. *The Anointing of the Sick*, Orthodox Liturgy Series, Book 1. Crestwood, NY: St. Vladimir's Seminary Press, 2009.

Mitchell, Brian Patrick. *The Disappearing Deaconess: Why the Church Once Had Deaconesses and then Stopped Having Them*. Alexandria, VA: Eeremia Publications, 2021.

Morosan, Vladimir. *Choral Performance in Pre-Revolutionary Russia*, Russian Music Studies no. 17. Madison, CT: Musica Russica, 1986.

Moscow Patriarchate. Basis of the Social Concept of the Russian Orthodox Church. https://old.mospat.ru/en/documents/social-concepts. Accessed August 30, 2024.

Moscow Patriarchate. Наказ XXB Всемирного русского народного собора «Настоящее и будущее Русского мира»." https://www.patriarchia.ru/db/text/6116189.html. Accessed July 26, 2024.

Moscow Patriarchate. "Постановление Архиерейского Совещания (Свято-Троицкая Сергиева лавра, 19 июля 2023 года, день Собора Радонежских святых)." https://www.patriarchia.ru/db/text/6043699.html. Accessed September 4, 2024.

Muksuris, Stelyios. *Economia and Eschatology: Liturgical Mystagogy in the Byzantine Prothesis Rite*. Brookline, MA: Holy Cross Orthodox Press, 2013.

Namee, Matthew, et al. *Converts to Orthodoxy: Statistics and Trends from the Last Decade*. Houston, TX: Orthodox Studies Institute, 2024.

Nikodemus of the Holy Mountain, St. Makarios of Corinth. *The Philokalia,* 3 vols. Trans. and eds. Phillip Sherrard and Kallistos Ware. New York: Farrar, Straus and Giroux, 1983.

Nikodemus of the Holy Mountain, St. *The Philokalia,* vol. 4. Trans. and eds. Phillip Sherrard and Kallistos Ware. New York: Farrar, Straus and Giroux, 1998.

Orthodox Church. *The Horologion or the Book of the Hours, The Daily Offices.* Trans. St. Tikhon's Monastery. South Canaan, PA: St. Tikhon's Seminary Press, 2000.

Orthodox Church. *Hieratikon,* vol. 2: *Liturgy Book for Priest and Deacon.* Rev. edition, eds. Hieromonk Herman and Vitaly Permiakov. South Canaan, PA: St. Tikhon's Seminary Press, 2020.

Orthodox Church in America. "Guidelines for Clergy." 2023-OCA-Guidelines-for-Clergy.pdf. Accessed October 2, 2024.

Orthodox Church in America. "Statement on Same-Sex Relationships and Sexual Identity." Holy Synod – Encyclicals – Statement on Same-Sex Relationships and Sexual Identity – Orthodox Church in America (oca.org). Accessed August 30, 2024.

Orthodox Church of Ukraine. "Conciliar Letter." https://www.pomisna.info/uk/document-post/lyst-arhiyerejskogo-soboru-upts-ptsu-vselenskomu-patriarhu-varfolomiyu/. Accessed July 26, 2024.

Orthodox Joint Commission. First Agreed Statement (1989) « Orthodox Unity (Orthodox Joint Commission) (wordpress.com). Accessed September 6, 2024.

Pan-Orthodox Council. "Autonomy and the Means by Which It Is Proclaimed." Autonomy and the Means by Which It Is Proclaimed – The Holy and Great Council of the Orthodox Church (holycouncil.org). Accessed September 9, 2024.

Pan-Orthodox Council. "The Importance of Fasting and Its Observance Today." https://www.holycouncil.org/fasting. Accessed September 9, 2024.

Pan-Orthodox Council. "Relations of the Orthodox Church with the Rest of the Christian World." Relations of the Orthodox Church with the Rest of the Christian World - The Holy and Great Council of the Orthodox Church (holycouncil.org). Accessed August 12, 2024.

Pan-Orthodox Council. "The Sacrament of Marriage and Its Impediments." The Sacrament of Marriage and Its Impediments – The Holy and Great Council of the Orthodox Church (holycouncil.org). Accessed August 30, 2024.

Papadakis, Aristeides. "Hesychasm." https://www.oxfordreference.com/view/10.1093/acref/9780195046526.001.0001/acref-9780195046526-e-2276. Accessed September 30, 2024.

"The Papal Selection Process for the Coptic Orthodox Church." The Coptic Orthodox Church UK: Search Results for Altar Ballot (copticcentre.blogspot.com). Accessed September 4, 2024.

Papanikolaou, Aristotle. "Liberating Eros: Confession and Desire." *Journal of the Society for Christian Ethics* 26, no. 1 (2006): 115–136

Parry, Ken. "Serbian Christianity." In *The Blackwell Dictionary of Eastern Christianity*, eds. Ken Parry et al., 442–446 Malden, MA: Blackwell, 2001.

Patriarch Kirill. "Патриаршая проповедь в Неделю сыропустную после Литургии в Храме Христа Спасителя." https://www.patriarchia.ru/db/text/5906442.html. Accessed September 4, 2024.

Pelikan, Jaroslav. *The Christian Tradition: A History of the Development of Doctrine*, vol. 1: *The Emergence of the Catholic Doctrine*, 100–600. Chicago, IL: University of Chicago Press, 1971.

Pentcheva, Bissera. *Hagia Sophia: Sound, Space, and Spirit in Byzantium*. University Park: The Pennsylvania State University Press, 2017.

Pew Research Center. "Ethiopia Is an Outlier in the Orthodox Christian World." https://www.pewresearch.org/short-reads/2017/11/28/ethiopia-is-an-outlier-in-the-orthodox-christian-world/. Accessed July 8, 2024.

Pew Research Center. "Orthodox Christianity in the 21st Century." https://www.pewresearch.org/religion/2017/11/08/orthodox-christianity-in-the-21st-century/. Accessed September 4, 2021.

Pew Research Center. "Religious Belief and National Belonging in Central and Eastern Europe." Religious Commitment and Practices in Central and Eastern Europe | Pew Research Center. Accessed September 11, 2024. https://www.pewresearch.org/religion/2017/05/10/religious-belief-and-national-belonging-in-central-and-eastern-europe/

Pino, Tikhon. *Essence and Energies: Being and Naming God in St. Gregory Palamas*. Abingdon: Routledge, 2023.

Pius XII, Pope. "Apostolic Constitution Munificentissimus Deus." https://www.vatican.va/content/pius-xii/en/apost_constitutions/documents/hf_p-xii_apc_19501101_munificentissimus-deus.html. Accessed August 8, 2024.

Plekon, Michael. "Church, Society, Politics: Perspectives from the 'Paris School'." *Logos: A Journal of Eastern Christian Studies* 53, nos. 3–4 (2012): 198–219.

Plekon, Michael. *Living Icons: Persons of Faith in the Eastern Church*. Foreword Lawrence Cunningham. Notre Dame, IN: University of Notre Dame Press, 2002.

Plested, Marcus. *Wisdom in Christian Tradition: The Roots of Moder Russian Sophiology*. Oxford: Oxford University Press, 2022.

Plokhy, Serhii. *Lost Kingdom: A History of Russian Nationalism from Ivan the Great to Vladimir Putin*. New York: Penguin, 2017.

Popova, Maria and Oxana Shevel. *Russia and Ukraine: Entangled Histories, Diverging States*. Hoboken, NJ: Polity Press, 2024.

Pospielovsky, Dimitry. *The Orthodox Church in the History of Russia*. Crestwood, NY: St. Vladimir' Seminary Press, 1998.

Pro Oriente. *The Vienna Dialogue: Five Pro Oriente Consultations with Oriental Orthodoxy*, bk. 1. Horn: Ferdinand Berger and Sohne, n.d.

Pro Oriente. *The Vienna Dialogue: Five Pro Oriente Consultations with Oriental Orthodoxy*, on Primacy, bk. 4. Horn: Ferdinand Berger and Sohne, 1993.

Purpura, Ashley. *God, Hierarchy and Power: Orthodox Theologies of Authority from Byzantium*. Orthodox Christianity and Contemporary Thought Series. New York: Fordham University Press, 2018.

Purpura, Ashley. "Innovating 'Traditional' Women's Roles: Byzantine Insights for Orthodox Christian Gender Discourse." *Modern Theology* 36, no. 3 (2020): 641–661.

Radle, Gabriel. *Marriage in Byzantium: Christian Liturgical Rites from Betrothal to Consummation.* New York: Cambridge University Press, 2024.

Rahner, Karl. *Theological Investigations*, vol. 17: Jesus*, Man, and the Church*. Trans. Margaret Kohl. New York: Crossroad, 1981.

Ravenna Document. "Ecclesiological and Canonical Consequences for the Sacramental Nature of the Church: Ecclesial Communion, Conciliarity and Authority." Ravenna Document | Ecclesiological and Canonical Consequences of the Sacramental Nature of the Church. Ecclesial Communion, Conciliarity and Authority (christianunity.va). Accessed August 26, 2024. https://www.jacobsmag.org/riccardiswartz

Riccardi-Swartz, Sarah. *Between Heaven and Russia: Religious Conversion and Political Apostasy in Appalachia.* New York: Fordham University Press, 2022.

Riccardi-Swartz, Sarah. "Orthodoxy and the E-Spirit of Radicalism." Sarah Riccardi-Swartz: Orthodoxy and the E-Spirit of Radicalism—Jacob's Well (jacobsmag.org). Accessed September 30, 2024.

Roman Catholic Church. *Rite of Christian Initiation of Adults.* Washington, DC: United States Conference of Catholics Bishops, 1988.

Roudometof, Victor. "Invented Traditions, Symbolic Boundaries, and National Identity in Southeastern Europe: Greece and Serbia in Comparative Historical Perspective (1830–1880)." *East European Quarterly* 24, no. 1 (1999): 429–468.

Russell, Norman. *Fellow Workers with God: Orthodox Thinking on Theosis.* Yonkers, NY: St. Vladimir's Seminary Press, 2009.

Russell, Norman. *Gregory Palamas and the Making of Palamism in the Modern Age.* Oxford: Oxford University Press, 2019.

Russo, Nicholas. "The Origins of Lent." Ph.D. diss, University of Notre Dame, 2009.

Saggau, Emil. "Checkmate: Serbian Orthodox Diplomacy in the Shadow of the Ukrainian War." https://publicorthodoxy.org/2022/09/21/serbian-orthodox-diplomacy-ukrainian-war/. Accessed August 17, 2024.

Savin, Olga, trans. *The Way of a Pilgrim and the Pilgrim Continues His Way*. Intro Thomas Hopko. Boston, MA: Shambhala, 2009.

Schmemann, Alexander. *The Eucharist: Sacrament of the Kingdom*. Trans. Paul Kachur. Crestwood, NY: St. Vladimir's Seminary Press, 1984.

Schmemann, Alexander. *For the Life of the World: Sacraments and Orthodoxy*. Rev. ed. Foreword Edith Humphrey. Yonkers, NY: St. Vladimir's Seminary Press, 2018.

Schmemann, Alexander. "The Idea of Primacy in Orthodox Ecclesiology." In *Primacy in the Church*, vol. 1, ed. John Chryssavgis, 339–366. Crestwood, NY: St. Vladimir's Seminary Press, 2016.

Schmemann, Alexander. *Liturgy and Tradition: Theological Reflections of Alexander Schmemann*, ed. Thomas Fisch. Crestwood, NY: St. Vladimir's Seminary Press, 1990.

Second Vatican Council. Lumen gentium (vatican.va). Accessed October 2, 2024.

Second Vatican Council. Unitatis redintegratio (vatican.va). Accessed August 30, 2024.

Secretariat for the Preparation for the Holy and Great Council of the Orthodox Church. *Synodika XII: IV Conférence Orthodoxe Préconciliaire, Chambésy 6-13 Juin 2009*. Chambésy: centre Orthodoxe du Patriarcat Oecuménique, 2015.

Shevzov, Vera. "Petitions to the Holy Synod Regarding Miracle-Working Icons." In *Orthodox Christianity in Imperial Russia: A Source Book on Lived Religion*, ed. Heather Coleman, 229–248. Bloomington: Indiana University Press, 2014.

Skobtsova, Maria. *Essential Writings*. Trans. Richard Pevear and Larissa Volokhonsky, intro Jim Forest. Modern Spiritual Masters Series. Maryknoll, NY: Orbis, 2003.

Skouboulis, Anna, trans. *The Philokalia of the Holy Neptic Fathers*, vol. 5. n.p.: Virgin Mary of Australia and Oceania, 2020. https://search.worldcat.org/title/1291631709

Slagle, Amy. *The Eastern Church in the Spiritual Marketplace: American Conversions to Orthodox Christianity*. DeKalb, IL: Northern Illinois University Press, 2007.

St. Phoebe Center for the Deaconess. "Proposed Guidelines for the Revival of the Ordained Female Diaconate in the Orthodox Church Today." https://orthodoxdeaconess.org/proposed-guidelines/. Accessed September 4, 2024.

Stewart, Columba (2018). "Jesus Prayer." https://www.oxfordreference.com/view/10.1093/acref/9780198662778.001.0001/acref-9780198662778-e-2487. Accessed September 30, 2024.

Streza, Ciprian Ioan. "The Mystery of Marriage: Mystery of Human Love Crowned in Glory and Honour. An Orthodox Perspective." *Review of Ecumenical Studies Sibiu* 10 (2018): 388–411.

Subtelny, Orest. *Ukraine: A History*, 4th rev. ed. Toronto: University of Toronto Press, 2009.

Suslov, Mikhail. "The Russian Orthodox Church and the Crisis in Ukraine." In *Churches in the Ukrainian Crisis*, eds. Andrii Krawchuk and Thomas Bremer, 133–162. New York: Palgrave Macmillan, 2016.

Symeon the New Theologian. *On the Mystical Life: The Ethical Discourses*, vol. 2: *On Virtue and Christian Life*. Trans. Alexander Golitzin. Crestwood, NY: St. Vladimir's Seminary Press, 1996.

Sysyn, Frank. "The Third Rebirth of the Ukrainian Autocephalous Orthodox Church and the Religious Situation in Ukraine, 1989-1991." In *Religion and Nation in Modern Ukraine*, eds. Serhii Plokhy and Frank Sysyn, 88–119. Edmonton: Canadian Institute of Ukrainian Studies, 2003.

Taft, Robert. *Beyond East and West: Problems in Liturgical Understanding*, 2d ed. Rome: Pontifical Oriental Institute, 2001.

Taft, Robert. *The Byzantine Rite: A Short History.* Collegeville, MN: Liturgical Press, 1992.

Taft, Robert. "Comparative Liturgy Fifty Years after Anton Baumstark (d. 1948): A Reply to Recent Critics." *Worship* 73 (1999): 521–40.

Taft, Robert. *A History of the Liturgy of St. John Chrysostom*, 4 vols. Orientalia Christiana Analecta 200, 238, 261, 281. Rome: Pontifical Oriental Institute, 1975.

Taft, Robert. "Holy Week in the Byzantine Tradition." In *Between Memory and Hope: Readings on the Liturgical Year*, ed. Maxwell Johnson, 155–181. Collegeville, MN: Liturgical Press, 2000.

Taft, Robert. "The Liturgical Enterprise Twenty-Five Years after Alexander Schmemann: The Man and His Legacy." *St. Vladimir's Orthodox Theological Quarterly* 53, nos. 2–3 (2009): 139–77.

Talbot, Alice-Mary. "A Comparison of the Monastic Experiences of Byzantine Men and Women." *Greek Orthodox Theological Review* 30, no. 1 (1985): 1–20.

Tanner, Norman, ed. *Decrees of the Ecumenical Councils.* Washington, DC: Georgetown University Press, 1990.

Theophan the Recluse. *The Path to Salvation: A Manual of Spiritual Transformation.* Trans. Fr. Seraphim Rose and the St. Herman of Alaska Brotherhood. Platina, CA: St. Paisius Brotherhood, 1996.

Thomson, Robert. "Armenian Christianity." In *The Blackwell Dictionary of Eastern Christianity*, eds. Parry et al., 54–59. Malden, MA: Blackwell, 2001.

Toroczkai, Ciprian Iulian. "The Orthodox Neo-Patristic Movements as a Renewal of Contemporary Orthodox Theology: An Overview." *Review of Ecumenical Studies* 7, no. 1 (2015): 94–115.

Ukrainian Orthodox Church. "Resolutions of the Council of the Ukrainian Orthodox Church on May 27, 2022." Resolutions of the Council of the Ukrainian Orthodox Church of May 27, 2022 – Ukrainian Orthodox Church (uoc-news.church). Accessed September 6, 2024.

von Gardner, Johann. *Russian Church Singing*, vol. 1: *Orthodox Worship and Hymnography*, trans. Vladimir Morosan. Crestwood, NY: St. Vladimir's Seminary Press, 1980.

Ware, Kallistos. *The Inner Kingdom*. Crestwood, NY: St. Vladimir's Seminary Press, 2001.

Ware, Kallistos. *The Jesus Prayer.* London: Catholic Church Society, 2014.

Ware, Kallistos. "Man, Woman, and the Priesthood of Christ." In *Women and the Priesthood*, ed. Thomas Hopko, 5–54. Crestwood, NY: St. Vladimir's Seminary Press, 2000.

Ware, Kallistos. "The Orthodox Church and the Primacy of Peter: Are We Any Closer to a Solution?" In *The Primacy of the Church*, vol. 2: *The Office of Primate and the Authority of Councils*, ed. John Chryssavgis, 861–888. Crestwood, NY: St. Vladimir's Seminary Press, 2016.

Wilken, Robert Louis. *The First Thousand Years: A Global History of Christianity*. New Haven, CT: Yale University Press, 2012.

Wynot, Edward. *The Polish Orthodox Church in the Twentieth Century and Beyond: Prisoner of History.* Lanham, MD: Lexington Books, 2015.

Zheltov, Michael. "Обзор истории чинов благословения брака в православной традиции." In *Православное учение о церковных таинствах, v. 3, Православное учение о церковных таинствах,* ed. Michael Zheltov. 109–126. Moscow: Synodal Biblical-Theological Commission, 2009.

Zizioulas, John. *Being as Communion: Studies in Personhood and the Church*. Foreword John Meyendorff. Crestwood, NY: St. Vladimir's Seminary Press, 1985. 2002 reprint.

Zizioulas, John. *Eucharist, Bishop, Church: The Unity of the Church in the Divine Eucharist and the Bishop during the First Three Centuries*. Trans. Elizabeth Theotikroff. Brookline, MA: Holy Cross Orthodox Press, 2001.

Zizioulas, John. "Symbolism and Realism in Orthodox Worship." Trans. Elizabeth Theokritoff. In *Synaxis: An Anthology of the Most Significant Orthodox Theology in Greece Appearing in the Journal Synaxe*, vol. 1: *Anthropology, Environment, Creation*, trans. Peter Chamberas, ed. Liaidan Sherrard, 251–264. Montreal: Alexander Press, 2006.

INDEX

academia *see* education, theological
Afanasiev, Nicholas 170, 213
Alexandria 4, 33, 41–2, 198–9, 248, 253; in Apostolic Age 6, 11, 12, 14, 15, 21; Clement of Alexandria 22; Coptic church 35–6, 171, 218; and deaconesses 232, 235, 255; and gnosticism 22; as learning center 6, 14, 21–5, 30, 40–1, 185, 195; Mark, apostle 11, 42, 198; Origen 22–4, 98, 253; Orthodox Patriarchate of Alexandria 35, 51, 199, 201–3, 232, 255; *see also* Antioch; Egypt; Oriental Orthodox churches; Valentinus
anaphora 86–8, 178–9; inclusion of deceased 200–1; "Only-begotten Son" hymn 85–7, 174; Orthodox interpretation of 179–82; of St. Basil 87–8, 178–9; of St. John Chrysostom 86–7, 178; *see also* Divine Liturgy; liturgical tradition
anointing of the sick 148–9
Antioch 4, 42; Antiochene theology 15, 19, 248; in Apostolic Age 6, 12, 14, 15, 19, 24, 25, 195, 198; the Didache 17–9, 24; Ignatius of Antioch 15–9; as learning center 6, 25; patriarchate of 35, 51, 64, 199, 202–3, 216; Peter, apostle 15, 24, 198; Polycarp 19–20, 24; St. John Chrysostom 168; Severus of Antioch 81–2; *see also* Alexandria; Christology; Irenaeus of Lyons; missionary activity; Nestorius
apostles 2, 5, 10–12, 111, 185, 253; apostolic teaching 6, 11–12, 18, 21, 24, 39, 210, 234, 253; and Church communities 2, 5–6, 13–14, 42, 89, 195–8; and the Didache 18; and handlaying rites 11, 141, 143; and Holy Spirit 11, 185, 213; and Nicene-Constantinopolitan Creed 80; *see also* Apostolic Age; Luke, apostle; Mark, apostle; Paul, apostle; Peter, apostle; patristic tradition
Apostolic Age 14, 89, 182, 240; Alexandria 6, 11, 12, 14, 15, 21; Antioch 6, 12, 14, 15, 19, 24, 25, 195, 198; Ephesus 195; Rome 14, 21, 195, 198; Palestine 23, 24; *see also* apostles; Luke, apostle; Mark, apostle; Paul, apostle; Peter, apostle; patristic tradition
architecture 7, 156; exterior 157–9; and iconography 157, 159; and interior design 156–7, 159
Arianism 39, 40, 90; *see also* Arius
Arius 25, 29, 39, 83, 88, 89, 253; *see also* Arianism; Nicene-Constantinopolitan Creed
Armenia 33–5, 42; Church of 34; Armenian genocide 36

Athanasius 31, 33, 36, 39, 41, 89; "divine dilemma" 84, 111; *On the Incarnation* 9, 83–5, 134, 210; and Orthodox Christology 83–5, 87–8; and theosis 95, 111; *see also* Christology, Nicene-Constantinopolitan Creed

autocephalous church 3, 7, 195, 199–202, 213, 229; in Bulgaria 49; challenges to 204–10; in Constantinople 49–50; in Georgia 4, 12, 35, 42, 64, 200; in Greece 49–50, 206; in Moscow 51; in nation-states 62, 64, 202–4, 206, 251–2; in North America 66, 207; in Poland 59, 205–6; in Russia 206; in Serbia 43, 49; in Ukraine 59, 62–4, 203, 204, 206, 209

autonomous church 3, 203–4; in Bulgaria 42–44, 49; in Finland 203–4; in Japan 204; in Ukraine 54, 203, 209

baptism 134–8, 140, 170, 213, 241, 250; in Antioch and Alexandria 19, 22; baptismal waters 135, 136; Baptism of Rus' 43, 61, 184; Chrism 128, 136, 137, 209; and exclusivism 200; and exorcism 135; and handlaying rites 11, 141; and Holy Spirit 95, 112, 249; ideal setting and timing of 138–9, 186, 188; and John the Baptist 112; and marriage 229; and Maximus Confessor 96–7; and Nicene-Constantinopolitan Creed 77; and non-Orthodox 225; rituals in 138; and St. Maria 130; and theosis 111; *see also* Chrismation

Basil of Caesarea 28, 39, 127, 167, 253; hypostasis 89; teachings of 95–97; *see also* anaphora; Divine Liturgy

Bolshevik persecution *see* Soviet Union

Bulgakov, Sergius 6, 98, 101, 104, 130; *see also* Sophiology

Bulgaria, Orthodox Church in 2, 64, 200, 203, 218; in America 66, 207; history of 42–4, 48–9, 236; music 161

burial, rites of 134, 149–50, 174

Byzantine Orthodox 9, 28; architecture 156; and Byzantine Empire 49, 52, 144, 169, 240; chants and hymns 160, 164; and iconoclasm 83; and monasticism 43; and Oriental Orthodox 35, 36; rites and rituals 29, 45, 168, 182, 232; and Russia 55; and St. Basil 167, 178; *see also* Taft, Robert

Chalcedon, Council of 3, 51, 66, 199, 219, 248; and Chalcedonian vs non-Chalcedonian Christianity 3, 32–41, 44, 81–3; and Tome of Leo 32, 34; and Zeno, emperor 34, 40

Chrismation 112, 135–41, 147, 170, 209; *see also* baptism

Christian socialism 129–30

Christology 15, 33–4, 39, 66, 174, 248; and Athanasius 83–5, 88, 248; Chalcedonian vs non-Chalcedonian Christianity 3, 33–5, 81–3; and Justinian, emperor 34, 37, 85, 174; miaphysite (or monophysite) 35, 81, 82, 250; and Maximus, monk 38; monoenergism 38; monothelitism 37–38, 40; in Orthodox liturgy 85–100; and Pontius Pilate 15, 78–9; and Theodore of Mopsuestia 40, 253; and Tome of Leo 32, 34; *see also* Athanasius; God, Orthodox conception of; Nicene-Constantinopolitan Creed; pneumatology; Valentinus

Chrysostom, John 127; anaphora of 86, 92, 178; Divine Liturgy of 28, 86–7, 92, 127, 154, 167–8, 189; Pascha service 122

confession 112, 137, 140–3, 155, 211, 232; and penance 140–3

Constantine, emperor 29, 31, 40, 76, 140, 195; Edict of Milan 196; St. Helen 233
Constantinople 168, 198–202; canon 28, 33, 41, 66; fall of 6, 45–8, 66, 169, 203; and iconoclasm 38; and inter-Orthodox Church relations 63–4; as "mother" church 207, 216; as new Rome 29–31, 40–1, 195, 198, 207; patriarchate of 4, 43, 51, 59, 61–2, 102, 130, 146, 199, 203, 205, 208, 227, 236, 238, 252; and Poland 59, 61, 205–06; and Roman church 224–5; Studite monastery 38; and *taxis* 199; and Ukraine 43, 50–1, 54, 59, 63, 208–9, 216; *see also* Constantinople, Council of; fifth ecumenical council; sixth ecumenical council; *see also* Constantinople, Council of; fifth ecumenical council; Ottoman Empire
Constantinople, Council of 41, 198–9, 249; and Gregory of Nazianzus 30; Nicene-Constantinopolitan Creed 9, 32, 76, 90, 104; *see also* Constantinople
Constantinople, second council in *see* fifth ecumenical council
Cyril, bishop of Alexandria 31–3, 81–2; *see also* Nestorius; Ephesus, Council of
Cyrillic alphabet 42; *see also* missionary activity
Cyril of Jerusalem 111, 127, 134

daily cycle 182–3; *see also* fixed cycle; liturgical year; movable cycle; weekly cycle
Didache, the 18–9, 24
diptychs 12, 114, 199, 200; and autocephaly 209
Divine Liturgy 3, 7, 19, 155, 165, 200; and the anaphora 86, 92, 179–82; at baptism and Chrismation 138–9; and burial rites 149; and Christology 85–8; and confession 141; epiclesis of the 179, 249; and fasting 120–1, 181; and fixed cycle 183; and the Great Entrance 176–7; and iconography 157; Liturgy of Communion 175–9; Liturgy of the Word 170–5; ministers of 169–70, 198; and monastic traditions 169; and movable cycle 188–9; and pneumatology 92–5, 112; and St. Basil the Great 87–8, 92, 94, 167, 168; and St. James of Jerusalem 167–8; and St. John Chrysostom 87, 92, 122, 154, 167–8; and saints 123–5; and Schmemann, Alexander 156; *see also* anaphora; liturgical tradition

ecumenical councils, Christ in 88; Nicene-Constantinopolitan Creed 76–80; hypostatic union 80–1
ecumenism 225–6
education, theological 6, 52, 60, 253–4, 256; Fordham University, Orthodox Studies 103–4; International Orthodox Theological Association (IOTA) 103; and Irenaeus of Lyons 21–2; and Ostrozky, Prince Konstantin 52; Volos Academy of Theological Studies 103; *see also* political theology
Egypt 11, 22, 72; and Council of Chalcedon 33–5, 39, 41; and monasteries 30, 182; *see also* Alexandria; Chalcedon, Council of
Ephesus, Council of 30–4, 80, 248; Mary as Theotokos 80; *see also* Cyril, bishop of Alexandria; Mary, Virgin; Nestorius
Ephesus, second council in 32
Ephrem the Syrian 81–2
eschatology: hell 98–9; judgment 97–99, 104, 149; purgatory 47, 98; universal salvation 98; *see also* Paul, apostle

Eucharistic Prayer *see* anaphora
exclusivism 5, 7, 10, 28, 41, 195, 218, 224–5, 250–1; and baptism 200

fasting 18–9, 63, 74, 116–22, 130, 141–2; and Holy Communion 117–18; and Lent 181, 186, 189; and monastic life 119; and sex 226; and weekly cycle 163
fathers, legacy of the *see* patristic tradition
feasting 121–3, 130, 163, 164; and Eucharist 121; and holidays 121–3; *see also* fixed cycle; liturgical year; movable cycle
fifth ecumenical council 37, 40
first ecumenical council *see* Nicaea, Council of
fixed cycle 7, 183; feasts 184–5; *see also* daily cycle; liturgical year; movable cycle; weekly cycle
Florence-Ferrara, Council of 46–8, 51; and Metropolitan Isidore of Moscow 47; *see also* pentarchy
Fourth Crusade 44–6, 66, 224–5; violence against Greeks 46, 225

gender, views on 7, 226, 239, 241, 252, 254–5; deaconesses in Zimbabwe 201–2, 232, 255; of God 73; and marriage 228–29; and women 103, 218, 228–9, 234, 236; *see also* political theology; sexuality; women in Orthodoxy
Gillet, Lev 74–5, 116
gnosticism *see* Alexandria
God, Orthodox conception of 25, 72–6, 150, 169, 178, 212; in anaphoras 86–8, 178–9; as Christ 77–81; apophatic theology 73; Holy Spirit 89–92, 179; Holy Trinity 6, 86, 88–90, 95, 174, 196, 249; and humankind 95–100, 226–31, 234, 241, 250, 255; kataphatic theology 73; as love 25, 74–5, 98, 134, 137, 147, 150; *perichoresis* 73; and St. Symeon 74–5; theosis 6, 95, 110–11; *see also* Christology; eschatology; Gillet, Lev; hesychasm; metanoia; pneumatology; Schmemann, Alexander; Sophiology; Valentinus
Great Schism of 1054 6, 45, 48
Greek Orthodox Church 11; autocephaly 49; and diaspora 65, 230; history of 35, 43–4, 46–7, 53, 82; and iconography 159; *kollyvades* movement 125; Philoptochos Society 233; Rum millet 48, 144, 236; traditions and customs of 122, 143, 165, 167, 174, 187; *see also* Zoe brotherhood; Ukrainian Greek Catholic Church (UGCC)
Gregory of Nyssa 95–8, 253

Hebrew Bible 4, 22, 36, 139, 175, 253; *see also* New Testament; Scriptures
hesychasm 6, 110–12, 115, 130; *see also* God, Orthodox conception of; Mount Athos; Jesus Prayer
hierarchy 103, 169, 255
Holy Roman Empire 45; Charlemagne 45
Holy Spirit *see* God, Orthodox conception of; pneumatology

icon veneration 6, 110, 130, 154; in churches 157–60, 166, 173, 176; in daily practice 56–7, 113–15, 252; diptychs and triptychs 114; and iconoclasm 38–9, 83, 156, 168–9; and John of Damascus 38–9; during Lent 186; and priests 234; in Rus' and Russia 44, 102; of saints 124, 249–50; and seventh ecumenical council 38–9, 83, 211; and St. Maria 130; and Theodora, empress 39; and Theodore the Studite 38, 168–9
International Orthodox Theological Association (IOTA) 103;

Gavrilyuk, Paul 103; *see also* political theology
IOTA *see* International Orthodox Theological Association (IOTA)
Irene, empress *see* women in Orthodoxy

Jerusalem 4, 28, 51, 168, 199; patriarchate of 199; *see also* Chalcedon, Council of
Jesus Prayer 6, 110, 112, 115–6; *see also* hesychasm, Mount Athos

Kyiv Metropolia 50–5; and Avvakum, Archpriest 53; Metropolitanate of Moscow 51; Moscow Patriarchate 52–5; Ostrozky, Prince Konstantin 52; and Roman church 52; and Russian imperialism 54–5; Zosima, Metropolitan 51; *see also* Kyivan Rus'; Orthodox Church of Ukraine; Russian empire; Russian Orthodox Church; Ukrainian Autocephalous Orthodox Church (UAOC); Ukrainian Orthodox Church-Kyivan Patriarchate
Kyivan Rus' 43–4, 50–1, 54; Baptism of Rus' 61, 64; Pechers'ka Lavra monastery 43, 61; *see also* Kyiv Metropolia; Orthodox Church of Ukraine; Russian empire; Russian Orthodox Church; Ukrainian Autocephalous Orthodox Church (UAOC); Ukrainian Orthodox Church-Kyivan Patriarchate

last rites *see* anointing of the sick
LGBTQ community 7, 242, 256
liturgical music 7, 52, 160–3, 170, 176, 252; chants 5, 7, 44, 154, 160–3, 166–7, 232; hymns 44, 81, 104, 160–1, 163–8, 173–5, 177, 180, 183; kontakion 161, 173; Kyivan tones 164; in Lent and Pascha 123, 186–9; Moscow Synodal Choir 162; responsorial psalmody 161–2, 174–5; *stichera* 165–7; in weddings 147; *see also* daily cycle; liturgical tradition; weekly cycle
liturgical tradition 7, 46, 85, 248; Divine Liturgy 167–9, 189; and epiclesis 93; of Hagia Sophia 161, 176; and Holy Communion 155–6, 171; and music and chanting 159–60; and "Only-begotten Son" hymn 85–6; and pneumatology 91–2, 95, 179; in Roman church 29, 128; scholarship on 129, 154–6; and Sundays 182; and the Typikon 165; *see also* Divine Liturgy; liturgical music; ministers; Mount Athos; Schmemann, Alexander
liturgical year 7, 113, 121, 167, 174–5, 183–9; *see also* daily cycle; fixed cycle; movable cycle; weekly cycle
Liturgy of the Hours *see* daily cycle
Luke, apostle 10, 15, 175

Mark, apostle 10–11, 42, 136, 198
Maronite church 36
marriage 63, 143–7, 228–9, 231, 250; authority in 228–9; contemporary decline of 230–1; and conversion 65; decrease in 147; and divine love 145; rites of 144, 146–7; same-sex marriage 129–30, 255–6; and sexuality 226–7, 239, 241
Mary, Virgin 10, 18; cult of in Constantinople 30–1, 80–1; iconography of 4, 157, 166; Marian feasts 121, 183–5, 226; veneration of 233; *see also* Ephesus, Council of
Melkites *see* Roman Catholic Church
metanoia 110, 112, 130
ministers: archbishop 4, 54, 197, 202, 212; bishops 4, 12–13, 16–17, 19, 157, 161, 170, 181, 196–203, 208, 211, 213–15, 217–18; community of people 134, 139, 159, 170, 213, 233, 254; deaconesses 5, 7, 58,

197, 201–2, 231–5, 255; deacons 5, 16–17, 19, 157, 161–2, 170–1, 176–7, 180–1, 196–8, 233–4; interim leaders 202; patriarchs 4; presbyters (priests) 4, 5, 16–17, 19, 139, 142–3, 148–9, 157, 159, 161–2, 170, 172–81, 187, 196–8, 201; protodeacons 5, 198; protopresbyters 198; readers 5, 197, 233; *see also* the Didache; primacy; women in Orthodoxy

missionary activity 6, 43–4, 232; and Antiochian Archdiocese of North America 66, 225; and Cyril and Methodius 42–3; and diaspora community 64–6; and Hilandar monastery 43; and immigration 62, 65; and Orthodox Church of America (OCA) 66, 207, 214; and Russian Orthodox Church Outside of Russia (ROCOR) 60, 66; and Saint Innocent 65; and Zoe brotherhood 126; *see also* Russian Revolution of 1917

Moscow Patriarchate (MP) *see* Russian Orthodox Church

Mount Athos 46–7, 75, 168–9; hesychia 112, 115; Palamas, Gregory 75, 127; *see also* hesychasm; Jesus Prayer; patristic tradition

movable cycle 7, 184; Holy Week 187–9; Lent and Pascha 186–8; Pentecost 189; *see also* daily cycle; fixed cycle; liturgical year; weekly cycle

nationalism 49, 50, 252; Russian 56

neo-conservative movement 129; and Schmemann, Alexander 104, 128–9, 134, 144–6, 154–6, 163, 207, 231; *see also* neo-patristic movement

neo-patristic movement 126–9; and Florovsky, Georges 101, 128; and Mohyla, Peter 53, 128; and Schmemann, Alexander 104, 128–9, 134, 144–6, 154–6, 163, 207, 231; *see also* neo-conservative movement; patristic tradition

Nestorius 30–4, 80; *see also* Ephesus, Council of; Cyril, bishop of Alexandria

New Testament: and Divine Liturgy 139, 164, 175; history of 10, 18, 22; and Jesus 79, 87, 118; and ministers 197; *see also* Scriptures

Nicaea, Council of: history of 29, 31–2, 39–40, 89; and Nicene-Constantinopolitan Creed 9, 78; and tradition 10, 211

Nicene-Constantinopolitan Creed: and Athanasius 33, 84; and Christ 76–80; filioque clause 29, 44–5, 47, 88–91, 249; history of 9–10, 32, 104; and Holy Spirit 90, 249; and liturgy 177, 201; and Only-begotten Son hymn 86; *see also* Athanasius; Constantinople, Council of; Nicaea, Council of

OCU *see* Orthodox Church of Ukraine

Old Testament *see* Hebrew Bible

Oriental Orthodox Church 3, 174, 219, 248, 251, 257; Armenian Apostolic Church 11, 33–4, 36, 42, 184, 215, 235, 255; Coptic church 35–6, 48, 102, 171, 218; ecclesiology of 215–16; Eritrean Orthodox Church 36; Ethiopian Orthodox Church 36; miaphysite Christology 3, 35–7, 40, 81–2, 251; Syrian Orthodox Church 11, 33–6, 81–2; Theodora, empress 34, 39

Orthodox Church of America (OCA) 66, 207, 214

Orthodox Church of Ukraine (OCU) 6, 64, 208–9; and St. Volodymyr 11; *see also* Russian empire; Russian Orthodox

Church; Ukrainian Autocephalous Orthodox Church (UAOC); Ukrainian independence; Ukrainian Orthodox Church (UOC); Ukrainian Orthodox Church-Kyivan Patriarchate; Ukrainian Orthodox Church under Moscow (UOC-MP)
Ottoman Empire 46, 169, 236; decline of 62, 126, 236; and patriarch of Constantinople 6, 52, 59; Rum millet 24, 48–50, 144, 203, 236; *see also* Constantinople

Palamas, Gregory 75, 112, 127, 186; *see also* hesychasm; Mount Athos; patristic tradition
Pascha *see* movable cycle
Paul, apostle: in Bible 10–12, 80, 85, 175, 248; on confession 140; and Peter 15, 24, 30, 195; on prayer 182; teachings of 95, 98, 118; *see also* apostles; Apostolic Age
Pechers'ka Lavra monastery *see* Kyivan Rus'
penance *see* confession
Peter, apostle 10; in Antioch 11, 15, 24, 198; in Rome 13, 30, 195, 198
Peter (the Great), *Tsar see* Russian empire; Russian Orthodox Church
patriarchate 4, 51–2, 199; *see also* Alexandria; Antioch; Constantinople; Jerusalem; Kyiv Metropolia; Rome; Russian Orthodox Church
patristic tradition 9, 82, 104, 127–8, 134; Church of the Fathers 9, 41, 80, 82, 88, 95, 126–8, 161, 210, 253; and Climacus, John 127; hymns of 161; and Palamas, Gregory 75, 127; *see also* apostles; Athanasius; Basil of Caesarea; Cyril of Jerusalem; Gregory of Nyssa; Mount Athos; neo-conservative movement; neo-patristic movement; Schmemann, Alexander
pentarchy 51–2, 199; *see also* Florence-Ferrara, Council of
pneumatology 88–92, 95, 249; epiclesis 93, 179, 249; Pneumatomachians 89; *see also* Christology; God, Orthodox conception of
Polish Orthodox Church 59, 61, 205
political theology 103, 242; *Basis of the Social Concept of the Russian Orthodox Church* (BSC) 239–40; *For the Life of the World* (FLOW) 240–2; Hovorun, Cyril 103, 210; Kalaitzidis, Pantelis 103; Papanikolaou, Aristotle 103; Volos Academy of Theological Studies 103; Fordham University, Orthodox Studies 103; *see also* education, theological; gender, views on; sexuality
Polycarp *see* Antioch
Pope Leo *see* Chalcedon, Council of
primacy 210, 212–16, 242; *see also* neo-conservative movement; neo-patristic movement; patristic tradition

Roman Catholic Church: and apostles 6, 13, 42; division with Orthodox 45, 225, 251; documentation of teaching 238; and Eastern Catholic churches 204; ecumenism 29, 48, 52, 224–26; Latinization of 45; liturgy and Holy Communion 113, 128, 234; and Melkites 35–6; and Nicene-Constantinopolitan Creed 9, 29, 249; on primacy 3, 210, 215, 242; and purgatory 98; and Sunday 164
Roman church *see* Roman Catholic Church
Roman Empire 29, 41, 80, 196; decline of 34–5, 38, 44, 46;

and Melkites 36; and Oriental churches 36; *see also* Holy Roman Empire; Roman Catholic Church; Rome

Rome: and Chalcedon, Council of 41–2; patriarchate of 4, 41–2, 195–6, 199–200, 204, 214–15; and Pope 3, 13, 29, 40, 47–8, 198, 210, 214–15; and Roman church 12–14, 36–7, 45, 47, 51, 128, 198, 215, 224

Rum millet *see* Greek Orthodox Church; Ottoman Empire

Russia, post-Soviet 62–3, 217, 219, 237–8; and Putin, Vladimir 63; Russian World ideology 63; and Yeltsin, Boris 63

Russian empire: All-Russian Orthodox Church Council 56; Bloody Sunday 56; decline of 49, 57; and Gapon, Gregory 56, 130; and Nicholas I, *Tsar* 56; and Nicholas II, *Tsar* 56–7; and Peter (the Great), *Tsar* 53–5, 57, 255; Revolution of 1905 57; Spiritual Regulation 53–5, 57, 255; synodal period 55–7; Treaty of Pereiaslav 54; *see also* Kyiv Metropolia; Kyivan Rus'; Russian Orthodox Church; Soviet Union

Russian Orthodox Church 4, 33, 52–6, 60; and Aleksy II, Patriarch 63, 203, 209; All-Russian Orthodox Church Council 56; and Anthony (Khrapovitsky), Metropolitan 60, 217; *Basis of the Social Concept of the Russian Orthodox Church* (BSC) 238–42; Bolshevik persecution 24, 58–60, 205, 207; and Kirill (Gundaev), Metropolitan 63–4, 236–7, 254; Molotov-Ribbentrop agreement 60; Moscow Council of 1917–1918 57–8, 62, 217–18; Moscow Patriarchate (MP) 50–5, 61–4, 101, 203–5, 207–9, 214, 254; and Peter (the Great), *Tsar* 53–5, 57, 255; revolutionary period 57; and St. Volodymyr 11; Spiritual Regulation 53–5, 57, 255; Soviet period 57–62; and Stalin, Joseph 60–1; synodal period 55–7; and Tikhon (Bellavin), Patriarch 58, 60, 218; and Trotsky, Leon 58; and Ukraine, invasion of 64, 236–7; *see also* Kyiv Metropolia; Kyivan Rus'; Orthodox Church of Ukraine; Russian empire; Russian Orthodox Church; Ukrainian Autocephalous Orthodox Church (UAOC); Ukrainian independence; Ukrainian Greek Catholic Church (UGCC); Ukrainian Orthodox Church (UOC); Ukrainian Orthodox Church-Kyivan Patriarchate; Ukrainian Orthodox Church under Moscow (UOC-MP)

Russian Revolution of 1917 57–8, 61–2, 66, 207; Living Church 58–9; and Russian Orthodox Church Outside of Russia (ROCOR) 60; *see also* Russian empire; Russian Orthodox Church; Soviet Union

St. Athanasius of Alexandria *see* Athanasius

St. Basil *see* Basil of Caesarea

St. Cyril of Jerusalem *see* Cyril of Jerusalem

St. Gregory Palamas *see* Palamas, Gregory

St. Maria of Paris *see* Skobtsova, Maria

saints, veneration of 39, 121, 123–5, 183, 249–50; icons 114–15, 250; Peter and Paul 117, 195; relics 124, 250

Schmemann, Alexander 3, 104, 134, 207, 231; autocephaly in America 207; *For the Life of the World* 1, 134, 145; on marriage 144–6; and

neo-patristic movement 128–9; on liturgy 154–6, 163; *see also* patristic tradition; neo-conservative movement; neo-patristic movement
Scriptures 22–3, 210, 212, 216; Hebrew Bible 4, 22, 36, 139, 175, 253; in liturgy 170; and music 160, 162; New Testament 10, 18, 22, 79, 87, 118, 139, 164, 175; scholarship on 127; *see also* New Testament
second ecumenical council *see* Constantinople, Council of
seventh ecumenical council 38–40, 83, 114, 211
sexuality 226–7, 238–41, 252; cohabitation, polyamorism, and pan-sexuality 230–1; contraception 227, 239; homosexuality 7, 129, 144, 226, 229–31, 239–40, 254–6
sixth ecumenical council 37, 83, 88
Slavic Orthodox Churches 11; customs and traditions 120, 142–3, 164–5, 174; history of 42–4, 46; Slavic cross 159
Skobtsova, Maria 102, 130; *see also* women in Orthodoxy
Sophiology 100–1; and Bulgakov, Sergius 101; condemnation of 101; and Florensky, Pavel 101; and Soloviev, Vladimir 101
Soviet Union (USSR) 57–62, 205; Bolshevik persecution 24, 58, 60, 205, 207; Council of the Ukrainian Greek Catholic Church (UGCC) 61; fall of 62, 219, 237–8; and Khrushchev, Nikita 61; and Molotov-Ribbentrop agreement 60; Stalin 60–1; and Trotsky, Leon 58; Ukrainian integration into 60; *see also* Russian empire; Russian Orthodox Church
Studite monastery *see* Constantinople

Taft, Robert 154, 156, 169–70, 176; *see also* Byzantine Orthodox
taxis 13, 199

telos *see* eschatology
Theotokos *see* Mary, Virgin
Toledo, Council of 88, 90
the Typikon 165, 183

UAOC *see* Ukrainian Autocephalous Orthodox Church (UAOC)
UGCC *see* Ukrainian Greek Catholic Church (UGCC)
Ukrainian Autocephalous Orthodox Church (UAOC) 59–63; and autocephaly 62, 236; and Metropolitan Filaret (Denysenko) 62–3; and St. Volodymyr 11; *see also* Orthodox Church of Ukraine; Russian empire; Russian Orthodox Church; Ukrainian independence; Ukrainian Greek Catholic Church (UGCC); Ukrainian Orthodox Church (UOC); Ukrainian Orthodox Church-Kyivan Patriarchate (UOC-KP); Ukrainian Orthodox Church under Moscow (UOC-MP)
Ukrainian Greek Catholic Church (UGCC) 61–2, 236; *see also* Orthodox Church of Ukraine; Russian empire; Russian Orthodox Church; Ukrainian independence; Ukrainian Autocephalous Orthodox Church (UAOC); Ukrainian Orthodox Church (UOC); Ukrainian Orthodox Church-Kyivan Patriarchate (UOC-KP); Ukrainian Orthodox Church under Moscow (UOC-MP)
Ukrainian independence: civil war (1917–20) 58–60; Russian-Ukrainian War (2022) 236–7
Ukrainian Orthodox Church (UOC) 203, 208–9, 236; and St. Volodymyr 11; *see also* Orthodox Church of Ukraine; Russian

empire; Russian Orthodox Church; Ukrainian independence; Ukrainian Autocephalous Orthodox Church (UAOC); Ukrainian Greek Catholic Church (UGCC); Ukrainian Orthodox Church-Kyivan Patriarchate (UOC-KP); Ukrainian Orthodox Church under Moscow (UOC-MP)

Ukrainian Orthodox Church under Moscow (UOC-MP) 63; and St. Volodymyr 11; *see also* Orthodox Church of Ukraine; Russian empire; Russian Orthodox Church; Ukrainian independence; Ukrainian Autocephalous Orthodox Church (UAOC); Ukrainian Greek Catholic Church (UGCC); Ukrainian Orthodox Church (UOC); Ukrainian Orthodox Church-Kyivan Patriarchate (UOC-KP)

Ukrainian Orthodox Church-Kyivan Patriarchate (UOC-KP) 63, 236; and St. Volodymyr 11; *see also* Orthodox Church of Ukraine; Russian empire; Russian Orthodox Church; Ukrainian independence; Ukrainian Autocephalous Orthodox Church (UAOC); Ukrainian Greek Catholic Church (UGCC); Ukrainian Orthodox Church (UOC); Ukrainian Orthodox Church under Moscow (UOC-MP)

Valentinus 21–3; and Gospel of Truth 21; *see also* Alexandria; Christology; God, Orthodox conception of

Virgin Mary *see* Mary, Virgin

weekly cycle 163; *octoechos,* hymns in 164–6; Saturday Vigil 165–7; Sunday 164–5, 167–9, 182; *see also* daily cycle; fixed cycle; movable cycle

women in Orthodoxy: deaconesses and ordination of women 5, 7, 58, 197, 201–2, 231–6, 255; Frost, Frederick Carrie 228–9, 232, 235; gender 103, 228–9, 239, 255; Irene, empress 38–40; Mary, cult of in Constantinople 30–1, 80–1; ordination of 231–6; Pan-Orthodox Council of Crete 103; Philoptochos Society of the Greek Orthodox Church 233; saints 233, 249–50; Skobtsova, Maria 102, 130; subordination of 228; Theodora, empress 34, 39; theologians 102–3, 253; *see also* gender, views on

World Council of Churches 61

Zizioulas, John 12–13, 115; *see also* icon veneration

Zoe brotherhood 126; *see also* Greek Orthodox Church

For Product Safety Concerns and Information please contact our EU representative GPSR@taylorandfrancis.com
Taylor & Francis Verlag GmbH, Kaufingerstraße 24, 80331 München, Germany

www.ingramcontent.com/pod-product-compliance
Lightning Source LLC
Chambersburg PA
CBHW050854160426
43194CB00011B/2156